PORTUGAL
AND MADEIRA

1   The Chapel of the Misericórdia at Viseu

From the painting by Tristram Hillier

PORTUGAL
AND MADEIRA

By

Sacheverell Sitwell

London
B. T. BATSFORD LTD

First published 1954

oc00491895

1000187754

MADE AND PRINTED IN GREAT BRITAIN BY
WILLIAM CLOWES AND SONS, LIMITED, LONDON AND BECCLES
FOR THE PUBLISHERS
B. T. BATSFORD LTD
4, FITZHARDINGE STREET, PORTMAN SQUARE
LONDON, W.1

To
TONY and ANN RUGERONI
With affection and gratitude

PREFACE

THIS book on Portugal is dedicated to Tony and Ann
Rugeroni as a token of affection and in gratitude for their
many deeds of friendship and acts of hospitality, not least
for having taken myself and my wife to Trás-os-Montes, to
Bragança, and the Minho in the summer of 1953, enabling me to
visit many picturesque and beautiful places which I had missed
before. I could never be sufficiently grateful to them for their
kindness and companionship, and I would like to include Mrs.
Rugeroni senior in this note of thanks.

Among Portuguese friends I would name, in particular, Dr.
Reynaldo dos Santos, of double personality, for he is both a
famous man of medicine and the greatest and most discerning of
his country's art critics. I must thank him, his distinguished son,
and charming family for happy hours spent in their hospitable
house in Lisbon. The various books of Dr. Reynaldo dos Santos,
especially his recent work L'Art Portugais, his great volume on
the sculptors of Portugal, and his superb volume on the Manoelino style, will be the monument of his taste and knowledge. It
can have been given to few critics to make so complete a record
of their country's art.

My friend Dr. Tavares de Almeida has given invaluable help
in procuring photographs. Certain of the illustrations in this book
were taken at his instigation. I am indebted to him for the pictures
in Santa Clara-a-Nova at Coimbra, and at the Convent of Jesus at
Aveiro, and for photographs of the beautiful statues at Arouca.
In addition, he placed at our disposal a large collection of other
photographs to choose from. This book could not have been
properly illustrated but for his participation.

I would like, also, to take this opportunity of thanking Luiz
Marques, who is a mine of information on all things Portuguese,
and his wife Susan Belloc Lowndes, a friend of long standing, and
co-author with Ann Bridge of The Selective Traveller in Portugal.
No English traveller can visit Portugal without their volume in
his hand, and an English writer on Portugal must be in constant
debt to them.

I would like to thank our Ambassador, Sir Nigel Bruce Ronald,
K.C.M.G., C.V.O., whom I remember 'on the square' at

Chelsea Barracks in the winter of 1916–17, in a previous existence, for his kindness and hospitality.

Among other friends whose hospitality we enjoyed in Portugal I would thank the Duke and Duchess of Palmela for showing me their palace in Lisbon with its portraits by Sir Thomas Lawrence, and the wonderful 18th Century wooden chapel on an upper floor. Thanks are, also, due to Visconde de Asseca and his wife for hospitality in their villa at Sintra with its painted rooms by Pillement; to the Visconde de Soveral; and to an old friend Mrs. Lally Horstmann, who wrote that fine and touching book *No Time for Tears*, for taking us on several expeditions from Lisbon including an afternoon in the beautiful Cadaval quinta at Collares. Senhor and Senhora José de Espirito Santo Silva invited us to their villa at Cascais, as did her sister Senhora Ricardo de Espirito Santo, whose husband has lately opened his palace in Lisbon as a private museum. On a previous visit I am indebted to Mrs. Schofield for showing me her famous Quinta da Bacalhoa.

In a final paragraph I would thank my friend Tristram Hillier, Messrs. Arthur Tooth Ltd., and Mr. Arthur Jeffress, the owner of the picture, for permission to make a coloured reproduction of his painting of the Misericórdia at Viseu for our frontispiece; the Clarendon Press, Oxford, for permission to reproduce the photograph of the church in Minas Gerais which serves as frontispiece to their *Portugal and Brazil*; Mr. R. C. Taylor for allowing me the use of some of his splendid photographs of Portugal; Mr. and Mrs. Max Graham for their kind invitation to visit the British Factory House at Oporto; Mr. H. V. Livermore for reading a great part of the proofs of this book; my wife, who has accompanied me on every journey to Portugal, and who has read through all my proofs; and Senhor Antero Fraga of Vidago, who gave me so much information concerning Bragança and Trás-os-Montes and whose proffered invitation to visit Mirando do Douro I shall always regret having been unable to accept. Everywhere we went in Portugal we were met with politeness and kindness for which we would like to express our thanks. This is, also, the opportunity to mention the excellent Government-owned *pousadas* of Portugal, some twelve or fifteen in number, where the traveller can rely upon good food, and comfortable beds with bathrooms. There is usually a *pousada* within reach of most places in Portugal, but not yet, which is a pity, in Trás-os-Montes, or near Bragança.

I made a special journey to Madeira in August 1953 for the purposes of this book, and would thank the officials of the Union Castle Line for facilitating this journey, and Mr. Foerster, the manager of Reid's Hotel at Funchal, for much kindness during our stay there. Finally, I must thank Mr. and Mrs. Graham Blandy for taking me to the Quinta do Palheiro, where for the first time in my life I saw sub-tropical trees and flowers growing in a garden.

My only regret, in writing the last sentences of this book on Portugal, is not to have been able to go to the Azores, where, besides the pineapples and the villages with hydrangea hedges, there are curiosities to discover, natural beauties apart, for there are few works of art. They could include a breed of fairy cattle, ninety centimetres high, coffee-coloured, and like miniature Jerseys, these in Corvo, smallest of the islands; a little race of horses the size of Shetland ponies; and the bulldogs or cães de fila of Terceira, a breed peculiar to that island. There is, also, the interest of a peasant population of Portuguese origin settled on islands in the middle of the Atlantic five hundred years ago. In a final postscript we would add that the jacket for this book is taken from a coloured print of the *quinta* at Bemfica, near Lisbon, that belonged to Gerard de Vismes, a rich Englishman who lived in Portugal in the 18th Century.

Mr. Peter Pitt-Millward undertook a special journey at my request in order to report upon Castro Laboreiro, and his account, which arrived just as this book went to press, will be found on pp. 235-237.

9 *April* 1954   SACHEVERELL SITWELL

CONTENTS

ACKNOWLEDGMENT

THE Author and Publishers wish to thank the following who
photographs appear in this book:

Club dos Caçadores Portugueses, for fig. 33; Julio Marqu
da Costa, for fig. 49; Gerti Deutsch, for figs. 25, 27, 29, 3
32, and 34; Marcel Gautherot, for fig. 2; Fritz Henle, f
figs. 3, 14, 15, 18, 19, 22, and 35; A. F. Kerstin
F.R.P.S., for figs. 7, 8, 10, and 11; A. Moreira, for figs. 3
56, and 68; Lettice Ramsey, for figs. 44 and 52; Paul Popp
Ltd., for figs. 5, 12, and 20; Secretariado Nacional da Info
mação, Cultura Popular e Turismo, Portugal, for figs. 6, 1
16, 17, 26, 28, 30, 37, 42, 43, 50, 51, 57, 59, 60, an
64–7; *Picture Post* Library, for fig. 4; R. C. Taylor, for fig
21, 23, 24, 40, 46–8, 53, 54, 58, 61–3, and 69–71.

Figs. 9, 38, 39, 41, and 45 are from photographs by tl
Author's wife.

LIST OF ILLUSTRATIONS

15

INTRODUCTION

THIS book is the result of visits to Portugal upon no fewer than five occasions. My first journey thither was in March and April 1926 when I came by boat from Italy in order to see the golden coaches of Belém and the Abbeys of Alcobaça, Batalha, and Tomar. It would be invidious to describe again the discomforts attendant on so simple a country sortie and contrast them with the convenience of the present. Beckford's *Letters* had inspired my visit, though I did not on that occasion see Queluz. I came again in 1931 or 1932, seeing Santiago de Compostela on the way, and embarking on the *Cutty Sark* at Vigo, whence we sailed for Leixões, visiting Braga, still fresh, then, from looking at the Rococo buildings of Lecce and of Noto, which enabled interesting mental and visual comparisons to be drawn, and so went down again to Lisbon, fog-bound and in a swarm of mosquitoes on the Tagus, but seeing the Abbeys once more and staying at Buçaco. My next visit must have been in 1936, when once again I came by way of Compostela, seeing Braga from Bom Jesus, going to Oporto for the first time, and to Aveiro, where the Convent of Jesus was an enchantment; thence to Buçaco once more for the Abbeys, and so to Lisbon. This was but one half of that journey, for it was continued to Setúbal, to Évora, and down to the Algarve.

After the War had ended and I was making journeys in order to write my book on Spain, I had intended, this was in 1949, to prepare a companion volume on Portugal, and went from Madrid to Lisbon, but was ill and unable to continue with it. The opportunity came again, though, in August and September of 1953, and I resolved to undertake a big and comprehensive journey to Bragança and Trás-os-Montes in order to visit a neglected corner of Portugal little known to the Portuguese themselves, and going to towns in the Minho like Guimarães and Barcelos, and their neighbours Amarante and Lamego, towns wherein a pastoral or Arcadian civilization of the 18th Century is to be admired. And on the way to Portugal I made a special visit to Madeira for the purposes of this book. I think it can be said that with the exception of one or two old towns like Castelo de Vide and Portalegre, and a convent or two like Arouca or Lorvão, I have at one time or another covered the whole country.

The writer on Portugal who has already any knowledge how ever superficial of the Spaniards and of Spain is confronted immediately by the difficulty of how vastly different are the two countries. It is not a question of those radical differences which divide ourselves from the French so much more effectually than the English Channel that a railway porter and his equivalent or opposite number at Calais are as unlike each other as a Red Indian and a Chinaman. But the contrasts between Portugal and Spain are divergencies of similarity. They are members of the same family who bear little or no resemblance to each other and nothing is more confusing than brothers and sisters of the same parents who are not alike. Persons of education from the one country can read a newspaper of the other; but a Spaniard would have to learn Portuguese in order to read a novel by Eça de Queiroz, and the two races cannot meet on common ground in conversation. It could be said, in paradox, that it is mostly where they are alike that they are different. Thus, the Manoeline buildings, though they spring from the same spirit, are in the finished result very dissimilar from the buildings of Ferdinand and Isabella. In a street in a little town in Portugal you only deceive yourself for a moment if you think you are in Spain. What a gulf of temperament between the sentimental *fado* and the music of Seville! And these differences have their revenges! For the Portuguese are fond of telling you that Velázquez was not a Spaniard but a son of Portugal. Was not his father da Silva and his mother Velázquez, the Silvas being of gentle Portuguese origin and only settled in Seville since the beginning of the 16th Century, so that the painter ought rather to have been known as Silva than a Velázquez? They will carry the argument further by explaining that *Las Meninas*, the name of his famous painting in the Prado, one of the miracles of art, is a Portuguese and not a Spanish word. Where, they will say, in Velázquez are the morbid fantasy and the love of death; the cold austerities of Ribera and Zurbarán, or Goya's nightmares? The cool tones in *Las Meninas* are of Portugal: and so, they add, are the sanity and restraint that paint things as they are and know when to curb their hand. But this particular discussion is of inflammable nature, and only likely to widen the differences between the two countries!

It is true that what is lacking in Portugal is the tragedy in Spain. That, and its sombre magnificence. Instead, there is pastoral or Arcadian poetry, whether of whispering pinewoods, or of vine-clad valleys. The Minho is one of the most beautiful regions of the world, with enough of early churches and old convents, painted *solares* and flowering orchards to render it, once seen, for ever memorable with its slow-moving peasant women, who become grape-bearing caryatids at the time of the wine harvest, and wide-horned oxen. In Portugal you are never far from the Atlantic, even in Bragança and Trás-os-Montes that are behind the mountains, but it is not entirely the same Atlantic which breaks on the coast of Cornwall, which is ever rough and angry off Brest and Finistère, and is only lulled treacherously and unaccountably, as by a mirage, at lush and arbutus-bearing islets and promontories along the coast of Kerry. The Atlantic is, in fact, the power of Portugal, and the mouth of the Tagus not so much a terminus or end of Europe as a port of embarcation for further worlds across the seas.

It is no wonder that the population of Portugal was sea-faring, but the marvel is the spate of energy that carried them within the span of two human generations to the far corners of the earth. Their Empire consisted in a fantastic collection of forts and islands, in theory as far-fetched and improbable as ever the maritime city of Venice that rose on shoal and sandbanks out of the Adriatic. São Tomé in the Gulf of Guinea in 1471; The Azores in the middle of the Atlantic; Sofala, Mozambique, and Mombasa on the route to India; Muscat and Ormuz in the Persian Gulf; Colombo in Ceylon; Diu and Cochin and Golden Goa in India; Amboina, Ternate, and Tidore, the spice islands, and Timor in the East Indies; with Macau in China as early as 1557; such was the trading Empire of Portugal in one direction only, towards the East. It must not be forgotten that Portuguese built the churches and forts of Gondar in Ethiopia, and may have taught the art of bronze-casting to the negro sculptors of Benin. The Portuguese Indies or *Estado de Índia*, comprised all their settlements between the Persian Gulf and the Cape of Good Hope on one side, and Japan and Timor on the other. Their great carracks were of over two thousand tons and the hugest ships afloat. Goa was the most splendid of all European cities built in the Orient, while at Macau the 17th Century churches were the work of Japanese converts crossed over to China at the bidding of St. Francis Xavier, the Apostle of the Indies. While the 'burghers' of Colombo to this day bear high-sounding names of old Portugal, boasting their drop of that blood and still speaking Portuguese, which is understood, too, in the Moluccas, at Malacca, and along the coast of Coromandel and Malabar, it is curious to reflect that the most distant, far-fetched appearance of the warriors and *fidalgos* of Portugal is upon the 17th Century painted screens of Japan. Here, on the *Namban Byobu*, *byobu* meaning 'screen', and *namban* meaning 'barbarians from the South', the direction from which carracks and caravels approached Japan, they are to be seen strutting in their top hats of Jacobean fashion, in odd contrast to the lacquered hats of the Japanese courtiers; with beards and long moustachios, long, thin faces, short doublets, and extravagantly wide breeches, their hands upon their sword hilts.*

Portugal slowly relinquished her 'Indian' dominion, though still retaining Goa, Macau, and Timor, while her great African colonies are only now developing. It is, however, her achievement in the Western hemisphere which is her lasting contribution to history, for having lost one half of the Empire the Portuguese turned with astonishing resilience to the other. It was the gold and diamonds of Brazil that made possible the extravagances of Dom João V. There was a steady, if small stream of emigration during three centuries from Portugal to Brazil. In matters of art, for we are not concerned with politics, there can be nothing in Brazil to compare with the churches and monasteries of Goa. Those, in fact, date from the 16th and early 17th Centuries, when there was more building activity in Goa than in Lisbon. Lamentably little is now left of Goa; and it could be said that it is more profitable to read of Goa than to go there. The Palace of

* A magnificent pair of six-fold screens, of this subject, painted in colours on gilded paper, and belonging to the Emperor of Japan, was shown at the Japanese Exhibition in the National Gallery of Art at Washington in 1953. Other painted screens of this nature are in the Musée Guimet at Paris, and in the collection of Prince Rupprecht of Bavaria.

the Inquisitors, of grisly memory, is a heap of ruins; and of all the churches only that of Bom Jesus, with the tomb and shrine of St. Francis Xavier, is still whole and eloquent of its old splendours.

In Rio de Janeiro, though there are old buildings, they must be overshadowed and outcountenanced by the new. No work, however, which extols the beautiful 18th Century buildings of Northern Portugal should fail to note their equivalent in Brazil, and in one particular State, that of Minas Gerais or the 'General Mines', in fact, the source of the gold and diamonds of Brazil. These are closely related in style to the buildings of the Minho and Trás-os-Montes, and are clearly influenced by emigrants from Northern Portugal. The graceful Rococo of the Minas Gerais excelled in oval plans, a further development of the Portuguese taste for the circular and the octagonal (see p. 214). One architect and sculptor of genius appeared, the mulatto Antonio Francisco Lisboa (1730–1814), called 'o Aleijadinho', or 'the little cripple', the victim of an obscure disease that covered him with sores and left him without the use of his hands. His masterpiece is in the church of São Francisco de Assis, at São João d'El-Rei, with a green soapstone doorway of great beauty and elegance (2), Brazilian relation to the Malheiros Reimões chapel in Viana do Costelo (see p. 190), which is among the delights of Portugal. He, also, carved the beautiful high altar in the church of the Franciscan Third Order at Ouro Preto, the capital of Minas Gerais, but the forte of o Aleijadinho was his carving of doorways and of windows. At the end of his life, when completely crippled and carried to work in a shaded litter under a cloak to hide his ravaged features, the Aleijadinho carved a set of twelve heroic statues of prophets, in soapstone, for the shrine of Bom Jesus, at Congonhas do Campo, the Brazilian counterpart to the sacred gardens of Bom Jesus at Braga, and of N.S. dos Remédios at Lamego (see pp. 154, 155). This retarded Rococo of Minas Gerais also found expression in the painted ceilings of the Manuel da Costa Ataide (1762–1837), whose work as late as 1810 recalls the frescoes by lesser Bavarian and Austrian masters of the sub-Venetian school, his best work being the ceiling of São Francisco de Assis at Ouro Preto completed as late as 1810. But, in fact, the doorways and altars of o Aleijadinho surpass their prototypes in Northern Portugal in elegance and fantasy despite their remote geographical situation, and the churches of the Minas Gerais must be included together with those of Cuzco in Peru and the two or three masterpieces in Mexico as the supreme works of the Iberian races in America, even if their creators were of mixed or *mestizo* blood. How different, though, are the churches of Minas Gerais from the golden churches of Mexico with their astonishing Churrigueresque altars! That is the Mexican style, *par excellence*, with all its glitter, compound of the Spaniard and the silver mines, the plumed *caciques* and the *marimba* bands. Minas Gerais, by contrast, is not Indian at all, but mulatto, and towns such as Ouro Preto were the Arcadian Portugal transported into a negro population who laboured in the gold mines. Life there must have been a picturesque spectacle for those who had the leisure to enjoy it, having at least a few advantages over the gold mines of the Rand.

It is to be noted that there were no monasteries in Minas Gerais owing to the Pombal government, constituting one great difference from Goa with its population of monks and nuns, while in minor matters there is a complete absence of *azulejos*, those blue and white tiles which are so typical of Portugal. One of the rare instances of reciprocal extravagance from the kings to their colonies is the magnificent gift of tiles from Dom João V to the Franciscan church in Bahia. They form 150 panels on the monumental stairway and round both storeys of the cloister, figuring the twelve months of the year, the four continents, the five senses, and a whole cohort of Roman soldiers. And we return from Brazil to Portugal conscious of one deficiency, at least, in this present work, which is that not much has been said upon the question of *azulejos*. But they are, indeed, charming and delightful enough without its being necessary to exaggerate their merits. I am aware, also, that bitter words are written here about the reparation of old buildings. If I have said harsh things of the 'restorers' it is for love of Portugal, and for what the wrecked monuments would have meant to future generations.

One of the fascinations of Lisbon is in trying to picture it before the fatal earthquake of 1755. The destruction of the Royal Palace is remarked upon in the chapter on Lisbon, but so much else perished. There was, for instance, Guarino Guarini's church of N.S. da Divina Providência, with an elliptical plan. But it is now as intangible as that visit of another great Italian architect, also a priest, Filippo Juvara, who came to Lisbon for six months in 1719 in order to make designs for the patriarchal church and for the Royal Palace at Mafra. Nothing was accomplished: and the earthquake left nothing of N.S. da Divina Providência. And there was the great Opera House by Giovanni Carlo Bibiena. This member of the famous family of theatrical architects came to Lisbon in 1753; the theatre was opened on 31 March 1755, and totally destroyed by earthquake in November of the same year.* It was the most splendid theatre of its day, and is in reminder that music was the besetting extravagance of the Portuguese Court. The Royal Chapel had twelve organists and one hundred singers on its payroll until the Royal Family fled from Lisbon to Brazil. Earlier, Portugal had been the chief warbling ground of the Italian *castrati* singers, and Senesino and Egiziello earned huge sums here. But the history of music in Portugal is not unclouded, and one of her most brilliant opera composers, Antonio José da Silva, was burnt at the stake for Judaism in 1739.

It must have been by little short of a miracle that the Jerónimos at Belém survived the earthquake undamaged. Had that gone, there would have been much less argument about the Manoelino! For it is the presence of this Abbey so near to Lisbon, and in a conspicuous position upon the bank of the Tagus, that draws attention to one of the most peculiar and original styles of architecture in the world. Were its only specimens in more remote and inaccessible places, as, for instance, the Convent of Christ at Tomar, the Manoelino style might have been looked upon as an aberration of taste of which there were only isolated

* Augustus Hervey, who saw the Opera House, comments in his *Journal* that it is "by the architect of the theatre in Siena". But the beautiful, oval Teatro dei Rinnovati on the ground floor of the Palazzo Pubblico of Siena (of all places!) is by Antonio Galli da Bibiena. On the night of 3 September 1758 an attempt was made upon the life of Dom José I as he rode through the streets of Belém, and Giovanni Carlo Bibiena was commissioned to build the Igrega da Memória in thanksgiving. The interior is as untheatrical and disappointing as his Opera House must have been magnificent. Bibiena brought with him a pupil, Giacomo Azzolini, who worked in the palace theatres of Queluz, Ajuda, and Salvaterra, and built the Picadeiro or Riding School of Belém, where are the coaches.

examples. But this Abbey with an interior looking more like the temples of Golconda or Coromandel, as those could be conjured up into the imagination, than a Christian church, stands contiguous to Lisbon, and from its scale and execution is not to be mistaken for the work of unrequited hands. In its fervour it must be the expression of the whole nation.

A nation of probably no more than a million souls in the time of this, her golden age. On the scale, therefore, of the cities and colonies of the Ancient Greeks; or the duchies of the Italian Renaissance. And of about the same magnitude as the population of Dutchmen who in the following century wrested much of their 'Indian' Empire from them, and obtained footholds in North America, the West Indies, and Brazil. It is, of course, obvious that the most adventurous spirits left Portugal, spent their energies out of the country, and in probably the majority of instances after a few voyages did not return. Four or five of the huge carracks left Lisbon every year for Goa; but of twenty-two making the voyage in 1590–3 only two came back, and out of thirty-three vessels leaving Portugal for India in 1606–8 only three returned to Lisbon from the round voyage that took up eighteen months. Three or four hundred men would die on the outward journey out of a complement of six or eight hundred.* Goa for our particular purpose was settled just a little late. Had it come but a decade or two earlier the churches and convents of Goa would have been built in Manoelino style, and a yet more curious city have risen on the Indian coast. Instead, it was in the secondary Italian, or, in fact, the Roman Renaissance at several removes, in a style that in the critical language of last century "betrays the degraded taste of the Jesuits". It is an idle dream to wish that it were otherwise; and the vision of cloisters and palaces drugged by the Orient to just the degree that Milton's imagery took fire at the thought of Ormuz, of Malabar, or of

* *The Portuguese in the East*, by C. R. Boxer, in *Portugal and Brazil*, Oxford, The Clarendon Press, 1953, pp. 217–219. This book of essays by various hands is a compendium of interesting and necessary information upon Portugal and Brazil. In particular, there is the essay on *Architecture in Portugal* by J. B. Bury, and that on *Baroque Architecture in Brazil* by Professor Robert C. Smith; and it has essays on *Portuguese History* by H. V. Livermore, and on *Music in Portugal* by Ann Livermore.

2   São João d'el Rei, Minas Gerais, Brazil: the Church of S. Francisco
de Assis, by 'o Aleijadinho' (1730–1814)

3   Queluz: part of the Garden Façade

Deccan, is as vain as it is to pretend to oneself, as I have sometimes done, that the Venetians during their golden age put
statues by their great sculptors to rise up out of the blue waters
of the Canale della Giudecca and the Canale de San Marco.

The mention of Milton and of his metaphors drawn from the
Orient makes it lamentable that so great a poet as Camões should
be as little read, outside Portugal and Brazil, as are Tasso or
Ariosto in the world at large. We are to imagine that Camões
(1524–80) and Gil de Vicente (1476–1536) are the great poets
of Portugal, but the narratives of her explorers and navigators
are the crude ore of poetry. It is probable that there are unpublished masterpieces of this sort, describing forgotten Hindu king-
doms, and perhaps early visits to China and Japan. Their second
or alternative 'Indies', when they had lost the first, was in
Brazil; and now, although separated from each other, the two
countries realize more and more clearly that they are branches
of the same nation. For the reason that there is only one Portu-
guese-speaking republic in Latin America, and because of their
amicable separation, the links are stronger than between the
Spanish-speaking republics and Spain. Thus, the Luso-Brazilian
entity is likely to endure and become more binding. If the
Portuguese had, as they assert, one of the great novelists of
Europe in Eça de Queiroz, Brazil had the novelist Joachim
Machado de Assis, his genius not obscured by his father having
been a negro house-painter. The *saudade* or gentle melancholy
which defines the Portuguese *fado*, their popular song, and
inhabits their whole national temperament, at such an antithesis
of difference from the finger-snapping, castanet-playing Andalusian, when comparing Lisbon to Seville, must permeate Brazil
as well as Portugal in the past as well as now. There is a passage
in Beckford's *Letters* indicative of this, which I have quoted at the
end of the account of Queluz (see p. 108), describing the soft
modinhas of Brazil that he wishes to learn to play and sing. In even
so small a thing as the reciprocal influence of popular music, in
comparison to most other nations of the world that are drowned
and deafened by the juke-box, the Portuguese have to be envied
who make their popular music for themselves, or import it from
Brazil.

The years of Spanish domination (1580–1640) weighed heavily

on Portugal. It covered the life span of two or three generations of Portuguese, and we can perhaps only conceive of its heavy and dull impact by transferring its dragging length into our own times and imagining that it lasted from 1890 until 1950. Portugal, like Catalonia, was the unwilling partner of Madrid. It must have seemed most improbable that she would regain her independence. The restored King Dom João IV, first of the house of Bragança, had to ally himself with the Dutch; and there followed twenty years of uncertainty and danger until, on the death of Cromwell, the old alliance with Great Britain was renewed again, a marriage was arranged between Charles II and Catherine of Bragança, and recognition of the independence of Portugal was at last secured from the Spaniards in 1668. The Methuen Treaty of 1703, besides other advantages, secured for Portugal almost a monopoly in the sale of wines to Great Britain; Spain was now falling asleep and no longer a danger; and first of all gold was found in great quantities in the Minas Gerais, and then in 1728 diamonds were discovered in the same province.

There followed something equivalent to a second Renaissance in Portugal. The gold and diamonds of Brazil, of which a fifth share went to the Crown, enabled Dom João V to indulge in glittering, if insensate extravagancies, most of which are touched upon in the pages that follow. The golden coaches of Belém are relics of that; but the vast sums spent on music in the Court Chapel and Royal theatres went on intangibilities of which hardly more is left than the names of operas and masses. However, the true vitality of Portugal was humbler, if more robust in nature, and its evidences are to be seen in so many small towns, scarcely bigger than villages, in Northern Portugal. Indiscriminate enthusiasm, though, is to be distrusted and they should be judged, soberly, after comparison with their equivalents in other lands. Churches and convents of the 18th Century, after all, are part of a lesser or silver age, when in many lands besides Portugal it would seem that the hand of man could not go wrong. Churches, of which so many are unlocked and entered in these pages, become more, and not less graceful and charming when the wonderful old convents in Bavaria and Austria are recalled to mind.

The Portuguese is a light and fanciful architecture not inspiring

30

the same epithets in praise that are evoked by the titan solemnity of Durham Cathedral or the carved and coloured miracle of Chartres. Such comparisons are pointless and the architecture of Trás-os-Montes and the Minho must be judged within its own field, which is that of the Baroque and Rococo. But, in the world of music, the church cantatas of Johann Sebastian Bach were succeeded in another generation by Haydn's masses. Those have their architectural equivalent in Rococo churches beyond number, of which the names would but impede and clog our text. When we consider the beauties of Northern Portugal, an Arcadia with, it could be said, Arcadian buildings, altars that are like dressing-tables out of fairy stories, gilded organs upheld by tritons, mermaids, satyrs, the *settecento* in Venice must also be taken into account. A little *ridotto* or gambling saloon, such as the Casino Venier, with its *stucco* birds upon the walls, low arabesqued ceilings, and inlaid floor of coloured marbles, compares, if there is courage to say so, with more than one sacristy in Portugal. What is lacking in Portugal, where the decorative painting is nearly always bad, is the brush of a Tiepolo. There are moments, as there are surfaces and ceilings, when one longs for even a third-rate Italian painter. But Italy is the land of painting, and Portugal is no more to be reproached for want of that than England, for here, too, it is no part of our native genius.

This characteristic, regional style of Northern Portugal is achieved with lines and ornaments of black-green granite and walls of white plaster. The granite is local equivalent to the Roman *travertine*, or the blue-green *pietra serena* of Florence. Braga is centre of the region; and it must be considered as being altogether distinct from Oporto, and in closer contact with Minhas Gerais in Brazil than with Lisbon. This has the sound of improbability, but, yet, is true. The Rococo of Ouro Preto is a direct importation from the North of Portugal, with perhaps the main difference that of soapstone in place of granite. In towns in Northern Portugal that are near the Spanish frontier there is no influence from Spain. For an Arcadia it was inward looking, unconcerned with anywhere more distant than a day's journey over the vine-clad hills. The link was one of language, and they were nearer in spirit to their own relations who had gone as emigrants to Brazil than to the Spaniards. This is the more striking because of the nearness to Northern Portugal of Santiago de Compostela, a town and shrine where are to be seen the culminating splendours of Spanish architecture. But there is no trace of that in towns in Northern Portugal; even where, albeit we exaggerate a little, it is near enough on still nights to hear the church bells of El Obradoiro—the west façade of the cathedral of Santiago, built of golden stone, loaded with statues as a Hindu pagoda, nodding on a summer night with snapdragons and flowering weeds—and watch the fireworks on the *fiesta* of St. James.

There may be nowhere better than at a Portuguese bull-fight to mark the difference between Portugal and Spain. The Lisbon bull-ring or *Campo Pequeno* is a peculiar building in mixed Mauresque and Russian (samovar) style, at first sight an unpropitious setting for the most thrilling and chivalrous spectacle that can be imagined. After the stampeding to buy cushions, general trampling, and mounting excitement that prelude a bull-fight it opens with a trumpet call and the parade into the bull-ring or *redondel*, a word in which the bloodstained drama of the Spaniards is missing. At the first bull-fight I attended, in 1949, one *cavaleiro* only, Simão de Veiga, rode into the ring; but at a bull-fight in September 1954 both Simão de Veiga and Nuncio, a younger *cavaleiro*, took part. They paraded into the ring upon their beautifully trained ponies, wearing Court dress of the reign of Dom José I; long, black coat, gold embroidered, with black tricorne hat and long boots for Simão de Veiga, and a long, scarlet coat in the case of Nuncio. It is, in fact, Court dress of the time of Louis quinze. The ponies of the pair of *cavaleiros* advance towards the president's box—and the President of Portugal was at the second bull-fight—performing the motions of the *haute école* as performed by the white Lippizaners from the Spanish Riding School at Vienna, except that these are manoeuvres that are still used in combat and are not entirely formal. When they have made their *cortesias* or salutations to the president and public the ponies are put through one or two more tricks, as though to enlist the sympathy of the spectators and prove that they are both highly trained and undefended, as indeed they are.

The dress of the other bull-fighters is, also, unlike that of the *toreros* of Córdoba and Seville. These are the *campinos* of the

Ribatejo, in knee-breeches, white shirts, *barretes verdes* or green stocking-caps, and armed with tridents. They are herdsmen from the plain of the Tagus, equivalents for Portugal of the horsemen of the Camargue, also carrying the trident, who round up the young bulls for branding at the annual *Ferrade*; and perhaps there are no others in Europe like them except the mounted cowherds of the *puszta*. But the *campinos* in their stocking-caps seem to carry an echo of Naples. Tridents apart, they could be dancers of the tarantella. We shall see them running to and fro at speed to herd the bulls, balancing their tridents (17).

But there is a fanfare on the trumpet and a bull is let into the ring. It is *embolado*, that is to say its horns are sheathed in leather, but it is a huge, vicious-looking brute, with a crest or ridge of muscle on the back of its neck and shoulders, bigger and heavier, on appearance, than the Spanish bulls, and it should be added that the bulls in Portugal seem generally to be brown in colour and not black. The horseman, meanwhile, has been handed his lance, which is no more lethal than a long *banderilla*, called in Portugal *farpa* or *ferro*, with a small point. He gallops towards the bull, with the lovely, close gallop of the *manège*, allowing the bull to come after him, then reining in and turning on the ground his pony stands on, close up against the barrier. It is a phase of the fight; and galloping away he now turns towards the bull once more, and halting at some distance, while the bull looks and waits for him, taunts the bull and cries, "Hah, Hah, Hah, Toro, Toro", several times repeated; and the bull standing his ground, gathers his horse and himself, and charges. This is the moment of drama, for the bull turns and runs head down towards him. The *cavaleiro*, just passing the bull and turning, plants the dart in the bull's shoulder. The bull comes after him in a fury and just fails to catch him. This process is repeated again with variants, and with passes, *cadeiras*, *gaiolas*, and so forth, of which the import is lost upon us.

The first stage is over, and the bull is, then, generally, played on foot with *bandarilhas*, the slight difference in the Spanish and Portuguese form of that word being indication of the more harmless nature of the pairs of darts in Portugal. When this is finished, the bull's death is often simulated with a wooden sword, or the *matador* feigns the kill with a sword wrapped round with cloth. Sometimes, as was the case upon the second occasion, *toreros* from Spain fight alternate bulls, and there is the excitement of the Spanish bull-fight without the bloodshed. But now comes the final feat of strength and skill when eight strongly built young men, the *moças de forcado* and heroes of the town, step into the ring. Their leader puts himself first of them, and they advance in Indian file. He may be ten or even twenty paces in front of the others, and with arms folded meets the rush of the bull and allows himself to be lifted off his feet upon the horns. The others then close in upon the bull in a wrestling, struggling mass, and after a moment or two the bull is upon its back, or brought to a dead standstill with the stoutest of the young men holding to its tail. That is the end; the oxen are then driven in with bells at their dewlaps, and after some manœuvring by the *campinos*, who have often to execute something nearly equivalent to a dance with their tridents, having a sort of running walk conditioned by the way they hold the trident in either or both hands, the bull trots out of the ring in the midst of the herd, uninjured, and the round is over.

Eight bulls were let in that evening, for the *corrida* took place at nine o'clock at night. Simão de Veiga and Nuncio each fought two bulls, changing their ponies at least once, and giving a graceful and impeccable display of horsemanship. Did one know more of the subtleties of the Portuguese bull-fights there could be discussion of their different styles. Both *cavaleiros*, who have the look of cavalry officers, perform their feats of daring with a smiling face, which must be the tradition in Portugal, and gives to the entire proceedings a courtly, aristocratic air, connecting it in rules and manners to the equestrian statue of the King Dom José in the square at Lisbon. The moment of death is lacking. It is light-hearted and chivalrous. There are none of the harrowing scenes that stain the Spanish sands. The ponies obviously enjoy their prancings. Again and again they are in mortal danger, but with so skilful a hand upon their bridle, and being the faster animal, they always get away. In any event the bull's horns are padded. But the Spaniards cannot have the drama without the bloodshed, the sound of the sword driven in to its hilt, so often in the wrong place, the mortally wounded bull being made to turn round and round with the flaunting of cloaks in order to increase its bleeding, the toppling to its knees, the last bellowings, and lolling tongue. The bull-fight in Portugal in all things is more chivalrous and gentle.

But so skilled is the art of the *cavaleiros*, and it involves such years of training, that there are never more than three or four of them in a generation. The population of bull-fighters is nothing comparable to that of Spain. It is only in towns in Southern and Central Portugal that there are bull-rings. The Spanish *toreros* make their fortunes in Mexico and South America; but the Portuguese bull-fight is confined to Portugal and has no following in Brazil. You could be in Portugal and not know they had bull-fights, unless you drove through Vila Franca de Xira and passed the bull-ring. It is true that the *rejoneado*, or fighting of bulls from horseback with the lance, is now increasing in popularity in Spain, but it is not really the style of Portugal, for it involves the kill. *Carmen* would lose its point with a last act set outside a bull-ring in Portugal. The spangled suits of the *toreros* belong to a different tradition. Or, in parenthesis, we could say that they are to the design of another composer, and one who is in love with death, which is the Spaniard. But not the Lusitanian. So the appurtenances are not so heavy with drama. But we would mention in a last sentence certain painted wooden boxes, standing upright, in which the lances of the *cavaleiros* are carried, boxes decorated in 'narrow boat', canal-barge manner with the insignia of the bull-fight, a thing only seen in Portugal and never in Spain; and recall once again, contrasting them with the sequins and pink stockings of Spain, with the *trajes de luce* and mantles, or *capas de paseo*, embroidered with roses and carnations of the *toreros*, the graceful and calm horsemen of Portugal in plumed *tricornes* and long, embroidered coats, smiling in face of the bull and crying, "Hah, Hah, Toro, Toro''; the wrestlers who shed no blood; and *campinos* who, were their Phrygian caps but red instead of green, might be dancing tarantellas to the tambourine in view of Vesuvius and Capri.

It is difficult at all times, in Lisbon, not to be reminded, in some things, of Naples. There is just that same amount, and no more, of Spain. But Lisbon has not the ferocious poverty of the slums in Naples. It is a town of Latins, but of Atlantic Latins. And the Spaniards are either inland, of the high table land; or

Mediterranean. For the Bay of Biscay is the sea of the Basques, and not the full Atlantic. As port of embarcation for the ends of the earth neither Bilbao nor Santander can compare with the mouth of the Tagus. They are harbours which send iron-ore to England, or fishing fleets to the fogs of Newfoundland, but not now, or ever, were they in communication, direct or spiritual, with Muscat or Ormuz, with Goa or Macau. That is something which cannot be forgotten in Lisbon; and in evidence there may be a family from Macau with a Chinese nurse to look after the children staying in the hotel, and one remembers that Macau has been a colony of Portugal since 1557 and that Hongkong has been a Crown Colony of Great Britain since 1841. It is only a pity that in Lisbon there should not be anything with so fine sounding a name as the Archivo de Índias, which stands along one side of the cloister at Seville, looking down on the orange trees beneath the Giralda, a library founded by the son of Columbus. The Torreão, or great tower of the Royal Palace at Lisbon, to which the sobriquet 'Indian' was attached and which was completely destroyed in the earthquake of 1755, must have contained relics and documents of the Portuguese conquests in the East, and may have been as much more valuable and interesting than the Archivo de Índias, as Lisbon, itself, is more important than Seville for its traffic with the Orient.

It becomes a subject of perfect fascination for anyone who knows Spain to carry his predilection as far as the land mass of Iberia will allow of it, which is to the Atlantic, and find Portugal of another taste altogether. A little country in comparison with the vast distances of Spain, though it is perhaps impossible to find oneself in the cloister of the Jerónimos at Belém in the shade of its Indian or quasi-Indian traceries, or within that grove of tall Golcondan palm-trees which is the abbey church, and not allow one's mind to travel over the burnt hills and stony immensity to the granite Escorial, which is but the middle of Spain; and for as long a journey again in either direction to the court of orange-trees at Córdoba, or to golden Tarragona, all within the peninsula. I have, I know, been singularly fortunate in the opportunites that have been afforded me of going from end to end of both countries. There can be hardly a town or village containing works of art, or a church or convent worth entering in either land, that

4 Grape Harvest in the Douro Valley

5　A Peasant Girl of Mafra

6　A *Sargaceiro*, or Weed-collector,
of Apúlia

has not fallen my way during the years since 1919 and 1926, respectively, when I first came to Spain and then to Portugal. It is another stroke of good fortune to have been allowed to complete this task.

Portugal is one of the most lovely countries of Europe, with its musical pinewoods, its vineyards, and Hesperidean orchards. There are valleys in Northern Portugal that are pure Arcadian vales. Little towns, Lamego, Barcelos, Amarante, contain beauties altogether out of proportion to their population. This is fair Lusitania; and in the South it is torrid without the heated blood of Naples, without the vendetta and the volcano. If a golden age lasts but a lifetime there are the extraordinary buildings of that same generation who sailed from the Tagus to India and China, and sailing into the West had their first landfall in Brazil. Now, it is a land awakening from long, but not dreamless slumber. It slept during the industrial age which blackened so much of Europe. If it has woken, unspoiled, into a happier present it is because that has been the project of benevolent and wise hands.

I

A TRIP TO MADEIRA

AMONG the divisions of the human spirit where pleasure
and anticipations are in prospect there is one dividing line
or watershed as true in application as any other and con
veying the closest testimony to individual character and tempera
ment. It can be stated in a sentence. There are those person
to whom the ideal of comfort and relaxation is a warm drink
coming in out of the cold; and those others who prefer a
draught, thrillingly and deliciously chilled, on a noon of blazing
sun.

The bypaths of this argument lead into infinity. There are
lovers of tropical nights, or of the midnight sun, just as, reversing
the order, there are those who admire the music of Sibelius, or
Mozart. There was the Norwegian naval officer, a man of
experience, who told me nothing on earth was so beautiful as the
Arctic in flower. He was speaking of Greenland and Spitzbergen
He had seen a dead whale a hundred feet long towed beside a
ship; and he told me of how polar bears at the approach of a
human being hide their noses with a paw, knowing their black
muzzles will betray them in the snow. He could never, he told
me, shoot a polar bear again. Others may tell you of the delphin
ium and larkspur in blue Alaska during the few weeks of spring
or of the wild flowers, crocus and cyclamen, in Sicily and Cyprus
There are lovers of the Alps, or of Dutch canals; devotees of the
Romantic or Classical in works of art; lovers of Gothic cath
edrals, or partisans of the Baroque and Rococo; and admirers of
single flowers who abominate the doubles. Argument is endless
but the thesis is the same.

Moreover, the appetite, once whetted, is not satisfied. In
which sense, Vesuvius and the milky waters of the Bay of Naples
lead directly to the coral seas. But, for this is to travel in imagina
tion, time and money are no limitations. It is certainly true that
the first taste of the Orient is something never forgotten, and
that stands out for ever in the memory. And the same thing is
true of a first experience of the tropics. The aridity of Upper

40

ypt, as of the Valley of the Kings at Luxor where at times it
s not rained for fifteen years, the heats of the Sudan and the
haran wastes, those, all, are equatorial. They are neither
opical, nor sub-tropical. For those terms imply an intensity of
wering. The tropics have tropical flowers and flowering trees.
has been the writer's good fortune to see Mexico and Florida
r the first time within a year of writing this. Who would forget
e gardenias of Mexico, or the scarlet poinsettias ten feet high in
ecember at the doors of the golden churches? I saw the camellias
Louisiana and South Carolina, wax-like and perfect, virgin
petal, or the marbled and the mottled; and in Florida palm-
aded avenues lined with hibiscus hedges, sands where there
ere pelicans instead of seagulls, and in the gardens Milton's
obab:

> "The fig-tree; not that kind for fruit renown'd
> But such as at this day to Indians known,
> In Malabar or Deccan spreads her arms
> Branching so broad and long, that in the ground
> The bended twigs take root, and daughters grow
> About the mother tree, a pillar'd shade
> High over-arch'd and echoing walks between:
> There oft the Indian herdsman, shunning heat,
> Shelters in cool, and tends his pasturing herds
> At hoop-holes cut through thickest shade."

is a sensation one will not forget to be for the first time in a
arden where a humming-bird has its home, even though in
ecember it was not visible and one but felt its little presence.
ow temptingly near the Bahamas lie to Florida; while Bermuda
but three hours' flight from the mainland! From the tropics,
st touched, one is drawn to Yucatán and Guatemala, did the
pportunity but present itself. One can no more be sated with
me avenues but must have the flamboyant and the jacaranda.
isbon is perhaps the only capital city in Europe where there are
owering jacarandas in the open streets. Four years ago the sight
f those, for they have not long attained the flowering stage, was
first invitation to the tropics. That was satisfied, we have seen,
n Florida and Mexico; and probably enough of predilection
as been shown already in these few lines to make it evident

how welcome was the chance that offered of going to Madeir
early in August 1953.

For Madeira is altogether exceptional among islands. It doe
not lie in the path of those who travel to see paintings or fin
buildings. They will go to Italy and Greece and Spain. Wher
the cactus and prickly pear come down to the Mediterranean
where the wild narcissi grow out of the cliffs of Capri, and at si
o'clock in the February morning as you are rowed ashore from
the little steamer coming from Amalfi you may float along an
pick them with your hand, there you get the taste and intima
tion of what an isle can be. But how pale are the flowers!—th
pallor of the narcissi even though they smell of honey!—the pale
ness of the plain of asphodel at Paestum growing up to the foc
of the temples!—in fact, that siren shore and the island of Capri
beautiful, intrinsically, but now clouded in demi-fashionabl
notoriety, are better relegated away from the present into th
misty past, removed from the cheap excursions, the cafés an
the carnations and the mandolines, till the Blue Grotto is but
legend of Tiberius and the shape of the island but conjectured
as in the background of a Claude painting!

Nevertheless, Capri, with its Greek shadows, has some hint i
it of the Hesperides, "a name", the classical dictionary tells us
"common both to Italy and Spain, and derived from Hesper, th
setting sun, or the evening, whence the Greeks called Italy
Hesperia, because it was situate at the setting sun, or in th
West; and the same name for similar reasons was applied t
Spain by the Latins." Hesperia, concludes Dr. Lemprière, autho
of the classical dictionary and 18th Century divine, being a
island of Africa, "once residence of the Amazons, a celebrate
place or garden abounding with fruits of the most deliciou
kinds." It was one of the labours of Hercules to procure some o
the golden apples of the Hesperides; and the hero, "ignorant o
the situation of this celebrated garden, applied to the nymphs i
the neighbourhood of the river Po for information, and was tol
that Nereus, the god of the sea, if properly managed, woul
direct him in his pursuit." So Hercules seized Nereus, "generall
represented as an old man with a long flowing beard, and hai
of an azure colour", as he lay asleep, and the sea god, unable t
escape from his grasp, answered all his questions.

Is Madeira, then, to be identified with the Hesperides? It is
onjectured that the Fortunate Islands mentioned by Pliny, the
oman geographer, in the 1st Century, A.D., may have been
he Canaries. He talks, also, of the Purple Islands, by which he
ould mean Madeira, and voyagers blown off their course may
ave caught sight of the island. But the Romans were not the
rst sailors in these regions. The Phoenicians had been here
efore them. All that can be said is that there were legendary
lands off the African coast, and one or other group of islands
as the Hesperides.

However, one of the beauties of Madeira is that, compara-
vely, it has no past. The Ancients may have known of the Cape
erde and the Canary Islands, but no one had ever set foot on
Madeira. It was reconnoitred in 1419 from Porto Santo, its
eighbouring isle, by one of the expeditions sent forth by Prince
enry the Navigator, and annexed in the name of Portugal in the
ollowing year. It was a virgin island. There were no aboriginal
hhabitants to exterminate. Colonists were quickly sent from
ortugal; and Prince Henry the Navigator, son of Philippa of
ancaster, and nephew, as we shall know later, of our John the
aunt, introduced plants of the Malvoisie vine from Crete and
gar-canes from Sicily. In so doing he laid foundations for the
ture prosperity of the island. Hercules, whether well directed
r no by the nymphs of the river Po, would have preferred the
land when terraced and laid out with vines. But in Madeira
ere is no breath of antiquity, no trace of Hercules or of the
mazons, and the history of the island is only contemporary
ith that of Eton College or the older colleges of Oxford and
ambridge.

It is an island to which you go for the flowers and the climate,
its most seductive and captivating, alike to those who have
avelled much and come at last to Madeira, and to persons who
rrive here for their first experience of being abroad and never
esire to go anywhere else again. They may have been again and
gain to Madeira without troubling to go ashore at Lisbon, not,
ideed, that the two places are coefficient and in easy communi-
ation with each other, because, although Madeira is so near to
ortugal it is surprising, also, how few Portuguese have been
ere. Perhaps they are content with their own climate. But

there is, too, the perpetual and aggravating anomaly that it is ea
enough to arrive at Madeira but next to impossible to retur
thence, by way of Lisbon at the date required. This seems alwa
to have been the besetting problem of a visit to Madeira. Yo
may even be told that there is no guarantee whatever of accomm
dation for the return journey, and that on the smaller Portugue
vessels all the cabins are reserved for officials returning from tl
Portuguese colonies in Africa. The Union Castle and Royal M.
Lines sailing from Southampton for The Cape and for Sou
America may call at the Canaries instead of Madeira on tl
homeward journey, but the traveller who trusts to luck and
not too pressed for time can often return home, comfortably ar
cheaply, on a cargo boat. In the interests of Madeira it is a pi
that this whole question of landing and taking off passenge
cannot be co-ordinated between the shipping companies, b
cause it is to some little extent a deterrent when planning a vi
to this most lovely of all islands.

Or you can arrive and go back by air. The flying boats of tl
Aquila Airlines make the entire journey in a summer night, takii
off from the Solent about midnight, coming down at Lisbo
and reaching Madeira in time for breakfast. During wint
months the flight takes place by day. It is a question of temper
ment as to whether you prefer to go by air or sea. To be waft
in a summer night (an English summer!) to a tropical or sem
tropical island is sensational enough, but it must be almost mo
magical to be taken there in as few hours of uneasy daylight ov
a lead-grey sea. This method of travelling has every advantag
There is no trouble, no bother, and no tipping; though it lacks tl
sea air and the restfulness of the sea voyage. It was just tho
considerations that persuaded us to make the outward journ
in the *Stirling Castle*, of the Union Castle Line, a ship whic
ten days or so after we had disembarked from her, having cross
the Equator would sight Table Mountain and cast anchor in tl
bay, after which comes the leisurely journey from port to port
Durban along the warmer waters of the Indian Ocean. How mai
tens of thousands of Englishmen have made the voyage to,
from, India and the Cape during two centuries and more, ar
landed at Madeira. This is perhaps the classic way of going ther
It gives a particular flavour to a journey to be on board a sh

hat is outward bound and but at the beginning of its voyage. While the rest of the passengers are playing their deck games one looks in the ship's library for books or papers from that further shore, willing to read hotel advertisements or even railway timetables during the long, lazy hours. But there were, too, the Cape wines to taste; and impossible while drinking them not to journey in imagination to the vineyards, stopping off for a few moments at the wine cellars of Groot Constantia, that old and beautiful whitewashed building in Dutch Colonial style, with sculptured pediment of bacchanalian scenes, standing in the cool green shadow of the oak trees, but steeped in the bright sunlight of another hemisphere.

Although it was early in August, there was mist and fog in the English Channel, which delayed our journey, and as well the ship developed engine trouble, so that instead of reaching Madeira on the afternoon of the third day out from England we arrived late at night, it was past midnight, and picked up the first lights on Porto Santo, Madeira's satellite island, just before eleven p.m. But the delay, though contrived by accident, was working in our favour. The lights of Porto Santo gave place gradually to those upon the mainland, and at last a whole galaxy disposed as in an amphitheatre announced Funchal. Rounding a headland, the whole town glittered before us at one o'clock in the morning, climbing up from sea level with lamp-lit roads zigzagging up into the hills. The ship slowed down, gliding noiselessly and with no apparent motion, and from nowhere an armada of little boats came out just as we cast anchor.

Each boat carried a naphtha flare like a bright torch, and had for occupants a rower and a boy to dive for pennies. There were thirty or forty of these little boats, as lively as fireflies, which had now to manœuvre in order to ride the wake and afterwash from our reversed engines, all heading with their bows in the right direction, and rising one after another as the waves reached them. It could be the arrival at some South Sea Island, and there is perhaps no other amphibious white population that comes out in this manner to meet passing vessels, ignoring night or day. This is an island habit and one that belongs, climatically, to the Fortunate Islands or Hesperides.

Now came the disembarcation. Customs and passport officials

swarmed aboard, and there were one or two owners of villa
with bunches of orchids for their friends. But it was remarkabl
how the feeling of arrival altered. Funchal was no longer a port
The armada or regatta of little rowing boats at half-past one i
the morning had some hint in it of arriving in Venice at th
height of the carnival, but as if that Adriatic city had been take
up bodily and set down in the parrot waters of the tropics. W
stepped into a launch, and saw that most of the inhabitants c
Funchal who were still awake were in those rowing boats
Funchal is not a big town. This was not an arrival at a city i
carnival, but a landing for the first time in our lives on a semi
tropical island in the middle of the night. It is this which is th
sensation of Madeira coming out from England. Not even th
first sight of the blue Mediterranean can rival with it. Fo
Madeira has its own climate. A few hours' sail away there wa
grey sea and sky. But here in a day or night's flying, or afte
three days at sea, is a sub-tropical island, and the balmy airs c
the tropics touch you and seem to brush against you as you com
ashore.

There is some novelty of sensation in landing from a big line
on an empty quay. It is a private and clandestine arrival, like
king stepping into exile and finding no one there to mee
him. Only a beggar or two, and a few of those late idlers who i
warmer climates seem to talk all night and never go to sleep
Now we were under the stone quay, jumping out on to th
weedy steps, and had set foot in Funchal. The town which a fe
moments ago looked from the sea as big as Naples or as Venic
dwindled into a country town upon a little island, and as quickl
grew into its own character and identity as we came under th
street lamps and saw the palm trees and the painted houses. W
were at the end of the pier where the taxis were waiting, an
two or three flower women dressed in the pretty local costum
with red skirts came forward with bouquets in their hands. Bu
it was too late to buy flowers and no one had small change. Th
flower-sellers were old women, good looking, but of an age tha
sanctioned them to be abroad so late at night. We were to knov
them very well, for they sold flowers in daytime at the door o
the hotel (8, 9). They greeted some of the other traveller
who landed with us as old friends from former visits t

7   A Distant View of Funchal, Madeira

8 Flower-sellers at Reid's Hotel, Funchal

9 Hydrangea-bearers

Madeira, and with artful innocence pressed the unsold bunches into their hands, waiving payment, a trick which was never, certainly, in the repertory of Italian beggars and street vendors. But this is an unspoilt population, perhaps the least tainted and contaminated of all peoples of European stock. The Madeirans are still in the age of innocence. In the hotels none of the servants wait about hoping to be tipped. The hotel manager will tell you that, when scolding them, he has to think seriously how not to hurt their feelings or he will get no work from them. If this giving of the flowers was kindness, not calculated cleverness, it certainly succeeded in that warm, unsullied night, for it seemed entirely in keeping with the first breath of Hesperidean air.

It would be difficult to imagine any experience more beautiful than the drive up from the harbour of Funchal, late at night, through avenues of palms and along streets planted with tropical trees and flowers. The night was warm and balmy; and there was little of architecture, but enough to show quickly the hand of Portugal which in touch and feeling is so different from the hand of Spain. It reveals itself in prettiness; being neither solemn, nor tragic, nor having the full gaiety of the South. This is the South in soft washes of colour, and buildings of basalt and whitewash. But one was too tired to take note of anything but the tropical trees and flowers and the tufted richness in the shape of all things growing. We climbed a long, broad avenue lined with villas, crossed a deep ravine, and were at the door of the hotel.

The windows of the bedrooms had gauze over them to keep insects away, and what a sensation it was to look out through that netting and see the moonlight falling on the sea and harbour and on the lights of Funchal; and then throw open the whole window, like an augmentation from minor into major in this Southern music, so that the unfamiliar and exotic forms of palm and cactus stood out against the moonlit sky! The lights of Funchal were still glittering. You could hear the waves, and then the noisy lifting of the anchor as the liner turned and headed for the Southern seas. That night it was a treat to sleep entirely luggage-less, not waiting for the baggage to be brought in the early hours of the morning and dumped inside the door. One fell asleep intending to think of tropical trees and flowers, of gardens in Honolulu,

49

tropical gardens that it is now practicable to lay out and plant
and that for the first time in history are within the arts of man
Inspired by the moonlight pouring through the window, I ha
wanted to think of gardens in Brazil where special play is mad
with the shadows of leaves and cactuses upon plain walls, o
Pacific gardens upon the blue bay of Acapulco, of the flowers o
Tahiti and the Marquesas, but with no more than the intentio
one fell fast asleep.

At six o'clock in the morning it was irresistible to get up from
bed and look out of window at this new world of the nigh
before. The dawn was completely golden, dropping in gold upo
the terraces and hills. I unhooked a shutter where it lay bac
along the wall, feeling that with life in it still warm from yester
day, and stayed there for a moment because the morning was s
beautiful; the huge arching firmament as blue as a bird's egg, bu
shaded like the dove's throat, as though you could touch it wit
your hand and stroke it back again to night.

Closing that one shutter, and leaning out to reach the other
the first light struck upon a building in the garden, and th
heavenly heat like a hot shadow crept along the earth. Then
went back to bed in the darkened room, and turned over, an
though the shutters were shut heard the dawn wind in the palm
boughs and the waves breaking, and fell into another kind o
sleep like that of coming home late from a party. It was te
o'clock in the morning when I woke, and for the rest of my firs
day in Madeira I felt I was an hour behind.

The gardens of Reid's Hotel lead down in terraces to the se
(7, 8), as far as an open air dining-room half-way down th
cliff, whence a lift takes you deeper through the rock down t
the bathing pool. Whole mornings and evenings go by, doin
nothing more than looking at the trees and flowers.

Geraniums and mesembryanthemums are easy of recognition
though nowhere else will you see such massed geraniums, lik
military bands, and the scented-leaved kinds growing, in variety
as high as a hedge of sweet briar. The mesembryanthemums, a
thick upon the ground as bindweed or ground elder, and in fac
much denser with their spines and lobes, were not in flower
This was August, one of the worst months in the year fo

Madeiran gardens. There were roses, too, but it was nearly
impossible to look at them.

For the hibiscus grows here in unimaginable colour and vitality.
It even appears to be not so much growing as hovering or
hanging upon the air, its pronounced stamens giving it the look
of a nectar-drinking bird, or humming-bird. It could be a flower
become a bird, and feeding on the air. There are not so many
kinds of hibiscus as I saw growing in Florida, where twenty-five
or thirty different varieties, all hybrids, grew in one garden.
But there was the pure white hibiscus; an apricot or nankeen
yellow; the dark red and the orange; and a hibiscus which was
pale rose-coloured and peculiarly lovely.

It is often said that the pæony takes the place of the rose in
Chinese gardens. In the gardens of the mandarins it was grown
and hybridized for many hundred years. It is probably true that
we have as yet little conception of what Oriental gardeners have
accomplished over many centuries with the pæony. But the hibiscus is the rose of tropical gardens. Like the modern rose it is
scentless; better scentless, though, than half-scented. For it is
one of the most flaunting of all flowers. It may never attain to the
refinements of the rose. Because that is not within its nature.
Perhaps it has already run the gamut of its possibilities. But
those, at least, are not yet widely known. No other flower but
the hibiscus flaunts its flamenco colours at such an angle in the
air. It is shameless and unafraid, not hiding in the leaves. It is not
long before you know the hibiscus to be the flower in Gauguin's
South Sea paintings. Those are his wild rose-bushes of the
Marquesas and Tahiti. His colours are conditioned by the
flowering hibiscus. It plays the rôle of the ilex in Claude's landscapes, where even if an ilex is not in the picture you feel the
dark glitter of the leaves. There is a hibiscus in every painting
by Gauguin where there are Polynesians, or 'Maories', as he
called them, and it is the flower of his Elysium or Hesperides.
Not less, we say, is it the rose of tropical or sub-tropical gardens,
flaunting, here in Madeira, its *Kanaka* colours.

There is nowhere within three or four thousand miles of
Europe where you may see the bougainvillea growing as in
Madeira. It is not to be known from its pale shadow in our con-
servatories. Here it climbs in all the profusion of the Polynesian

islands, and in different colours. The ordinary purple bougain
villea may grow beside one that is plum-coloured, or a maroon
or darker purple, and another that is terracotta or brick-red
This is the rarest, and not more than an occasional plant of it i
to be seen. But, also, the *Plumbago capensis*, the other 'exotic' o
the British glass-house, grows here on trellises, or covers a long
wall, its pale-blue stars as luxuriant as wistaria, and as thick a
jasmine. The rose-pink plumbago of Indian origin, lovely to thin
of, is apparently disappointing.

Geranium and mesembryanthemum, we say, are easy of recog
nition, because there are so many other flowers to which it i
impossible to put a name. But there are the pale-blue or whit
trumpets of the 'morning glories', always to be preferred to th
purple in which the undertone of red is too vibrant. In Portuga
'morning glories' 'swarm' over the kilometre cottages along
the railway lines, giving a lovely effect until you begin to tire o
this red constituent or under colour. The pale blues are much
more beautiful; and it becomes a fascination to watch the indi
vidual flower unfold early in the morning like an entire firma
ment, a blue empyrean of its own, and in the evening sag and lik
a celestial parachute droop down to earth. At night there will b
an entire palisade of 'falling glories'.

And there are the passion flowers; blue, or rosy mauve, o
blue and white.* Being August, the oleanders were in flower
'Laurier-rose', which is their French name, is as lovely soundin
as 'oleander', and perhaps oleander is more descriptive of th
white flower. A snowy whiteness seems to be spelt forth in th
syllables of oleander, and they quickly become lauriers-rose an
oleanders in the mind. But there are bignonias, too, red or cora
or orange trumpets, and it may be here for most persons tha
the unknown flowers begin.

Palm trees and cactuses grow as if the earth belonged to them
and have become so crossed and intermingled that you canno
tell which is palm and which is succulent. There is the form, fo
instance, that having a central trunk or stem appears to suppor
itself upon a bunch of sticks. It looks exactly as though an od

* The blue passion flower comes from Brazil and Peru. There is an ivory
white from Patagonia; and one would like to know the colours of Impératric
Eugénie, a hybrid of the Second Empire.

umber of sticks, mostly of the same length, had been leant
gainst it. They do not seem to grow out of the trunk, but to
ave been just put there. This can be no tropical rarity, for it
rows in many gardens in Florida. I do not know its name and
ave no idea of its country or origin. There is the sort that comes
ut of the soil on stilts and then converges to one stem. There
re candelabra cactuses, taller than seven-branched candlesticks;
nd as regular; and organ cactuses in a frenzy of self-protection,
ristling with spikes. Huge star cactuses grow by the stone steps.
hey have the look of giant fireworks; set pieces ready to burst
nto fire this one night only and hurl their sparks into the tropic
eas. Some must be Mexican, or South American; others
African, or from the jungles of Borneo, or Celebes.

But it is enough for one morning. We must go down to the
own and have a look at Funchal (7), not even stopping on the
way, for it is one long road of flowers. Funchal is a town with
ot much of distinction or interest yet that satisfies. Perhaps it is
ot quite as I pictured it with ten or fifteen thousand inhabitants,
ut a quarter of its real size, down in a shady hollow, with
treets and squares paved with pebble mosaic, and shaded by
all magnolia and jacaranda trees. The Portuguese, most roman-
ic minded of the colonizing races, were more interested in Goa
nd Macau. Madeira was too near home. For this reason there
re more and better buildings in The Azores than in Madeira.
Nevertheless, there are some pretty things in Funchal. It is worth
while entering the cathedral for the sake of the ceiling, which
overs aisle and both naves, and is work of the 16th Century of
edar wood inlaid with ivory, in Mudéjar style. Or is it of
Madeiran juniper? For it is variously described. A little higher
up the hill are the best buildings in Funchal, in the Praça do
Município, which has at one side the Câmara or Town Hall, a
ormer palace, and at the next corner the Jesuit church or
Colégio, with gilded altars. Both buildings are whitewashed, with
windows and corner stones of black basalt, and the Câmara has a
courtyard and a pleasing stair. There is little else in Funchal
except souvenir shops and wine lodges.

But, indeed, in Funchal every prospect leads to flowers. It is
ime wasted to stay away from them. The streets are lined with
acaranda trees; not in flower, of course, in August except for a

stray blossom here and there, lacking the jacaranda blueness, an
giving no idea at all of their beautiful and incredible flowering i
spring. For the jacaranda blossoms before it comes into leaf.
is a tree which turns blue in a single night. A blue like that c
the heliotrope, but with a touch in it of 'powder blue'; and t
see a tree as big as a fair-sized oak-tree covered with individu.
flowers shaped like the trumpet of a fox-glove or a gentian, an
yet, as a whole, light and feathery in effect, as 'powdery' an
graceful as a spray of mimosa, later, indeed, when the leave
come, they much resemble mimosa leaves, is one of the beautifu
sights of the world.* But there are now plantings of jacarandas i
tropical cities all over the world, in East and South Africa an
the Congo, in Egypt, India, Malaya, and Australia, and perhap
no one realizes the full beauty of the jacaranda who does no
experience it, consciously, for the first time.

But there are more sensations in store in Funchal. Half-wa
down the main street there is a little public garden. Till recently
this was bigger in size, but in order to widen the avenue muc.
of it was swept away. It is a sub-tropical garden of transcendenta
interest which to flower lovers 'is, alone, worth the journey t
Madeira. Few, if any, of its trees and flowers are indigenous t
the island. They have been brought from all quarters of th
tropics and sub-tropics. So unique is this exotic garden that it ha
been made the subject of a special little book or brochure b
Madeira's learned and 'old style' botanist and historian in th
second generation, Mr. Grabham, who explores it, pains
takingly, in quarters, and in fact the entire garden must no mor
than cover the area of four tennis courts set side by side. In on
corner, making it smaller still, is a dark pond shaded by dan
ferns and banyan trees, an impenetrable jungle through whicl
19th Century explorers in sun-glasses and pith-helmets should b
hacking their way as in old illustrations to stories by Jules Verne

---

* The jacaranda is of Brazilian origin. It is a fine and valuable timber wood
and it may have been with the feeling that the jacaranda tree was worthy of th
Temple of Solomon that the community of Portuguese Jews in Amsterdam
built the great *hechal* or cupboard to hold the rolls of the law in their synagogue
For it is built like an architectural frontispiece, with pillars supporting obelisks
all of jacaranda brought from Brazil, and one of the remaining relics of Dutcl
rule in Pernambuco.

could be in skit or parody upon the stove-houses of Victorian days, dimly remembered with their steamy heat and wet, damp doors.

But this lilliput of the tropics, for the rest, is more brilliant than if flowering in a hundred climates of its own. In the middle of one plot there grows a tufted, rounded tree of shining leaves, as compact as a bay-tree, twenty or twenty-five feet high, protruding red-orange flowers, in quantity, some dropped upon the ground, that, when handled, are open cups the shape and size of tulips. This is *Spathodea nilotica*, the Uganda flame tree, habitat, Lake Victoria basin in Uganda, reputed among the most beautiful of flowering trees, though one authority remarks that it can look common and vulgar if the flamboyant, *Delonix regia* (syn. *Poinciana regia*) is in flower beside it. But the flamboyant will not come into flower in Madeira. And where the jacaranda and the flamboyant flower, side by side, as at Durban and in East Africa, there, we may be certain, some other flowering tree will fail and not reach maturity.*

For the flamboyant with its scarlet flowers is said to be the only worthy rival of the jacaranda, both of them being suited particularly for planting in long avenues. Having seen the jacaranda one is the more regretful of missing the flamboyant, which must be one of the beauties of the world not personally experienced. There are differing opinions of their merits; but knowing the jacaranda, the sight of which is like a divine revelation of a new world of harmony and proportion, one may guess the flamboyant to be hard hitting and exultant like loud music. It must, however, be exact in pitch and of the purest tone or it could not put to shame the Uganda flame tree, *Spathodea nilotica*, which with its trimmed shape and cupped red-orange flowers looks like a park tree, but from a celestial game preserve. It reminds one of Hieronymus Bosch's *Garden of Earthly Delights*, a panel of his great triptych in the Prado, where figures of naked innocence, a black man and a negress among them, walk in the earthly paradise. Just so would be one of the flowering trees in paradise.

* There is ever a shortcoming even in the most favourable climate. At Palm Beach, in Florida, in midst of the only sub-tropical climate in the United States, camellias will not grow, although they are prolific, or even endemic, at Charleston, South Carolina, and in Louisiana.

Another wonder is the frangipani. This is a low tree, not muc
taller than a human being, entirely formal, even artificial i
growth, shaped like a coral tree, or it more nearly resembles
tree carved, painstakingly, out of sandalwood. The branche
that is to say, look as though they should be of fragrant woo
and it is curious to the touch, being neither wood, nor vegetabl
as if formed from some sea-substance. It is twiggy and brittle
though it would snap into little pieces, most intricate of patter
and nearly crustacean in the manner of its growing. Leave
large, and long and glabrous, flat, but not hairy, more resem
bling fins, or penguin or turtle flippers, except that they ar
flatter still and could be palmate fans. Moreover, the leaves ar
disproportionately few. As though the frangipani kept all i
energies for flowering.

The habitat of the frangipani is in Mexico and Guatemala.
is somewhat of a rarity in Madeira, always an object of intere
as though there were legends attaching to it, and looking
though it had the power of motion like one of the race of spe
trally thin and elongated spiders, or could be blown over th
ground towards you like a ball of thistledown. This, in a tre
six or eight feet high, and as static as a twig of coral. Cou
Frangipani is reputed to have been a Florentine nobleman famou
in the 17th Century for inventing scents, and somehow the nam
suits both Florentine and flowering tree. It is now a legend, an
become the sister to patchouli and opoponax. All know its nam
but few have touched a frangipani tree. The flowers are
though formed of seashells, as unreal as the tree that bears then
and indeed inspiring some other name than flowers; of a textu
like double cream, vegetable, withal, and leathery, but lik
leather of underbelly, and of elusive scent. There appear to h
two sorts of frangipani, a pure white and a yellow with othe
tints in it, as there could be in seashells. It is the yellow that ha
the stronger scent. You may have the feeling that the race
frangipanis is so old that the scent has nearly gone out of then
or that they need the spiced airs of their own hot valleys, but th
scent is something ineffable, when you get it, older, deepe
warmer, than tuberose or gardenia, a scent that fulfils its nam
and paints the legend.

Hibiscus, agapanthus, oleander, all were in flower; and ther

56

10   Fishing Boats on the beach at Câmara de Lôbos, Madeira

vas 'Pride of India', blue-mauve or pale crimson, like a livelier, ut scentless lilac tree. *Spathodea nilotica* was fading from one day o another. We were but in time to see it. So many other trees nd flowers were not in season. It was the first taste of a world nknown. But there were palm trees and cactuses; and the grass elow them was 'Kikuyu' grass, from East Africa, stitched into he soil, blade by blade, as though sewing a fleece rug, but it then nakes 'runners', springy to the step, with a consistency like hat of the mattresses used by acrobats when they alight from one rapeze or set of parallel bars and bounce up into another. This arden must be uniquely wonderful in the early months of the ear. There is probably no other garden in the temperate world vhere are to be seen so many tropical and sub-tropical trees and lowers. Civilization, should it continue, with cheapening air ravel coming into prospect, may be but at the beginning of an ra of tropical gardening, in Africa, Central and South America, nd many other regions, and what an opportunity is here for a ainter to produce a book of tropical trees and flowers! This was ot beyond the capabilities of the Victorians, when we remember ould's *Humming Birds*, undertaken with so few facilities over a eriod of so many years. But there is no comparable book on ropical flowers; no coloured plate of jacaranda, flamboyant, or Iganda flame tree!

Where the bridge crosses the ravine coming out of Funchal 1 the direction of Reid's Hotel a richness of vegetation begins hat is quite tropical. You look down on banana palms and caranda trees, and close by, waiting in the shade of some tall ld plane trees, there are a bullock sledge or two, relics of what vere not long ago the only vehicles up and down the cobbled treets. Here are walls on which bougainvillea and plumbago run iot. But many of the villas have allamanda growing on them, a ellow hibiscus-like climber, but with no stamens, a plant oming from Brazil and tropical America, superbly bold and andsome with big wide flowers. How warm and languorous are he images it calls to mind! The allamanda is another colour of auguin in this tropic scene, one of the *Kanaka* colours of his 'olynesians, rubbed yellow with tumeric oil and crowned with owers.

Walking away from Funchal along the coast road you come to

59

banana groves and groves of sugar-cane. The tropical richness
nearly indescribable, the forms are as thick as figures in mediaeva
tapestry, and the Hesperidean orchards come down and touc
upon the sea. Here and there, with aerial gourds hung in thei
branches, are paw-paw trees. And walking for half an hour yo
reach a corner and look down on the small fishing port o
Câmara de Lôbos (11), where you see the boats drawn up an
beached in the little harbour overhung with painted houses
Câmara de Lôbos has exactly the proportions of a stage setting
as though it could be transferred and set down upon a stage. Th
boats are in the harbour during the day, but towards evening th
nets are put up and in the language of the theatre you may watc
this from the wings. They are hoisted like tents or pyramids int
the boats ready for the night's fishing (10), the catch bein
espada, "a sort of large pitch-black eel having the whitest fles
inside", as tender as sole or whiting, and much eaten i
Madeira. Just at this corner, looking down upon the fishin
village, a road climbs steeply up, as it were, 'into the flies', an
in a moment or two you are in the mountains.

Now are to be seen the extraordinary system of terracing, an
the *levadas* or water courses by which the hillsides are irrigated
Tall reeds or *canas* grow along the sides of the ravines. Banan
glades and groves of sugar-cane are left below, and we are in th
territory of the trellised vines. They overhang both sides of th
road and must be twelve or fifteen feet high, taller than any vin
but those in sight of Vesuvius in the *campagna felice*, which is th
plain of Naples. But the grand vines of Madeira, giving tente
shade, slope back from the road. They are like rows of ope
booths with low entrances where you can but crawl inside, the
trellises heavy with the black grapes; grapes, grapes, to left an
right, and every way you look, so that with a loaf of bread a da
you could live in luxury for days on end and eat nothing else bu
the black bunches. Hereabouts, on the wall of a villa, the fou
or five sorts of bougainvilleas are growing all together, and th
road climbs high enough to see the water coursing and bubblin
in the *levadas*, a few inches or a foot or two across. Each terrac
or 'landing' has water laid to it with ant-like industry, and ther
are flights of steps cut in the soft volcanic rock or tufa; 'landings
of wheat, or orange or lemon 'landings', for the terraces ar

often no bigger than when you step out from the lift-door in a block of flats. Before long the road has climbed so high that it is the region of fir trees, and we are nearing Cabo Girão, the highest headland in the world except for one in Norway. The car stops, and you have to get out and walk a few steps towards a balcony built out over the cliff. It is a fall of two thousand feet, not a slope or glacis, but a sheer drop down to a narrow strip of sand, just too far to throw a stone into the water, but near enough to look down a great depth and see a great fish, or the shadow of a fish, gliding in the deep. Begging here in the high air was an old crone, bent with age and walking with both hands on a stick. She was barefooted, and wore a black cloak and frayed skirt of white homespun, the only person we saw wearing this traditional dress of the Madeirans during our stay in the island.

A drive in another direction takes you to Camacha, where grow the willows and where the baskets and wickerwork are made. It is also the village of the flower-sellers, who walk all the way down to Funchal carrying baskets of flowers upon their heads. The roads are bordered with blue and white agapanthus, and beyond lies another and different landscape, not terraced, for it is a high plateau. This is towards the North coast of the island, where there are excursions that can take five days by foot, or three days, partly on foot and part by car. Some of the population here have never been to Funchal and must be the least spoilt of European peoples. It is this North coast which has the finest scenery. Arco de São Jorge is a village with a golden church in Dom João V style, the only one on the island, and it is famous, too, for its wild pineapples. Another village, Queimadas, has a special repute for its pink orchids. Many of the cottages in these villages have handlooms and every district had, once, its subtle differences of costume. Such villages are written of from hearsay, not having been visited personally, but the road from Camacha took us on towards the North coast, for we wanted to see the villages that are surrounded by hydrangea hedges. By some botanical or, rather, mineralogical contradiction, that I do not understand, these hydrangeas have coloured themselves in the inverse sense to their behaviour in European gardens, where sulphate of iron is put into their soil to turn them from pale pink to blue. Here, they are blue naturally, and it is said that sulphate of iron has to be put into the soil to make them pink again. Santana has the tallest hedges of hydrangeas, they are ten feet high, but although we saw other villages with hydrangea hedges and earthy banks planted with geraniums and arum lilies we could not penetrate as far as Santana because the new road was under construction. Begonias and huge heliotropes and mesembryanthemums grow round the peasants' cabins. It is even said that arum lilies are scythed and thrown for straw into the cow byres.

We were rewarded, however, by seeing something exceptional even in this flowery island. Where the road ended short of a bridge that was being built we scrambled up the bank and looked over it in the direction of Santana, down to the sea and over to some pinnacled, fantastic mountains, and as we looked there passed a few feet under us along the road three men running with the peculiar steps of those who carry loads down from the hills, and they were entirely buried and weighed down with blue hydrangeas. You could not see their heads, or faces, and the flowers came down below their waists (9). They looked, not like feathered Indians but like flowery messengers, or running *caciques*. The Mayan Indians had men who ran in this manner for incredible distances along the raised causeways carrying gifts for their kings or chiefs, and the three men who were on their way to a flower festival in one of the villages along the coast resembled Indians from a carved monolith, conventionalized, as in the sculptures, to a hieroglyph of flowers and feathers.

There are no vineyards in this part of the island, and August is too early anyway for the pressing of the grapes. This is done in the villages, and then the new wine or must is brought to Funchal by ox-sledge, or in small boats along the coast. However, the Lodge of the Madeira Wine Growers can be visited all the year round. The interior courtyards with their wooden galleries recall the *fondouks* in Moroccan towns. There are giant barrels, some of them a hundred and fifty years old and worthy of wine cellars in the Abbey of Thelema. Part of the building with cobbled paving was, once, one of the main streets of Funchal; there are carpenters' shops where wooden staves for the pipes or casks are shaped, and a room half-bar, half-refectory, in which to taste Sercial and Boal and the nectarous Malvazia of 1808 or 1833.

The Wine Lodge is reminiscent of old prints of Madeira. Those are mostly coloured lithographs of 1830–50 and of English origin, minor works of art that are delightful hung along a passage. Their value, aesthetically, is about that of the gouache paint-ings of the Bay of Naples, and it is of the old kingdom of The Two Sicilies that one is inevitably reminded. There is much of Naples, always excepting the Volcano and the taran-tella; maybe, a spike of flowering cactus in the foreground and a group of white-clad peasants. The men wore white, the white of Pulcinella, but it was homespun cloth, not linen; white shirts and breeches, and they affected a knitted cap with a peak or crown, little worn now, but still sold in the souvenir shops of Funchal, which exactly resembles the peaked cap of the *Roi d'Yvetôt* in Picasso's etching. This gives them in the prints the air of jugglers or acrobats, and you may still get the taste of this at sight of an old man in a peaked cap sitting in some remote village outside his cabin, or when a small boy wears one of the peaked hats and he is transformed, instantly, into a child harle-quin of Picasso's 'blue period'. The red women's dresses, subtly differenced for each village, are only worn now by the flower-sellers.

Island excursions in Madeira are still like those you may read of in old travel books on Naples of a hundred years ago. There are no railways on the island. Many villages are still inaccessible by motor, and the trips recommended by Mr. Grabham and other island *literati* must resemble those undertaken by English travellers to see classical ruins in Southern Italy and Sicily. There are rest houses in which to stay the night, and motors, where the road allows of it; but no antiquities, and perhaps the other main difference is that there are no monks. Old books on the island of a hundred years ago are already deploring that the excellent conserves and sweetmeats were no longer made by the nuns in Funchal. They were famed for these, as they were in Portugal, but this was a tradition coming down from the 18th Century and forming another parallel with Southern Italy and Sicily. All travellers noticed the skill of the nuns, particularly in the convents of Palermo, and have left appetizing accounts of

their conserves and ices. Country trips in Madeira, we say, are
reproductions in miniature of excursions into Magna Grecia.

Much more could be written on this subject; and of how not
only the making of wine and the growing of sugar-cane, but the
craft of basket-making and even the Madeiran embroidery were
started and given impetus from England. But, also, tropical
fruits, the guava and the avocado, were introduced by Englishmen, and it was our countrymen who brought trees and flowering
shrubs to Madeira from all over the world. Indigenous trees and
plants are few in number. The *til* or Madeiran ebony is probably
the most handsome of the native trees. But Englishmen have
brought plants and trees to Madeira for nearly two centuries. A
tulip tree planted by Captain Cook is still growing in the Quinta
do Val; and Veitch, the British Consul in Madeira, laid out
gardens and was responsible more than any other one person for
extending and altering the island flora. Many of the quintas are
a hundred and fifty and more years old, and the tallest magnolia
trees in the world are to be admired in Funchal.

The most famous and beautiful of the gardens is the Quinta do
Palheiro, laid out by a French landscape gardener at the end of
the 18th Century for the Conde de Carvalhal, who built the fine
palace in Funchal that is now the Town Hall. For five generations
since then, Palheiro has been the property of the Blandy family.
It lies high in the hills above Funchal, at an altitude that does no
permit of the flamboyant or the jacaranda. But other trees and
plants thrive in its temperate climate. There is a tulip tree close
to the house as big as a large plane tree, and this must be a
unique sight when it is in flower. *Clethra arborea*, the lily-of-the
valley tree, which is indigenous to Madeira, dangles its scentless
sprays which would deceive bees from a wood where the true
lily of the valley grows. There are 'bottle-brushes', as tall as oak
or sycamores, that must be marvellous in their season when lit
and burning with red cockscomb flowers; and another Australian
tree, a flowering eucalyptus, grown from seed brought from
Africa, thus much has it travelled, which, when examined in
detail, looks as though an olive, or a half-olive, had taken it in
mind to sprout into a tuft or wig or chevelure, much like the
flower of an artichoke, but of an indescribable carroty, but
cinnamon brick-red. The leaves of this eucalyptus are streaked

r even variegated, but have no eucalyptus smell, and it would
e an accomplished botanist who recognized the flowers. Other
ommonplaces of this garden are *Stanhopeas* or vanilla orchids,
owers more deserving to be called animal than vegetable for they
ppear to be possessed of beaks and eyes, are dappled or stippled
oft chocolate-brown on white, and smell, authentically, of
anilla. Palheiro, like so few gardens of great botanical interest,
as the beauties of formal planting to give it form and line. And
he care of its owners keeps it full of botanical splendours and
uriosities, among the most recent of them being an agapanthus
rom one of the lakes of Central Africa which is darker blue than
he normal flower.

Towards the end of our few days in Madeira more flowering
rees came into season. It was sensationally beautiful to walk
ack from Funchal on a particular evening and notice a tall tree
vhich was in flower. This was the bombax, with a flower like a
ose-pink starfish. It appeared from below to be shaped exactly
ike a starfish, for it was high up among the leaves. One writer
ays of the bombax that "in June some superb specimens, their
ew foliage the colour of flame or of daffodils, tower over the
valls and gardens of Funchal", and mentions the bombax next
o the delicate blue of the jacaranda. That would be in spring or
arly summer. During August the foliage was pale green, and
ooking up into the bombax, which was high as a tall acacia tree,
t was difficult to see the flowers for they lay so near the light,
apping against it like so many starfishes lying on the sands, now
ust to be seen in colour and outline against that golden ground,
nd then lifted entire and bodily into the blue empyrean. I did
ot know the habitat of the bombax and only conjectured it was
ndian. In the garden of another villa across the road there was a
ate flowering *Spathodea nilotica* or Uganda flame tree which, by
ow, was connected in my mind with images of Africa. In con-
rast, the flat pink flowers of the bombax seemed like emblems
of another continent. They were in the same tint of colour as a
ink *sari*. It is from the silk or floss of the bombax after its
lowering that kapok is made, and the waistcoats or 'Mae Wests'
hat kept so many sailors and airmen afloat in icy seas were made
of this vegetable substance deriving from the bombax tree.
omewhere there must be huge bombax plantings or forests,

perhaps where elephants dress the planks of teak wood and
arrange them in order with their trunks? Would there be
palaces of pink marble with latticed casements to look out on the
peacock waters; or does the bombax come from Burma, where
the women dress in bright colours, their mouths are stained red
from chewing betel, and they smoke black cheroots?

But a more particular treat was in store for our last night in
Funchal. The gardens of the hotel have in one place an outer
wall or ramp, at the edge of the cliff looking deep down into the
sea, and this wall was entirely covered with a thick growth of
jag-edged leaves, but they more resembled long, jointed vegetable
limbs with spiked or toothed edges. Their purpose must be that
of the spiked rail or the broken glass put on top of a wall to
prevent persons from climbing over. The vegetable limbs, which
suggested two-edged swords with toothed blades, or the
weapon of a swordfish (the blade of Xiphias), or even the
tentacles of an octopus, had so grown over and into one another
and were so entangled as to form a thorny hedge or protective
zariba along the length of the wall. The texture of the spiny
stems was pithy, like that of the green lobes of the mesembryan
themum, and it was a surprise to see, here and there, great buds
with tasselled and pointed ends. Was this an orchid or a cactus?
We passed it each time we climbed down to, or up from the sea.
A friend in the hotel, without telling us, each day cajoled the buds
trying to split the calyx and coax the flower to open. On our
last night he succeeded, and we saw the Queen of the Night, or
Night-blowing Cereus, in flower, a huge blossom like a phantom
water-lily, large enough to lie by itself in a cup or vase, and
looking, at once, like a chalice for drinking nectar, and like the
prototype of a starry constellation.

The Queen of the Night is of wax-like texture, thin as candle
wax that flakes off from the hand, and wholly incredible in the
elaboration of its petals, the cup or chalice of the flower having
its lower segments or flanges folded back to form a base or
socket out of which the goblet rises, shaped from row after row
of exquisite, white, glistening flakes or petals. The fragility of
this white flower is such that you hardly dare to touch it. In all
probability it is pollinated by moths, and for its lifespan of a
night only has created for itself this wondrous and ghostly shape

beauty to the end that those fluttering night-wanderers should
e drawn into the snowy chambers and stay long enough to
ecome, themselves, messengers of pregnancy from flower to
ower.

Early next morning the Queen of the Night had shrunk and
rivelled. It had gone in a single night from the bloom of youth
o dishonoured and decrepit age. For at six o'clock in the
morning, having stood for a last moment on the terrace outside
ur window in order to look once more at the tropical trees and
owers, at the hibiscus and frangipani, at the bougainvillea and
e bombax, it was time to go down to the harbour and climb into
e flying boat, and be off to Lisbon. Coming through the room,
e Queen of the Night had not outlived the dawn; it was quite
ead and faded. But the flying boat scudded along, raising with
a crest or mane of foam, and climbed into the sky. Madeira lay
eneath, and in a moment or two was left behind. So were the
ropical trees and flowers of that lovely and unspoilt island, and
was little consolation to be told in a letter that thirty of forty
ueens of the Night were in blossom the next evening, like so
any nectar cups or starry clusters.

II

LISBON

THE beautiful way to arrive at Lisbon is by flying boa
Coming by any of the other airlines you touch down
Portela Airport, and miss the sensation of gliding up tl
Tagus parallel to the city. Only four hours after leaving Madeir
we sight land along the South side of the river, not passing ov
Cascais and Estoril, but nearing Lisbon all of a sudden by tl
Tower of Belém a few hundred feet below, coming lower sti
past the long, white buildings of the Abbey, and yet lower alor
the wharves and by the painted houses, looking down upon tl
square with the statue of the King Dom José in plumed hel
and breastplate riding his long-tailed circus horse (13), low
still by the masts of the fishing boats, and still lower out of Lisbc
at the other end of the town to where there are only oil tan
and derricks, and now, down, down into the water with
ruffling of foam, and we are safe and sound in Portugal on
burning August morning.

It is a fine experience, too, to reach Lisbon by sea. There w
be more to say of this later, for Lisbon is the loveliest of all wat
towns and it is our intention to sail home from Portugal upon
liner. But the approach by flying boat only compares in complet
ness and rounded fullness of feeling to that moment when tl
aeroplane makes a half-circle round the dome of St. Peter's, ar
in another few moments you have arrived in Rome. Think
flying up the Thames from Greenwich, past St. Paul's and tl
Houses of Parliament, and over Chelsea and Hammersmith Read
as far as Hampton Court, and you will have the sensation of tl
arrival up the Tagus!

But Lisbon is more compact, and smaller. The traject is
matter of moments, and you see the history of Portugal out of
porthole. The Tower of Belém, with sentry boxes like stor
pepper-pots built out of the Tagus by an architect who had mac
toy forts just of this nature in Morocco, stands on the beac
from which Vasco da Gama sailed in 1497, doubling The Cap
reaching Calicut, and returning from India to Lisbon two yea

er with a cargo of spices which sold in the market for sixty
nes the expenses of the voyage. Oriental riches helped to build
e Abbey of Belém; while the statue of Dom José stands for the
her era of prosperity in Portugal, and reflects the 18th Century
ld and diamonds of Brazil. Behind his statue are the steep hills of
e city; and if you reach Lisbon by train, perhaps by the long
awn Sud-Express from Paris, you crawl slowly down a tunnel
ore than two miles long and emerge at a most peculiar railway
ation in neo-Manoelino style, disconcertingly small as a termi-
s, where the platforms are on the second floor and you have
descend to the street by lift, or down two flights of steps.
obably this is the best method to appreciate that Lisbon is a
lly town. But whatever way you arrive here, not least, coming
to the town by road, there is the knowledge that Lisbon is at
e end of Europe, faces on the Atlantic Ocean, and leads to
frica, India, and Brazil.

Coming out from the station we are in the Rossio or main
uare of Lisbon, deafened by the cries of newspaper boys and
llers of lottery tickets, and jostled off the pavement by the all-
ale crowds outside the cafés. This is not the attractive view of
isbon. To all the noise and hubbub is added the shrill clanging
d groaning of the trams. The shop windows are not particularly
aticing. You look everywhere for a restaurant and do not find
ne, even forcing a way into the cafés only to discover no corner
here you can eat. There is universal consumption of ices and
ttle cups of coffee, but solid food and drink are as difficult to
cate as in a country town in England late at night. Probably
ere is no foreigner of any nationality who does not regret his
rst experience of the Rossio. It lies in a pit or cauldron at the
ottom of the town, with not a breath of sea air, hemmed in by
uildings on steep hills. Moreover, it is an old-fashioned roar and
ubbub. Recently, the black and white mosaic pavement which
ave it character has been taken up and removed, "*pour la
acilité de la circulation*", which could be translated, in order to
hake the Rossio even uglier and more noisy still.

But there are, of course, excellent and first-rate restaurants
ust round the corner, two or three of them within a few yards
f the Rossio. The reaction comes quickly. In fact, the Rossio
s formed of plain 18th Century buildings, which no one takes it

into his head to notice, and it is only that the noise and t
immediate ugliness are that of Cannon Street or Charing Cr
Station, of the Gare St. Lazare, or of the overhead railway whi
runs down Fourth Avenue in New York City. And in a mat
of moments you can walk out of the Rossio in any direction a
regain calm and equilibrium, if not quiet, for Lisbon is nev
silent. It is perhaps the noisiest of all cities, after Brussels,* t
with this consolation and this much to explain it, that it is a c
in the sun.

The quickest way out of the Rossio is down one of the thr
streets leading to the Tagus; Rua do Ouro or Rua Aurea (Gc
Street), Rua da Prata (Silver Street), and Rua Augusta (which
the street in the middle, under the Triumphal Arch),
pointing to the river and to 'Black Horse Square', the old Engli
nickname for the Terreiro do Paço, with its statue of Dom Jc
I, seen, lately, like a toy soldier from the window of the aer
plane. But it is, in fact, a green horse; the bronze equestri
statue is verdigrised with age and the sea-breezes. Machado
Castro was the sculptor, a name that the Portuguese glide in
three syllables, Ma-Chad-Castr . . . , and numerous little carv
wooden figures of native types and holy persons from his hand a
to be seen in Lisbon, much resembling, indeed, the figures fro
Neapolitan *crèches* or *presepe* of the 18th Century. But, in th
equestrian statue, Machado de Castro is more grand and fo
midable. The King Dom José rides forward proudly, as in th
manège or *haute école*, his helm magnificently plumed, his cloa
falling from his shoulders to the horse's flanks, not too 'Roman
but a King of Portugal of the 18th Century, with a Hapsbur
mother, in fact, the Roman Emperor of the Riding School (13
It is to the theatrical masques and entertainments of the Cour
staged by Italian scenographers of the Bibiena school, that th
statue attaches, just as it is related, too, to the golden coache
of Belém. Perhaps it is the most beautiful equestrian statue c
the 18th Century, but the square, itself, though an admirabl
setting for the statue, does not deserve the encomiums tha
have been lavished upon it. The Piazza of St. Mark's is not to b
compared to it; nor the Place Stanislas at Nancy, nor the diamon
shaped square of the Amalienborg at Copenhagen. What is rar

* By day; but motor drivers are not allowed to hoot their horns at night.

inimitable, here, is the sunlight. You can walk down to the
rus at the far end of the square and not be able to look at the
bank in detail because of the glare and quiver of the heat. It
s here that the King Dom Carlos and his family landed from
Royal barge on that February morning in 1908, coming back
m shooting at Vila Viçosa, and a few moments later the King
l his elder son were killed by pistol shots at the far corner,
the General Post Office. Queen Amélie stood up in the
riage and tried to shield them with her body. It is undeniable
t some aura of that horrid scene clings to the square, even
on a blazing day in August.

Walking back along the narrow streets one can never entirely
get that murder, and absent-mindedly, or in the wrong mood,
y not notice Yardley's Old Lavender Water and the hundred
er products of England in the shops, or have been long
ough, perhaps, in Portugal to appreciate the smoked hams of
aves and Lamego hanging in the grocers' windows. But the
t shops in Lisbon are in the Rua Garrett, or Chiado, which
approach from a corner of the Rossio up the Rua Nova do
mo, climbing steeper and steeper, then turning dramatically
right-hand angle. The Rua Garrett, too, is hysterically pre-
itous and steep, with two or three late 18th Century churches
rcely worth the trouble of entering, although they have
ted ceilings. The interest of the Chiado is more human.
re is, for instance, the tobacco shop, the Casa Havanesa, "*où
flâneurs se portent de préférence*" in the words of the French
de-book, and indeed the "jeunesse dorée", past and present,
it includes some veterans, is on duty on the pavement. There
cafés where the most excellent ices are sold; and one of the
t shoe and leather shops in Europe with a little shop-front
l interior fittings that anywhere else would be termed Empire
Regency, but that, being Portugal, may date from much
er still. Among the major fascinations of 'window shopping'
Lisbon, especially in the Chiado, must be numbered the
cers and greengrocers, combined under one roof, and dis-
ying glorious bunches of grapes, melons, and the peaches of
obaça. There are, as well, all the different sorts of *marmelada*
conserve of quinces, and enough jars of jam and marmalade to
vince one that these are, in origin, a Portuguese invention.

71

But we will leave Bond Street or Fifth Avenue for the poo
quarters. The old market has been pulled down in the last ye
or two, and this was one of the picturesque sights of Lisb
because of its pineapples and sellers of caged birds; pineapp
hung up in hundreds, dwindling in the distance till they looked
bigger than fircones, and all coming from The Azores. In t
Lisbon restaurants there is a special instrument which will pe
a pineapple and present it to you, entire, without its skin,
emblem of this city where pineapples sell for as little as sixpen
The caged birds sold in Lisbon are chiefly parakeets. There i
beautiful variety coming from São Tomé, the island in the G
of Guinea, where the best chocolate in the world is grown, a
which has belonged to Portugal since 1470. The parakeet
green, with a scarlet head, though the hen bird's head is pal
with a square-cut tail of black and yellow, and lovely touches
a cerulean blue under the wings, when those are opened. 1
cock bird, like an acrobat, crawls along the roof of its cage w
beak and claws, which the hen bird will not do, reflecti
maybe, with its wise eyes that it is a 'man's game'. Both bir
however, have the habit of hanging head downwards in th
cage; and in the bird shops dozens of them are to be seen,
clusters, heads downward, as must be their habit among
tropical trees and flowers. How sad that with the rule agai
the import of parrots put into force again we could not br
the pair of these little birds back with us to England! T
would have been destroyed, we were told, instantly on arri
Another, and lovely variety of parakeet to be seen in the b
shops, comes from Mozambique, with nearly as much of ce
lean blue in its plumage as the São Tomé parakeet has green. '
flower and fish markets were not less wonderful, though
spectacular, now, in their new buildings. For no longer, in
phrase of the French guide-book, is this "un coin pittoresq
digne d'arrêter un aquarelliste." How beautiful, though, it u
to be! Much earlier in the year the flower-stalls have the magi
cent and sensational Iris Susiana for sale, huge silvery-g
flowers with black veins and dottings. But not even Iris Susi
looks at its most splendid in an ugly modern building.

All over the town touches of colour are given to the str
by the *varinas* or fishwives, walking, barefoot, with strai

cks, and balancing the creels of fish on their heads (15). Salted
d dried cod or *bacalhau*, the national dish of Portugal, is their
aple merchandise. They are called *varinas* because they come
om Ovar, a fishing town further up the coast, below Oporto.
hey have a marked physical resemblance to each other, are of
bust physique, and often wear round their shoulders a shawl of
at particular dark, olive green which is so popular with the
ortuguese that, in retrospect, it becomes the colour of Portu-
l. With fine clarion voices they cry out their wares. It is clear
at the *varinas* are a race apart, and one willingly agrees to the
eory that like others of the fishing population they are of
hoenician descent.

But their stentorian cries are not the only music of the
reets. There are the pan-pipes of the knife-grinders. Heard
ore often in the early mornings, and sounding like as many
apagenos, they become a lovely embodiment of the heat and
nlight, and always there is another knife-grinder piping at the
orner. One gets to recognize their flutings. Has each knife-
rinder his peculiar call? You look out of the window, and all
ou see is a nondescript young man in a beret, wheeling his
rrow, and holding the pan-pipes in his hand. As soon as one
ating moves out of earshot another begins. What a lovely
emory they are of hot mornings! All the knife-grinders are
aniards (*Gallegos*) coming from two small villages in Galicia,
d brothers or cousins to the knife-grinders to be heard in every
anish town, but more especially in Seville. Every now and
en you pass Gypsy women in the streets of Lisbon, to be known
once by their tawny skins, always of their own hue of smoky,
ltry darkness, by their walk which is different from that of any
her race in the world, and by their long skirts touching on the
vement. They do not dance or sing like the Spanish Gitanos,
t tell fortunes and are engaged in all the other Gypsy wiles. It
as interesting to pass in the Rossio a splendid Gypsy brother and
ster hurrying, flauntingly, among the crowd, beside them an old
ergyman, on holiday from England, hobbling, his summer straw
t in his hand, in a trembling agony of vacancy. His glance
sted upon them, in the true meaning of the phrase, and cer-
inly they looked at him; and who is to decide which was the
ore unlikely and improbable of these apparitions?

73

The steeper parts of Lisbon are what put it apart, almos
from other towns. Some of the streets could be compared t
switchbacks or mountain railways, paved with cobbles, but th
noisy trams climb indefatigably even here. The district calle
Alfama could be described as a rabbit warren on a steep hillsid
It is the old ghetto or Jewish quarter of Lisbon, which, becau
of its rocky foundations, was not injured in the earthquak
Except that none of its houses are painted that 'limelight' blu
Alfama is not unreminiscent of the Kasbah of Algiers; the sam
little archways, dark passages, and flights of stairs. But, wherev
space allows of it, there are lovely views over the Tagus; and in
fine old house on one of these sites a member of the Espírit
Santo family of bankers has recently opened his collection t
the public. A scarlet lacquer coach stands in the hall, and up
stairs there are furniture and china of the period of Quee
Maria I, who was daughter to the plumed Dom José of th
equestrian statue. This collection is among the pleasures of Li
bon on a Sunday afternoon. High over all this part of the city, i
mediaeval walls and battlements seen unexpectedly from man
windows in the town, stands the Castelo de São Jorge, wher
white peacocks and other rare birds roam at liberty.

The Sé Patriarchal or cathedral, also in this quarter of th
town, has been so hideously scrubbed and restored as to effect
ally remove all patina of age. Its Romanesque façade may b
strong and imposing, but how bare and disappointing is th
interior! That paragon of the 18th Century in Portugal, th
extravagant King Dom João V, paid huge sums to the Vatican i
order that the Archbishop of Lisbon should be elevated into
Patriarch and have the privilege of saying mass from a high alta
as in St. Peter's, facing the congregation. Moreover, the Patr
arch officiated in vestments resembling those of the Pope, an
his canons in imitation of those of the cardinals. So, at least,
was asserted by old writers, though the ritual now is muc
simplified, and perhaps the impression of a visit to the Sé is th
it is not a worthy setting for one of the three Patriarchs of th
Western Church. Any traces of Rococo splendour have bee
swept away. But it could be that the vestments and sacred vesse
in the treasury, even though late in date, might alter th
opinion. São Vicente de Fora, another big church, is not fa

74

12   Terreiro do Paço from the air

13   The Equestrian Statue of Dom José I (1775)

LISBON

14   The Palace of Fronteira in the suburbs of Lisbon (c. 1650)

way; and it was here that the embalmed bodies of the Braganças
om João IV (*d.* 1667), first of the dynasty, to the murdered
ing Dom Carlos and his son Dom Luiz Felipe could be seen till
few years ago through the glass tops of their coffins, a horri-
ying vision now wisely put an end to. More enticing, that is the
ord for it, is the Artillery Museum in an 18th Century palace,
ith painted ceilings, old and absurd uniforms, intimidating
eapons that can never, comparatively, have done much harm,
d a jacaranda tree of singular beauty growing at the door. It is
ell worth the trouble of continuing further into this outlying
art of Lisbon in order to visit the church and convent of
ladre de Deus, much more interesting than any of the churches
st mentioned, with a Manoelino doorway and nave lined with
zulejos which we will count as our first experience of this art
eculiar to Portugal. Some of the tile pictures at Madre de Deus
e set, delightfully, in formal gardens, showing the wide range
f subject of the *azulejos*. There is a double-storeyed Gothic
loister which you pass on the way to the upper choir, where
ere is gilded woodwork that is typically Portuguese, too, in
s richness, and primitive paintings, including portraits of an
rly king and queen. And the sacristy, again, with its mar-
ellously rich and sumptuous cabinets and vestment chests of
caranda wood, and their polished brass locks and hinges, is a
ature typical of Portugal.

A journey into an altogether different quarter of Lisbon takes
s to the Janelas Verdes, or 'House of Green Shutters', which
, in fact, the Art Gallery, but in order to arrive there it is
ecessary, when telling the taxi-driver, to try and elide the name
nelas Verdes, long as it is, into three syllables. It is of no use
be diffident about the accent. The only method is to embark
oldly, saying 'Yanells Verds'. The Art Gallery is on a vast
ale, many times too big for its contents, which could be put
to a building less than half the size. There are, in truth, many
o many primitive paintings on view; and the acres and acres
f indifferent pictures detract from the one or two masterpieces
f the early school. If indeed, there is any work of art of the
ortuguese school other than the double triptych by Nuno Gon-
lves. Flemish in influence, and related however remotely to
e visit of Jan van Eyck to Portugal a generation earlier, in

1428–9, these panels by Nuno Gonçalves perhaps rank as a wor
of art with the paintings of Jaime Huguet, greatest of the Catala
masters, or, to remove them for purposes of comparison outsid
the Iberian peninsula, with the altar-paintings (c. 1444) by Con
rad Witz in the museum at Basle that portray with so naïf
realism the lake scenery of Geneva and the snowy mass of Mon
Blanc. That is how the polyptych is to be rated as a work of art
and national pride in the golden age of Portugal must not b
allowed to exalt it above all early paintings of whatever statur
so that it becomes the peer of Giovanni Bellini or Fra Angelico
This polyptych of St. Vincent, the patron saint of Lisbon, hun
undisturbed for centuries in the monastery of São Vicente d
Fora but has now become, as it were, the banner of Portuga
for round the saint, who is the central figure in each triptych
are grouped the King Dom Afonso V, kneeling in a surcoat c
green velvet, a man in a wide-brimmed black hat conjectured t
be his uncle Prince Henry the Navigator, and courtiers, knights
beggars, sailors, in fact, all classes of the nation at the epoch jus
before their voyages to India when the Portuguese were buildin
forts and castles along the coast of Guinea and campaigning i
Morocco under this very King Afonso V, 'o Africano'. There i
a fisherman wearing his fishing net draped round him as thoug
it is a gown; and a bearded man, foreshortened in an extra
ordinary attitude as though prostrating himself, his rosary c
fish's vertebrae or backbones dangling on his wrist; there ar
monks of Alcobaça in their white robes, a knight in Orienta
helm typifying the Moorish citizens of Lisbon, and a Jew wit
the 'thora' to stand for the rich and important Sephardic colony
After this wonderful mediaeval vision in all its exactitude c
detail, helmets, sword hilts, coats-of-mail, it is difficult to tur
to the other Portuguese Primitives, except, perhaps, to notic
the one or two paintings in which ships of the time of th
Navigators, brigantines, and caravels with bellying sails, are i
the background.

There is one other great work of art in the Janelas Verdes, an
that is the triptych of the Temptation of St. Anthony, left to th
Portuguese nation by the late King Dom Manoel, and one of th
two surviving masterpieces by Hieronymus Bosch, the othe
being his great painting in the Prado, formerly in the Escoria

Both are of the same provenance for they belonged to Philip II of Spain. The Temptation of St. Anthony has wonderful and lurid conflagrations, a city on fire with figures outlined against the flames, and aerial monsters cruising in the skies. It exists in a world of its own, to which there is a missing key. The other primitive paintings in the Janelas Verdes are so poor and empty in comparison that it is better to turn to the rooms full of pottery and china, much of it from local factories, Rato and Vista Alegre, unknown outside Portugal. A portion, and it is but a small part, of the immense collection of French silver in Louis XV style made to the order of Dom João V is on view. This comprises more than twelve hundred pieces from the workshop of François-Thomas Germain (1726–91),* greatest of the French silversmiths; a gold breakfast set, a toilet service in gold and enamel, and innumerable salt-cellars, coffee-pots, jugs for chocolate, cutlery, and miscellaneous objects to ornament the dinner table, most of them in that whitened metal which marks the difference between French and English silver. The rest of the silver collection, some of it still in use and displayed upon official occasions, is in the former Royal Palácio das Necessidades, on its hill above the Tagus. Some of the simpler objects in showcases at the Janelas Verdes, cups and saucers, knives and forks, egg cups, are beautiful because of the Gallic care and logic put into their simple lines; but the involved centre-pieces of boars and stags struggling with hounds, and so forth, are ugly and in bad taste. They would have looked in place at the Great Exhibition of 1851, and one need not be an Englishman to prefer the silver of Paul de Lamerie, the Huguenot silversmith who worked in London. Other objects in the collection are by Antoine-Sebastien Durand; and four, of sixteen statuettes of the different countries of the world in gold and enamel, are on view by Ambroise-Nicolas Cousinet. This is the famous *dessus de table*, reckoned to be the masterpiece of the French silversmiths of the 18th Century, and once again the judgement of a Briton inclines heavily to his own country. But in a nearby room there is an

* Much of this silver, judging from the dates of Germain and of Cousinet (who made the statuettes referred to later in this paragraph in 1757–8), must have been to the order, not of Dom João V (*d.* 1750), but to that of Dom José I, his son.

79

undoubted masterwork, the chalice of the monastery of Belém, made to the order of Dom Manoel I of the first gold brought back from The Indies by Vasco da Gama. Let us keep in our minds its old attribution to the hand of Gil Vicente, who, besides being a silversmith, was a great poet and first of the playwrights of Portugal. [Gil Vicente is a partly mythical figure; no one knows yet for certain whether he was the one person, or two separate individuals, silversmith and poet.]

The noise of far off thunder, and not so distant, in the rooms of the Janelas Verdes comes from the trams in the street outside. Their screeching is so vociferous that it is only in the open space looking down on the river that we realize that this is one of the most beautiful quarters of Lisbon, near to most of the Embassies and Legations and not far from the Estrêla Church, the two towers and domes of which are one of the few architectural features of Lisbon, and could be described as giving through charm and fortuitous circumstance an effect out of all proportion to their merit as works of art. Inside is the tomb of Queen Maria I, the builder of the church, in Empire style; and also the tomb of Fr. Inácio de São Caetano, who began life as a circus clown at country fairs and ended as Archbishop of Évora and Confessor to the Queen. Even here, in this outer part of Lisbon, the *varinas* with their creels of fish and brightly coloured kerchiefs are met with, and perhaps it is only the sight of another *varina* in those warm colours of the South, or the act of walking under the feathery boughs of what you know next spring will be a blue jacaranda tree, one of many all along the street arching over the tramlines, but you feel an affection for Lisbon growing upon you. You begin to compare it in your mind with Naples or Istanbul; or, knowing neither, wonder if Lisbon is not the most beautiful city you have ever seen. By this time the beds of red and yellow cannas down the middle of many of the streets may be becoming as much of a commonplace as the platoons of tulips in Hyde Park. But, like the jacaranda trees, they are a tropical foothold on the mainland of Europe, the only tropical stronghold, for that term could not be applied to the palm trees of Monte Carlo. They are in reminder that the Navigators sailed from the Tagus round Africa to India, that they colonized Macau, in China, and Mozambique, and settled in Brazil. To the

me extent to which in Naples you know it was once a Greek
ty, or feel the touch of the Orient in Istanbul, there is this
ttle air from the tropics along the banks of the Tagus and up
ιe hills of Lisbon past the painted houses with their tilted eaves,
breath, no more than that, of India and China, of Africa and
razil.

As though with the same idea in mind, the Estufa Fria, which
something unique in Europe, has been laid out in the higher
ιrt of Lisbon, above the statue of Pombal, in the Parque
Juardo VII. It is a garden of tropical plants and ferns cunningly
sposed with winding paths and different levels in order to
ιpear even bigger than the reality, and all enclosed within high
alls and roof made from thin slats of wooden lattice. The in-
rior is twilit like a tropical forest, dank and damp and darkly
xuriant; there are walks high up under the roof; palms, and
ιnds of waterplants, and stepping-stones. Not having been
ιere, it reminded me of the headwaters of the Limpopo! Per-
ιps the pools should be deepened in order to allow of the
ppopotamus and crocodile. The effect is more natural than in
ιe hothouses at Kew. It is as though a section of tropical forest has
ιen taken up and brought bodily to Lisbon. The only other
ιings missing are the halcyons and sunbirds.

Plumage as glittering as theirs, but of religious purposes, is
be admired a little distance away at the church of São Roque,*
ι the side of a steep hill in the old part of Lisbon. The King
om João V, that paragon of extravagance, took it into his head
lavish insensate sums of money upon one small chapel in his
ιurch. He sent to Rome, and had the chapel clothed in porphyry
ιd lapislazuli and precious marbles to the design of Vanvitelli,
e architect of Caserta (the Versailles of the kings of Naples).
ιere are balusters of *verde antique*, incrustation of agate and
ory and amethystine, and magnificent hanging lamps of chiselled
onze, all the work of Roman craftsmen to whom Dom João
ιust have been a godsend. His prodigality, pushed nearly beyond

* The church, by the Italian Terzi, resembles the Gesù at Rome. Always one
the most popular of Lisbon churches, São Roque was the setting in 1642
a Marathon sermon, by Padre Antonio Vieira, who preached for two days and
ιight on end. His filibuster exploit is reported in *The Selective Traveller in*
rtugal, p. 49.

the limits of normality, is continued in the museum next doo
There may be seen the altar front for the chapel of chased silv
on a bed of lapislazuli, bronze candelabra of incredible richnes
sets of altar vessels in silver gilt, and other objects in met
which, taken in conjunction with his orders to Germain ar
other French silversmiths, just mentioned, must establish Do
João as the greatest patron in history of the arts of the goldsmitl
There are no collections in the world to compare with the
treasures, respectively, of French and Italian craftsmen of th
time. As well, in the museum of São Roque, are altar cloths
richest Italian lace, worked in the Roman convents, and ves
ments so glittering with gold that they are heavy with bullic
and appear to be raised like the old 'stump work' embroider
indeed, embossed in gold. There are, also, sets of vestments
cloth-of-gold with reflections of rose, 'shot' with rose, and
cloth-of-silver, all with mitres to match; and vestments of tw
shades of Tyrian purple or violet.

There need be no further lingering over Lisbon churches. B
one more, the Paulistas or Santa Catarina, on an even steep
hill than usual, where a taxi will not wait because of the doub
tramlines, offers a large space much like an old theatre on
steep hillside, with high golden proscenium arch in the Bibie
manner, golden female statues that could be angelic programm
sellers, and a golden organ high on the wall on the same tier
the nuns' singing gallery or choir. This was in order that the
voices and stringed instruments, some of the nuns playing tl
violin and viola or viol d'amore, could be conducted ar
accompanied from the organ loft. This gilded organ is so beaut
ful and graceful in composition, it has such decorative balanc
that it compares to one of Mozart's themes or subjects, as tho
were conceived by him to be subjects for variations, and tl
angel musicians of the organ, violin or lute in hand, could l
leading this terrestrial music, each in turn. In the churches
Northern Portugal, 18th Century organs are to be found su
ported or upheld by figures of mermaids, satyrs, or tritons, a
brilliantly painted. They are among the most wildly fantast
inventions of the whole age of Rococo. They are somethir
apart, seen nowhere else. One would like to know more abou
those organ-makers, and their theory of music. But this organ

e Paulistas is of another origin, half-sister to the opera, and
tuned to the Italian music schools of Rome and Venice.

Coming out into the street again with that invisible music
ing in one's ears, it is a precipitous, headlong walk down to
e docks and quays and painted fishing boats. Near the station of
ais do Sodré, where the electric trains start for Estoril and
ascais, is the headquarters of the *varinas*, where they are to be
en of all girths and ages, straight of back and firm of body,
fting their creels of fish on to their heads (15), and setting forth
climb the steep streets with wide Gypsy stride. Here, too, are
e ferry boats which take the motor-cars and passengers across
e Tagus in ten minutes while the bootblacks ply their business
board. Cacilhas is the other side of the river, with a famous
a-food restaurant, a staircase lined with seashells like a grotto
a folly, narrow canals beside the walls which are really fish
nks crawling with clams and other molluscs, and a menu with
erything from shrimps to cuttle-fish or squids, including many
fferent ways of cooking *bacalhau* (salted cod), a fish more often
an not 'difficult' for foreigners, but which is the national dish
Portugal. There are lovely views of Lisbon from this restaurant
an evening, but let us decide that this is the hour to talk of
her restaurants and return across the river.

Two restaurants opposite each other in the same street
ading out of a corner of the Rossio are Aquario and Tavares,
e first of them less expensive, and specializing in sea-food. A
eal at Tavares, or at the Chave d'Ouro, in the Rossio, will cost
lot of money, in spite of the astonishing cheapness of the wine
Portugal, which is never more than the equivalent of five
illings a bottle even in the more extravagant wine lists. As
en the smaller vineyards make several sorts of wine, and there
no attempt at uniformity, the diversity is endless. I must admit
not being drawn, myself, to the *vinhos verdes*, which are
esh, *not* green, young wines; often, indeed, they are rusty-red
colour, but all are a little acid to my taste. I prefer the many
owths of Dão, red wine from the centre of Portugal, rather
Burgundy type, but there are many other good red wines;
d the delicious *vins rosés*, the best *vins rosés* to be tasted any-
here. Among them are Mateus, from far off Trás-os-Montes;
e light and sparkling Faisca which comes from Setúbal; and the

vins rosés, pink champagne included, of Lamego. Now for th
dishes upon the menu. Rice is little eaten. There is nothing t
equal the Spanish *paella*; but soles and whitings and fresh sardine
are excellent. They are to be had in the smallest *bistros*, and ar
no better in the most expensive eating-places. But the Portugues
show little imagination in their cooking. It is only in a couple c
places in Lisbon and in Oporto that there is variety; elsewhere
is the eternal cod and mutton.

The one altar of gastronomy in Lisbon is the Hotel Aviz, in
former private house of astonishing decoration, and owing i
unique character among hotels de luxe to this, and to there nc
being bedroom accommodation for more than twenty-five c
thirty guests. All depends, therefore, upon the service and th
restaurant, there being a staff that outnumbers the residents i
the proportion of five to one. The Hotel Aviz is in the highe
part of the town beyond the statue of Pombal (which is no sillie
than the monument outside Buckingham Palace, or many othe
sculptures), and lies in the direction of the Campo Pequeno, c
bull-ring. It stands on an island site, surrounded by railings, an
with bougainvillea climbing to its third-floor windows. Withi
are thick pile carpets specially woven, tile pictures, dark woo
arm-chairs of formidable carving; a bar like the Herald
College, Portuguese version, redesigned for an Atlantic liner
many mirrors and golden coffered ceilings. The dining room
downstairs looking on the garden. Here, with any dish of inter
national renown for alternative, you may eat things of the Portu
guese chef's invention, adding his own country in this fashion t
the world's repertory of cooking; and such local specialities ;
smoked duck, to be had nowhere else; melon and smoked har
from Chaves, a little town to the extreme North of Trás-o
Montes, only six miles from the Spanish frontier, which prc
duces the finest smoked ham in the world, incomparably bette
than all others of whatever provenance; or the huge and tawn
peaches of Alcobaça to be eaten with sour cream, outdoc
peaches with almost the flavour of apricots, which melt in th
mouth, and must be a race of peaches apart, perhaps known i
the time of the white-gowned friars of Alcobaça, bigger, an
better than the outdoor peaches of Italy and California, and form
ing the perfect image of August in this sun-drenched, tawny lanc

15   *Varinas* unloading a Fishing Boat

16   Herding bulls

17   *Campinos*

ALEMTEJO

There is another memorable dish for those lucky enough to be
given an invitation, in Lisbon; and this is *bacalhau* (salted cod) as
served, on Fridays only, to members of the Circulo Eça de
Queiroz and their guests. This club, formed in honour of the
great Portuguese novelist of last century, is entirely consecrated
to his memory with its paintings of scenes from his novels, some
of them sketches by the King Dom Carlos who was his friend.
There is a ridiculous statue to Eça de Queiroz in Lisbon, one of
the silliest statues in the world, in which the frock-coated
novelist is embraced by his muse, a naked woman, making one
wonder how much this disciple of Flaubert suffered from the
lady's attentions during the many years he spent as Portuguese
consul in Newcastle-on-Tyne. Eça de Queiroz is said to be among
the greatest of European writers, and has been compared to
Chekhov or to Balzac, but is quite unknown in England and in
America. Some of his novels, however, are now appearing in a
translation by Mr. Roy Campbell. Probably this way of preparing
bacalhau, which is a carefully-guarded secret, was a favourite with
Eça de Queiroz. It certainly takes away the salt pungency of the
dried fish and can claim in its own right to be one of the best
dishes of its kind. Somehow the quiet interior of this club with
its faded paintings of thirty or forty years ago brings one near to
this writer, of whom one knows nothing at all; his portrait is
recognized, the workings of a mind as full as that of Dickens or
Kipling begin to be apprehended; and above all there is the
sense that Lisbon has living character of its own as much as
London or New York, as much as Rome or Naples.

How much of this went for ever in the terrible earthquake
of 1 November 1755 we shall never know. Half of Lisbon, and
that the old part of the city down by the Tagus, was destroyed,
and thirty thousand people were killed, it being no more, of
course, than a historical coincidence that this disaster happened
the day that Marie-Antoinette was born. There is not even an
inventory of the works of art that perished in the destruction of
the old Royal Palace, on the site where the equestrian statue of
Dome José I now stands. The Paços da Ribeira, or palace of the
river bank, the outline of which is known from old paintings and
engravings, was built by Dom Manoel I, and with its later modi-
fications rather resembled the wings and corner towers of the

Escorial.* It contained a marvellous library, rich in illuminate
manuscripts and in the musical collections of the kings of Portu
gal, wonderful tapestries, and who knows what lost paintings o
Spanish provenance, pictures by Hieronymus Bosch left in Lisbo
by Philip II, paintings, it is possible, done by Jan Van Eyck durin
his visit to Portugal, or portraits by Velázquez taken there durin
Spanish rule. It must, also, have had many of the extravagan
bibelots and gewgaws gathered in by Dom João V, who was
magpie for objects that glittered or sparkled. He died just fiv
years before the earthquake, so that his collections will hav
been intact. His golden coaches at Belém will give some ide
of what an extraordinary accumulation it may have been. Littl
of that period anterior to the earthquake is left,† one of the onl
exceptions being the garden of the Marquês de Fronteira a
Bemfica, just outside Lisbon, with a box-parterre of the earl
17th Century in Italian style, and ornamental water tank backe
with tile pictures of twelve plumed horsemen like equestria
figures out of Mortlake tapestries, precisely, that is to say, o
Velázquez date. The garden of Bemfica gives a momentary illusio
of Italy till you look again at the pavilions with pyramid roo
flanking the garden terrace and at their roofs of lustred tiles
After that, it is no longer Frascati or Villa Lante, but th
Atlantic country of Portugal that explored the seas to India an
fought the Moors.

It would be hard, indeed, to exaggerate the beauty of Lisbo
in the heat of August and early September. A city where
although the trams run, late and early, and motor traffic neve
ceases, you are woken by a cock crowing in some hidden back
yard or corner of a garden, and standing at the window you loo
down at the bank of geraniums in front of the house opposite an
they are glowing, in incandescence, like blind flowers, for th
dawn has not reached to them; the palm trees are but shadow

* Philip II built an addition to the Royal Palace at Lisbon with a great towe
called the Casa da Índia. Filippo Terzi was the architect. The corner towers o
the palace at Mafra were perhaps influenced by this.

† The church of N.S. da Divina Providência was entirely destroyed. It w
by Guarino Guarini of Modena (1685–1735), one of the leading Baroqu
architects of Italy, by whom there are many fine buildings in Turin. Anoth
great architect, Filippo Juvara (1676–1736), spent six months in Lisbon
1719 without results. He also worked in Turin. Both architects were priests

of themselves, and looking up over the roofs the morning just touches, that moment, on the white walls of a castle, high up, the Castelo de São Jorge, like a celestial city in a cloudless sky. The next sound may well be the pan-pipes of the knife-grinder at the street corner, for you sleep long in Lisbon on the summer mornings, going to bed late at nights and taking a long siesta in the afternoons. Altogether, there can be no lovelier summer city than Lisbon in late August or early September; and it is pleasant, as I think this anecdote will show, at all other seasons of year. For a Portuguese acquaintance tells me of being rung up, one winter morning, by a friend in Lisbon. "Have you looked out of the window yet?", this friend said; and my acquaintance, wondering what he meant, looked out of the window and saw to his astonishment that snow was falling. It was the first snow there had been in Lisbon for very many years!

III

BELÉM, SINTRA, QUELUZ

THE first move of most foreigners arriving in Lisbon is t
drive out of the town to Belém. A few years ago, befor
the War made the population more polyglot, even this fa
was not so easy. 'Belém', you could say to a taxi-driver, pro
nouncing it 'Balem' more or less as written, Belém being, o
course, the Portuguese for Bethlehem; and he would never hav
heard of it, for in any case it is pronounced 'Beleim', and th
Abbey is always called 'Jerónimos' after the Order of Hierony
mite monks that built it. How muddling! But, long befor
arriving at the Abbey, your thoughts were, and are, distracte
by the beauty of the drive along the Tagus past the dockyards
and by the pink and white villas and palaces. In one of them, now
a hospital, Marshal Junot had lingered in amorous dalliance wit
Comtesse d'Ega, before taking her back with him to Paris. I
another palace, we were told long ago, lived a bastard branch o
the Braganças descended from Dom João V, who were alway
dwarfs. This story was probably a folk memory of the Meninos d
Palhavã.* But, by now, we are at the door of the other attractio

* The Meninos de Palhavã, meaning 'children of nothing at all', or 'worth
less straw', sons of Dom João V, were three in number. Their Lisbon palace
now the Spanish Embassy, with huge stables and riding school, is still haunte
by them, and many are the stories told in Lisbon of bell-ringing and othe
poltergeist-like disturbances caused by this trio of brothers, who walk straigh
out of the pages of William Beckford. On the accession of their half-brothe
Dom José I, Pombal exiled them to Redondo, a little down beyond Évora. O
the stringencies of their exile to this bucolic setting I know nothing; but th
eldest brother Dom Gaspar survived to build one of the most lovely of Portu
guese country houses, the Quinta da Palmeira, near Braga, complete, a
might be guessed, with rooms painted in *chinoiserie* style. Their father Dom
João V, extravagant in everything, and philoprogenitive nearly on the scale o
Augustus the Strong of Saxony, had a famous love affair with the nun Paul
Teresa da Silva, called Madre Paula, of Odivelas. This was not as scandalous a
it sounds because the King had the right of entry into her convent. The nun
were famous for the excellence of their orange marmalade and sweetmeats
especially *marmelada* (quince), still known in Lisbon as 'Odivelas'. Madr
Paula was an excellent musician, and it is probable that a magnificent scarle
lacquer harpsichord and stool seen by the writer some years ago in Londo

' Belém, which is the Riding School, where are to be seen the
olden coaches.

This is the most astonishing collection to be seen anywhere of
lded coaches of the 18th Century. No one has ever explained
ow, or why, this should be in Portugal. The roads were no
etter there than anywhere else, and probably worse. But coaches
ould seem to have been a particular mania with the kings of
ortugal, and the rich nobles followed suit. We must look upon
as a playful aberration of taste, like that of Indian rajahs who
ollect Daimlers and Rolls-Royces, exotically painted, but have
owhere to drive in them. The writer remembers meeting a
ertain Indian potentate at a luncheon party. The host said to him,
May I ask you why you have had your new fleet of Rolls-Royces
uilt with such high roofs?" The Maharajah replied, "Oh! I
on't know. I might want to wear an aigrette!" Such, it could
e argued, must have been the spirit in which new coaches
ere built in Paris, in Rome, and in Vienna, to the orders of
om João V and Dom José I. It was the late Queen Amélie (d.
953), mother of King Manoel II, who first realized the unique

longed to her. The harpsichord had been given by Dom João to a nun who
as his mistress, and had only lately come out of the convent in Lisbon where
e lived. From her dates (1701–68) Madre Paula may have been a pupil of
omenico Scarlatti, who was in Portugal for eight years, 1721–29. There are
teresting accounts of the Bernardine nuns of Odivelas in Augustus Hervey's
urnal, edited by David Erskine Kimber, London, 1953. The convent contained
o professed nuns, and as many more novices, servants, and others. As the
itor of the Journal points out, "in the large unreformed communities, there
s a large floating population of lodgers and pensioners, ladies whose husbands
ere overseas and who wished to be chaperoned, wards in chancery waiting
l they came of age, and ladies who had been sentenced to a period of seclusion
a convent for moral escapades. The choir sisters, too, were probably selected
ore with an eye to their vocal than to their virtuous qualities. The atmosphere
Odivelas, in fact, was that of the Venetian 18th Century convents in Casa-
va's day. Dom João V had two mistresses who were nuns; Dona Magdalena
axina de Miranda, or Madre Paula, and a French nun, who were, respectively,
others of Dom Gaspar, Archbishop of Braga, Dom José, who was Grand
quisitor, and Dom António. It was the two latter who were visited by
ckford in 1787. Other relics of this pre-earthquake gaiety of living were the
o sons of Dom Francisco, brother to Dom João V. Their mother was Dona
ariana de Sousa; and the younger son, Dom João de Bemposta, friend and
on companion to Augustus Hervey, was legitimated in 1750, and appointed
ptain-General of the Navy and Grand Chamberlain to the Queen.

nature of this collection of Royal coaches and made the suggesti‹
that they should be grouped together in a museum. This w‹
formed out of the former Riding School of the Royal Palace.

The coaches are arranged in two rows down the whole leng‹
of a great painted hall, nine or ten coaches to each row (18‹
while three particularly enormous and golden coaches are dra‹
up facing you from afar as you walk down the hall. Earliest of
is the open, red velvet coach of Philip III of Spain, in which
rode to Portugal in 1619.* There follow the golden coache‹
high and towering, a half-dozen or more of them, being near
as magnificent as our own Coronation coach of George III. The‹
is the coach of Queen Maria Francisca Isabel of Savoy, wife
Dom Afonso VI, built in Paris. This king's brother drove hi‹
from the throne into exile in The Azores, became king himse‹
as Dom Pedro II, and then with Papal permission married ‹
brother's wife, a complicated history. The chariot of t‹
Queen Dona Maria Ana of Austria, wife of the paragon Do‹
João V, is of unparalleled splendour, made in Vienna, of gold
gesso. It is only surpassed by the Coronation coach of Dom Joã‹
built in Paris, slung in marvellous fashion between its scar‹
wheels, with windows on all sides, 'step' like a golden landi‹
at the back for the liveried footmen, and roof glittering wi‹
golden crowns. There is the golden coach in which the Patriar‹
of Lisbon drove through the streets; other equipages, one th‹
belonged to the Queen Dona Maria Ana Vitória, wife of Do‹
José I, and another presented by the Pope on the birth of Do‹
José I; the splendid coach, built by João V in Lisbon, in whi‹
King Edward VII and Queen Alexandra drove on their State vi‹
in 1904; and the row or 'coach rank' ends with a delightf‹
small vehicle, a 'one-seater', built for one or other of t‹
Meninos de Palhavã.

The three extraordinary pantomime 'floats', for that is wh‹
they look like, drawn up at the end of the hall, were triumph‹
cars made in Rome to the order of Dom João V for the embas‹
of the Marquês de Fontes to Pope Clement XI in 1716. Accor‹
ing to legend these coaches took two years to drive from Rom‹
round the Mediterranean, and eventually to Portugal. Th‹

* Generally referred to as the coach of Philip II of Spain, but there seems
be a misunderstanding.

ought back with them the precious permission for the Cardinal
Lisbon to become Patriarch, and for mass to be said in the Sé
triarchal as though before the high altar of St. Peter's in
ome. They are altogether too extravagant in design, but are
st seen in the large looking-glass that hangs behind them,
here their tangle of tritons and mermen is a little simplified by
flection and one can at the same time admire the golden
lendour of their wheels. The coaches then continue down the
her side of the hall; coaches of Dom José I; of the Infanta
aria Benedita; of Dona Carlota Joaquina, daughter of Charles
and the 'Goya' Queen of Spain, and wife of Dom João VI,
e king who, later, willy-nilly, found himself taking refuge from
apoleon's armies in Brazil. Last in the line is a neat and splendid
rriage of large size, built in London in 1824, upholstered in
hite satin, with splendid coach-lamps, body beautifully painted,
oor handles and roof ornaments of gilded bronze, and hammer-
oths with superb tassels and fringe of bullion. This carriage is
example of coach-building at its highest level of perfection, a
asterpiece of the applied arts from the London of George IV.
A few years ago yet another hall of coaches was opened to the
blic, and it is said that, even now, there is no room for some
teen to twenty more coaches or carriages which are not on
ew. The new hall has some carriages, berlins and cabriolets, so
autifully painted that they may serve to give an idea of what
rriages must have been when they came fresh from the *vernis-
artin* workshops and glittered in the streets of Paris. They are
inted in greens, and in fire-colour with metallic reflections, and
e quite unique. There is an elegant cabriolet belonging to Dom
iguel de Lima Barreto e Menêses, Bishop of far off Bragança,
d certainly an absentee living in Lisbon, for he could never
ve used this carriage in his rocky diocese. There are, also,
me beautiful little open, two-wheeled carriages in which the
fantes and Infantas of Portugal took the air in the park at
ueluz. Even this is not all. In the room, by the entrance, is the
vely little *carrinho de recreio* or play-cart of Dom Carlos, dating
om about 1850; more carriages of London provenance:
ainted sedan-chairs; and the graceful and curious processional
erlin (1740) in which the image from the pilgrimage shrine of
ossa Senhora do Cabo (see p. 141) was taken with solemn

ritual round the Lisbon churches, a little masterpiece, this, of Rococo design. On the wall behind it hang the scarlet lances carried by the riders (*cavaleiros*) in the Portuguese State bull fights, looking to be, as they indeed are, relics of chivalrous, no fatal combat. They have the appearance of tournament lances and are, indeed, a late survival of the tourney.

Upstairs, where few persons bother to go, there are showcases with many fascinating objects of minor interest; harness of wonderful elaboration; stirrups of the Royal princesses, worked like slippers of golden and intricate design, betraying Moorish influence; the side-saddle or *Amazone* of the Infanta Dona Maria Antónia; silver trumpets of the Royal bodyguard, with hanging banners elaborately embroidered; old scarlet and tabbied uniforms of the Royal bodyguard of Halberdiers; liveries of the grooms and coachmen, their powdered wigs and black *montera* jockey caps; and the saddle and saddle-cloth of Dom Pedro de Alcantara de Menêses, Marquês de Marialva, greatest of the grandees of 18th Century Portugal, who is mentioned on nearly every page of Beckford's *Letters*, but of whom, despite his contemporary riches and importance, for he was the Esterházy of his country and as full of possessions as the greatest of European nobles, few other relics are to be found.

No one can leave this astonishing golden vision from the past and not be a little dazed by it. The question recurs again, of why there were all these coaches and carriages in Portugal. The only answer is that coaches and Italian opera singers were the luxuries of the Court. The horses can have been not less glorious than the carriages. It so happens that there is a description by an 18th Century traveller Joseph Baretti, who saw one of the processions through the streets of Lisbon, and he mentions the piebald horses with long plaited manes and tails, trained to move forward at "so short a gallop" that they could keep pace with the footmen walking beside them. They were horses of mixed Spanish, Neapolitan, and German origin, the piebald and spotted ones deriving from the German principalities where they were much admired during the declining years of the Holy Roman Empire. Another race was kept for riding, and Dom José I in his equestrian statue is mounted on one of these horses of the haute école. When the Royal family returned from Brazil after the Napoleonic

18   Golden Coaches of Belém

19   The Tower of Belém (c. 1520)

Wars the strains were lost. The coaches remained, but not the
horses; though many persons in Lisbon remember the visit of
King Edward VII and Queen Alexandra, when they were rowed
ashore in the Royal barge by eighty rowers, and drove in one of
these coaches through the streets of Lisbon; and even now
under the Republic use is still made of one or more of the
coaches upon State occasions.

It is but a few hundred yards to the Jerónimos, as the Abbey
of Belém is always called, and the walk gives little time to recover
from the coaches. The Jerónimos, moreover, in this lovely climate is more often than not approached in blinding sun, and is
built of a white limestone which, itself, gathers and throws back
the light. Usually, it is almost painful to stand back and look up
at the detail of the carved doorway. I have seen it, too, on
pouring wet days, and again with a cold wind blowing up the
dust. Most persons visiting the Jerónimos for the first time are
disconcerted in any case by their encounter with the Manoelino
style. But there is another doorway, not less elaborately carved,
with kneeling figures of Dom Manoel I (1495–1521) and of his
second wife,* and after a moment we are seeking shade in this
strangest and most exotic of all abbeys.

The extraordinary effect of the interior of the Jerónimos is
due to the enormous width and height of the transept, supported
on only six huge octagonal pillars which hold up the vaulted roof.
The ribs of this vaulting and the gigantic pillars, themselves,
cannot fail to give an impression of huge palm trunks and ribbed
leaves. At the first moment of seeing it, and now again when
turning round to look back on it, the Jerónimos is an Indian
temple, a thousand or fifteen hundred years old, and not a Gothic
abbey. It is nearer the temples of Angkor than to Chartres and
Amiens. The tombs of the Cardinal-King and of the luckless Dom
Sebastião, supported upon black marble elephants, do nothing
to diminish this flavour of India. The Jerónimos, at first glance,
is immensely old and anonymous. It is difficult to believe that the
name of the architect is known. But Boytac was his name, though

* The kneeling figures of Dom Manoel I and his Queen are by the Frenchman,
Nicholas Chanterène, who carved the tombs of Dom Afonso I and his son Dom
Sancho I, and also the elaborate pulpit at the monastery of Santa Cruz in Coim-
bra.

little, if anything, had been discovered about his origin. He wa
a Frenchman, probably from Languedoc, as the last syllable c
Boytac suggests with its echoes of place names such as Figeac
Souillac, Aurillac, or Sévérac, and it is possible that his comin
to Portugal has some connection with the successive marriage
of Dom Manoel I to two daughters of Ferdinand and Isabella
for there were foreign architects working in Spain, particularl
the mysterious Juan Güas, to whom Boytac has definite affinity.

Both Boytac and Juan Güas* were foreigners intoxicated wit
the land of their adoption, Portugal being in the case of Boytac
if anything, more exciting, then, than Spain. But the Manoelin
style is no longer so much of a mystery to those persons wh
know Salamanca. There we may see buildings of an equal fantasy
but without that touch of India which was the result of th
voyages of the great Navigators. The romance of the great se
voyagers of Portugal is immediately evident in the Jerónimos
which stands on a site little more than a mile from where Vasc
da Gama started for India in 1497. Boytac was probably originato
of the Manoelino style, an invention which Portuguese architect
of his own generation, Mateus Fernandes, and the brothers Diog
and Francisco d'Arruda, were quick to seize upon. Or it was
mysterious ferment working in all of them at the same time
Nothing could be more fantastic than the twisted pillars of th
church of Jesus, at Setúbal, an early work of Boytac, and nothin
could be more eloquent of Portugal. Boytac was one of thos
foreigners who invent and give an idiom to their adopted land.

But the wonder of the Jerónimos is the double cloister an
here Boytac surpassed himself (20). A whole new mythology c
ornament makes its appearance; armillary spheres, ropes, an
anchors, the cross of the Order of Christ, and the coral an
marine *motifs* of the Manoelino, are all to be admired. Reynald

* Reynaldo dos Santos attributes the exceedingly curious church of Sã
Bras at Évora, with an exterior like a toy fort, to Boytac, and sees in its naï
pepper-box towers and turrets an influence of the cathedral at Albi, th
astonishing brick skyscraper to which there is no parallel in France. *Cf. L'A
Portugais*, Librairie Plon, Paris, 1953, pp. 14, 15. Juan Güas, if we woul
compare him to Boytac, should be seen in the cloister of the Infantado Palac
at Guadalajara, in San Pablo at Valladolid, and in San Juan de los Reyes a
Toledo. Boytac and Juan Güas are not alike, but there are curious paralle
between them and they, at least, balance each other in exuberance and fantasy

os Santos also attributes to Boytac the traceries of the cloisters
Batalha and the Unfinished Chapels at the same place; and on
e strength of this attribution Boytac is unsurpassed by any
chitect in sheer originality. This is not to say that his sense of
eauty or good taste put him among the greatest of all architects;
ut innovators of form and ornament like Borromini worked on
small scale beside the one mind that invented the cloisters at
elém and at Batalha. The corners of the cloister at Belém are
cut off' and arched over, giving an added exuberance and
tality to their quadrangular design. It is only the later hand of
ão de Castilho,* the architect who succeeded him, and who
orked in the ordinary Renaissance idiom of the Spanish Plater-
sque, that brings sanity and convention into this cloister. With-
ut an ancestry, unless in an opium dream of India, this double
loister at Belém is one of the most original works of architecture
the world. It was built on the proceeds of spices and peppers
rought from India, and there is no point in judging of it by the
aid standards of the Italians. The Manoelino was an *art nouveau*,
ore extreme than anything that came later in the age of the
aroque. Belém lies at the extremity of Europe, far from Rome.
uch a building would never have been allowed in 16th Century
aly. But it is natural, near to the landing stage of the first
oyagers to travel round Africa to India and back again.

The Tower of Belém, a little further on, is built out into the
agus almost at the point from which the voyagers set sail. Here
ain, nothing could be more different from the Italian. It is one
f the familiar landmarks of Portugal, built of white limestone,
d passed so often that no one looks at it (19). Yet you do not
orget it. The Tower of Belém forms a permanent image in the
emory, and the more closely you examine it the more curious
becomes. The entire building is tied in, tautened, as it were,
y a stone cable tied in sailors' knots, and there are little pepper-
ot turrets for sentinels which have domes like the many cupolas
f the Koutoubia mosque at Marrakesh. Indeed, the architect
rancisco de Arruda, one of the four master-minds of the
Manoelino style, had worked long on the fortifications at Safi
nd at Mazagan in Morocco, and had clearly been to Marrakesh.

* João de Castilho (1515–52) may be responsible for the vaulted roof of
elém, a formidable feat of engineering.

It is a Portuguese fort in romantic idiom, built in that same decade when they were building forts in Goa and in Ormuz, even if, in this instance, it is an echo of Morocco more than India.

The road from here to Estoril, before the motor-road was made, passed under an archway through the rose-coloured villa of the Marquês de Pombal, at Oeiras, where there is a famous garden with cascades and water-tanks, blue and white tile-pictures and many statues. This country palace, because of its tilted eaves and the theatrical look of its painted wings and flying arches, all rose-coloured, left a delightful impression. Twenty years ago, when travel in country districts was so difficult, Oeiras was like a foretaste of Arcadian Portugal.* But the new motor-road caters for other tastes. Estoril has to be reached in as short a time as possible, in violent competition; and having arrived, there is little or nothing to do except gamble, half-heartedly, if you have money, and look at the geraniums. For the massed geraniums outside the Casino are the colour equivalent to a full brass band. Their colours are loud enough to drown a conversation. Nevertheless, the rich Portuguese own villas at Estoril, all foreigners flock there, and it is the temporary home of every exiled Royal personage. There seems little to recommend Estoril except that it is near Lisbon. Even the train journey is just that much too long. A far more delightful place, only a mile or two further along the coast, is Cascais with its toy harbour where the little sailing yachts lie in summer. Cascais is still a fishing town which gives to it all that Estoril lacks in picturesqueness and in charm.

The unique advantage of Lisbon is the extraordinary diversity of scenery and climate within twenty miles of the town. Just beyond Cascais is the Boca do Inferno, where the waves break through a natural archway into a cavern in the rocks; and only a mile or two beyond that, even on a hot day in August, you emerge into another climate at the sands of Guincho. A cold wind is blowing, the sand gets into your eyes and hair, there is damp mist everywhere, and the blue sea of only three miles away has become a mill-race of curling, white-crested breakers. It is

* The palace of Oeiras is by the Hungarian architect, Carlos Mardel (1733-63). Those are the years in which he worked in Portugal. He designed some of the fountains in Lisbon, and more villas.

ngerous to swim here. A more dramatic change of climate it
ould not be possible to imagine. Round the corner of the next
eadland is the Cabo da Roca, with its lighthouse, the most
Westerly point in the whole mainland of Europe.

From here a country road, not, of course, the usual approach
om Lisbon, leads to Colares and to Sintra. It is only six or eight
iles, this way, to Colares. Nearing it, there is another entire
nange of scenery and climate. You have the illusion that this is
aly. It is a little enclave of Italy for it only extends for a few
iles. But the houses and the vineyards* and the cypresses are
ompletely Italian, and so is the milky view into the distance.
his could be some part of Tuscany, near Lucca, or the country
ound Verona. Presently, on the sloping hillside, the road passes
large old villa with a portico and flight of steps. It is a lesser
roperty of perhaps the greatest landowners in Portugal, a family
ho went into voluntary exile with Dom Miguel in 1833,
nd only returned to Portugal a hundred years later to find
neir old villas and country houses waiting for them like the
alace of *The Sleeping Beauty*. This particular villa at Colares,
isely left untouched, is a beautiful and romantic evocation of
ne past. Nobody seems to have come there while it was sleeping
or a hundred years. The family portraits of the end of the 18th
entury in the hall; the portrait of Nun' Alvares Pereira, the
oly Constable, a famous ancestor of the Middle Ages, one of
ne heroes of Portugal and victor of Aljubarrota, seen as a
inter of the early 17th Century imagined he must have been,
, that he looks like a wizard-nobleman out of an old fairy story;
ow-shaped rooms resembling those in English houses of the
me; and a 'conversation piece' by an unknown painter, prob-
ly a German, in which an ancestor of whom there is a portrait
the hall reappears in midst of a large family, all grouped in the
en air, and he is wearing, for some mysterious reason, the uniform
the Mecklenburg Dragoons; all these, and the old furniture
nd china, give the house an air. There are ghost stories, as there

---

* The wine of Colares became popular in England for a generation or more
er the Peninsular War. Another local wine, Carcavelos, from near Oeiras,
as a favourite in the 18th Century, and even earlier, in Elizabethan days.
arcavelos, more than a century old and still delicious to the palate, was in the
e at Ashburnham Place in 1953. This is a white wine.

should be, connected with it, chests full of old dresses, an
among other family treasures, Germain silver ordered from Pari
in the same years that Germain was patronized by the Kings Dom
João and Dom José. A little higher up the hillside lies anothe
villa belonging to the same family; with shuttered rooms, and a
old garden of great beauty which has busts that, Janus-like, fac
both ways. The terraces at this villa, and the view into th
distance, are entirely Italian. Perhaps there is nowhere, in a
Spain and Portugal, that is so Italian. Yet the tiled fountains ar
of Portugal; and what Colares really recalls are descriptions c
18th Century Portugal in Beckford's *Letters*. He mentions th
camellias of Colares, and says the landscape is 'Elysian'.

It is only three or four miles from here to Sintra, with charm
ing villas and languishing views in every direction. And, again
a change of climate. For in a moment you are in the mists an
damp of Sintra, with women and children selling bunches of re
and white camellias at every corner of the road. The Cork Con
vent or Capuchos, the 'sight' of Sintra, in perpetual mist, wa
raved over by a generation of romantic Englishmen who wer
not too old to have been told stories of professional hermit
living in grottos in English 18th Century parks. Although th
cells are lined with cork, the hermits who were here until 183
must have led lives of exemplary cold and discomfort, and t
judge from the doorways were no more than four feet high
There are no works of art. It would be possible to wander, an
get lost, for days on end in this damp and foggy Sintra whic
seems alone and isolated in a curious way, as though it is a
Atlantic island put down upon the mainland. There are villa
innumerable; some old and genuinely ruinous, others in hideou
neo-Maneolino style. The Royal Castle of Pena, a Portugues
Balmoral, built by the King-Consort Fernando II of Saxe-Coburg
and ante-dating its prototype like an ugly dream, towers up int
the mist upon its rocky crag. Knightly figures in armour crop u
out of the rocks, an inspiration of the awful Baron Eschwege wh
was the architect; while in the interior are rooms lined wit
porcelain, and of cement imitating wood. The arm-chair mad
of coal, now at Osborne, and bought by our own Prince-Consor
of Saxe-Coburg, would look happy in this setting. The view i
splendid from this ugly eyrie.

Far below, on the road from Lisbon, lies the Quinta do Ramal-
ão, wherein the 'Caliph' Beckford, it would be almost true to
say, set up his tent, for he hung its echoing and empty rooms with
Oriental silks and cottons. If Beckford does not haunt Ramalhão,
now a convent school, its other ghost should be Dona Carlota
Joaquina (wife of Dom João VI), who conspired here while in
political and marital disgrace. At the end of the long enfilade of
rooms, overlooking the road, is Beckford's dining room frescoed
with Brazilian trees, and with a cork dining table that it must
have been uncomfortable to eat from. The frescoed walls are
said to be by Pillement (1728–1808), though Beckford, who
writes of this artist at work on other villas in Sintra, never
mentions him in this connection. This much can be said: if
the frescoes are by Pillement he was an indifferent painter. In
Portugal, a land of few painters, there is much talk of him, but
few works to justify his reputation. At least one other villa,
an old house in extreme, romantic dilapidation, seen from
the road behind its railing, the Quinta de Seteais, is said to
have a room painted by Pillement, but the writer during
visits to Portugal extending over twenty-eight years has never
yet heard of anyone who has been allowed inside its shuttered
rooms.

A sudden view of two huge conical chimneys, Oriental relations to that of Glastonbury, and of the same date, means the
Royal Palace. The interior has been so restored that it is nearly
spoilt; except for rooms that have ceilings painted with magpies
in one instance, and with swans in the other, and for some old
and beautiful *azulejos*. There is much 19th Century furniture; yet,
in spite of everything, the palace of Sintra is a Moorish palace,
and in its beauty of situation it is the most Moorish building in
the whole of the Iberian peninsula after the Alhambra at Granada.
But it is seen best from below, where you can look up to it; and
since the whole of the valley under it is full of villas and their
gardens not everyone has admired the palace of Sintra when it is
outlined against an evening sky. There is one particular villa of
square shape, in two storeys, a house which is painted green to
match the clipped terraces that frame its hedges. It has fountains
and water tanks, and the garden climbs down the hill in little
green rooms all laid out for summer coolness and in order to get

the view. This villa, which was built in the 1790's, belongs t
the age of pleasure and it is almost too good to be true that fou
or five of the prettiest rooms in Portugal should lie within. Th
dining room is painted with looped curtains and slender column:
and landscapes, so as to represent the inside of a pavilion or tent
The work is of a skilled hand that must have had experience i
painting theatre scenery. Another, higher-ceilinged room h.
slighter but graceful painted decorations; while next door is
room, probably from its character an alternative dining room
entirely frescoed with birds and landscapes by Pillement, so
is said; but the painting has so much more character than any
thing else attributed to him that, either this is the only roo:
painted by Pillement while he was in Portugal, or all others ar
genuine but this is by a better hand. A little boudoir, howevei
painted with *chinoiserie* figures is so charming that it is an apothec
sis of the art of the tea-canister; this is grocers' and tea-mei
chants' *chinoiserie*, but as though the painted decorations wer
from the brush of Boucher. This enchanting little room, prettie
than anything in the Royal palaces, gives the date which it :
difficult to guess from the other painted rooms, and, I think
yields the clue, which is that both rooms, this and the secon
dining room, are by Pillement. It must certainly be the prettie
house in Portugal.

That epithet could never be applied to Mafra, which lies nc
many miles away. This was the culminating extravagance of Dor
João V, and his effort to emulate the Escorial. It would be tediou
to repeat again the stories of the chimes of bells he ordered fror
the bell-founders of Malines, doubling his order when they drev
his attention to the expense. His architect was the German
Frederico Ludwig or Ludovice of Ratisbon. The façade is lon
and heavy, spun out, and looking as though it might collaps
sideways like a card house (42). It was a palace-monastery; th
king's apartments lay to the South, the queen's to the Nort
with the church between them, and the monastery lay behind
What are fine at Mafra are the local marbles, the embroidered vest
ments, and the bronze grilles and lamps. Trevisani, an Italia
painter, covered many feet of canvas and ill spent his time. Mafi
is a monument to the monotony of Royal palaces. The dullne:
is nearly intolerable, and can have been no better when king

20   Belém: Cloister of the Jerónimos, by Boytac (c. 1510)

21   Queluz: part of the Garden Façade

22   Queluz: the Neptune Fountain

d monks were there.* There is practically no furniture in the
alace, and accounts of Portugal in the 18th Century make it
nlikely that there were ever more than those few pieces which
ie Royal family carried round with them. The ladies-in-waiting
ere accustomed to sitting on the floor, and chairs were not
uch more in use than in a Moorish palace. Mafra is disappoint-
ig except for the library and for the atrium to the church with
s fine marbles.

Few tastes, however, could resist the charms of Queluz, the
vely country palace a few miles from Lisbon. They begin to
sert their fascination from the moment its dependent buildings†
id semi-circular wings, all colour-washed pale pink, are seen.
nfortunately, the interior was gutted by fire in 1934. Among
uch else that perished was an apparently unique pictorial wall-
iper, probably of French manufacture, which had for subject
ie Greek Wars of Independence. Lord Byron appeared in this
nong the white-kilted Evzones. A charming room survives, un-
ouched by the fire, that has *azulejo* wall panels of palm-trees
id negroes and Chinamen, in blue upon a yellow ground. There
little else, except a fine romantic portrait of Dom Miguel. At
ueluz it is, above all, the gardens that are lovely. They are by
ie Frenchman, J. B. Robillon. Nothing could be livelier or more
eautiful than the double staircase leading to the lower garden,
ith its balustrade and spreading flights of steps. The garden
çade, especially that of the side pavilion near to the garden
arapet, is of exceptional beauty, and so well suited to a garden
1). The great parterre is beautiful also, and so, in poetical
nagery, is the canal lined with blue and white tile panels of
ips in sail. The palace was built by Dom Pedro, younger son
Dom João V, later husband and Regent to his own niece, the
ibecile Queen Maria I. But the spirit of this beautiful country

* This seems, too, to be the impression locally, for when a friend of the
riter, a British Museum official, went to Mafra a few years ago he heard the
rillon in the distance and found the authorities were welcoming him with
e *Merry Widow* waltz. Tastes change, and it would seem, deteriorate with
ne. Baretti, visiting Mafra on 13 September 1760, found the bell-ringer
aying Handel "and the most difficult lessons of Scarlatti" on a xylophone of
s own invention. *A Journey from London to Genoa*, Vol. I, pp. 254, 255. What
usic, we may ask, will the bells of Mafra be playing in 2054–5?

† An excellent, if expensive, restaurant has been installed in one of these.

palace is to be had in William Beckford's *Letters*. Here, he r
races with the maids of honour of Dona Carlota Joaquina at h
bidding, during the few months that may have been the happie
period in his troubled life. He tells of the music of Quelu
hearing, or so he says, the warblings of Italian *castrati*, and tl
oboe and flute players posted "at a distance in a thicket
orange and bay trees"; not forgetting the soft *modinhas*
Brazil, that he wished to learn, "languid, interrupted measure
as if the breath was gone with excess of rapture, and the so
panting to meet the kindred soul . . . with a childish careles
ness they steal into the heart." There is yet an echo of Itali
music in the Court chapel at Queluz, and dying echoes of mus
among its thickets of orange trees and woods of myrtle (3, 21, 22

IV

A JOURNEY TO THE ABBEYS

Alcobaça, Fishing Village of Nazaré; Batalha; Tomar

THE classical journey in Portugal is to set off for the Abbeys, which is nothing of an undertaking nowadays. But it was not always so. As late as 1926 conditions of travel were no better, and probably in many ways very considerably worse, than in the time of Beckford. It would be difficult to tell the truth about this without being accused of exaggeration. But Beckford could stay in satrap luxury with the Cistercian monks of Alcobaça and had not to endure the discomfort of the country inns. On the occasion of which I am thinking I had spent the winter writing at Amalfi, and just before catching the ship from Naples to Lisbon a jar of *foie gras* arrived from an address in France which had been advertised in the *Continental Daily Mail*. As there was not time to eat it at Amalfi we took the *foie gras* with us, and it accompanied us as far as the Abbeys where, but for it, there was no other food that we could touch. I have a memory of roast pork with the hog bristles still adhering to the skin and served up with it, to the accompaniment of wet sheets upon the beds and damp air from the river Liz streaming in through the windows of the hotel. The climax of the expedition came on the morning when we went to Tomar and the roads were so bad that we had to motor *backwards* for half an hour in order to rest our necks.

Leiria could in those days be called the storm centre of the Abbeys, a country town with a history, and an old castle on a hill built by the King Dom Diniz (Denis) and his wife, St. Elizabeth of Portugal. It is interesting to read in the staid pages of Baedeker that the banishment of the Jews deeply injured Leiria. There are churches and monasteries on hills all round, and miles and miles of pine trees of balsamic breath. It is, in fact, the forest of Leiria, which was planted by Dom Diniz. The other attraction of the neighbourhood being the dress of the peasant women who still wear the little round black pork-pie hats with velvet ribbon

and pompom on the top, as though they had been shown por
traits of the Empress Eugénie at the height of her beauty, while
the older peasant men wear mutton-chop whiskers and the black
stocking cap. On the road between Alcobaça and Batalha little
children knelt in the dust begging with clasped hands as though
in prayer, a custom which one may be right in thinking was
taught them by the monks, though now, in the multiplicity of
motor-cars, they no longer do this, for it has become dangerous
and absurd. The air along the road whined and creaked from the
wheels of the ox-carts, which were solid rounds of wood, and
the slowness of the pace wore on the nerves and seemed to be
the measurement of heavy peasant minds. To be told that the
peasants loved the whining of those wooden wheels, and that the
oxen would not work so well without it, made one comprehend
how countrymen can sleep all night long while dogs bark and
howl outside. The other memory of that road between the
Abbeys is of an old blind beggar singing a song of which the
refrain rang 'os Senhores de Portugal', making one wonder if
that, too, dated from five centuries of monkish landlords.

It is now an easy run of some two and a half hours from Lisbon
to Alcobaça along a first-rate road, and there are inns in the town
which are famous for their good food. The peaches of Alcobaça
are nowhere visible for they are all sent off to the Lisbon market
but they are grown in the surrounding orchards. It would, indeed
seem more than likely that peaches were grown here while
monks lived in the Abbey. Much hideous pottery is made and
sold in Alcobaça,* but what gives the town its character are the
chintzes and printed cottons. Many of these are printed from the
early 19th Century English wooden blocks, 'remaindered', we
imagine, about a hundred years ago, and now printed with native
colouring added. Nowhere, not even on the odd island of Marken
in the Zuyder Zee, is there such a repertory of coloured chintzes
and where they excel particularly is in floral patterns. The shops
selling these cottons in the main streets of Alcobaça are a great
stimulus to eye and mind.

The Abbey stands in the middle of the town as though, as if
the truth, the chintz shops were dependent on it. There is a wide
terrace in front of it with floreated obelisks and flights of steps

* More correctly, the kilns are at Caldas da Rainha, twenty miles away.

23 The Main Front

24 The Capela do Destêrro

ALCOBAÇA

25   The Tomb of Dom Pedro I

26   'Manoelino' Doorway of
the Sacristy (c. 1520)

ALCOBAÇA

he original Gothic doorway and rose window above it still
emain, although embedded in a 17th Century façade with a pair
f towers. The effect is pleasant and not incongruous, even if not
articularly distinguished (23). Unfortunately, the hand of the
estroyer has been allowed unlimited play at Alcobaça. Under the
retence of restoring the interior to its original Cistercian purity
here has been a holocaust of objects accumulated down the
enturies. It is one of the worst and most disgraceful works of
andalism of our times. All the golden woodwork has been re-
noved and the whole edifice is now stripped and bared. Where
he rest of the civilized world has learned to leave well alone,
he steady destruction continues all over Portugal. There used to
e, immediately inside the entrance in the Sala dos Reis, delight-
ul and entirely imaginary statues of the kings down to Dom José
, in armour and plumed helms, and if these have been spared
nuch else has been smashed to pieces and thrown away. The
ottery statues of Dom João V and Dom José are particularly
nteresting for the details of their costume. All the magnificence
f Alcobaça has gone, and the naked altars are the last stage in
his wilful descent into disgrace.

Bare white columns apart, there is the chapel where Dom
'edro I is buried with Dona Inês de Castro, his murdered mis-
ress.* Their tombs, which were damaged by Junot's soldiers, are
till beautiful; the King and his ladylove being buried foot to
oot in the romantic notion that, thus, his eyes would behold
er on the day of Resurrection. Romantic mottoes, *ate o fim do
iundo* among them, heighten the poetic air. Each body is attended
n its tomb by six small figures of angels. Their functions must
emind all, who went to Westminster Abbey for the Coronation,

* After the death of his wife, the Infanta Constance of Castile, Dom Pedro
ell in love with Dona Inês de Castro, who was her Spanish lady-in-waiting.
he belonged to a great and noble family of Castile, and some of the Portuguese
obles, fearing the influence of her brothers, persuaded Dom Pedro's father,
fonso IV, to have her secretly beheaded at Coimbra. Dom Pedro rebelled
gainst his father, and two years later on his father's death (1357) secured the
xtradition of her murderers from Castile, proclaiming that she had legitimately
een married to him. The tombs of Dom Pedro and Dona Inês de Castro may be
he most beautiful sepulchres in all Spain and Portugal after the tombs by Gil de
ilóee in the Cartuja de Miraflores at Burgos. They are a hundred years earlier in
ate than the tombs at the Cartuja.

of the maids of honour, for they hold the crowns in place and smooth down the robes of the King and his mistress, their wings, in the meantime, folded neatly at their backs (25). The wheel of fortune on the tomb of Dom Pedro, although most of its little figures are mutilated and headless, is most beautiful in execution. Coming away from the tombs the great empty Cistercian church looks more than ever as if it had been decided just to finish it, put nothing inside it, and leave it looking as though brand new.

What are exceptional are the pair of Manoelino doorways to the sacristy and to a chapel opposite, of a brilliant and flashing whiteness as though made of *meerschaum* or sea foam. They are absolute models of their kind, composed from trees and snapped boughs of coral, which have been given appropriate foliage as of seawood, the pilasters coming up out of the ground with roots of coral, the whole doorway being noble in proportion and set off by a dado of bright tiles (26). Their only defect is that the door joints have a band of Renaissance ornament which detracts from the original conception, and but for which they would be unique and original works without a counterpart. The little detached chapel of N.S. do Destêrro, near the sacristy, has a nice façade of 1690 with Salomonic pillars (24). The band of spring cleaners, to call them by the kindest name that comes to hand, has descended also upon the monastery buildings and scrubbed the cloister of Dom Diniz and the chapter house. Even their impious hands have failed, though, to destroy the beauty of the well house in its corner, or to dim entirely the splendour of the refectory.

On the whole it must be said that Alcobaça is disappointing. Everyone, who can, should see it first, and afterwards, Batalha. But we have to remember that it is nothing without the monks, who were expelled in 1834. It was the monks who gave it life, and a terrible contrast was achieved with the turning of Alcobaça into a cavalry barracks. Batalha, as we shall see, can stand by itself, but Alcobaça demands that the monks should return again. The kitchen, which Beckford wrote was the greatest temple of gluttony in Europe, was completely desecrated. The library is ruined since the stucco ceiling fell down and it has lost its book cases. Some parts of what is now the town of Alcobaça formerly belonged to the monks and had been formed into two courts

hich housed pharmacies, cellars, barber's shops, and stables.
lass, we must remember, is said to have been celebrated night
nd day without intermission by nine hundred monks. The monas-
ic estates comprised thirteen towns, including three sea ports,
nd the Abbot ranked with the highest peers of the realm. He
vore the robes of a bishop, and under Pope Pius V in 1580 Alco-
aça was made into the head monastery of the Cistercian Order.

It would seem certain that the thriving fruit industry of Alco-
aça, famous for its pears, apples, plums, peaches, and melons,
a direct legacy from the monks. Behind the chapel with the
alomonic pillars stretched a great formal garden and a lake with
tatues and obelisks; but what were more famous were the
itchen-gardens. The Marquês de Fronteira in his memoirs speaks
f entering a huge enclosure next to the monastery and being
truck with admiration at seeing it so well cultivated. All was to
e found there; a garden full of ravishing flowers, an orange grove
vith the trees all in rows and looked after with such care that
hey yielded fruit which was famed all over the kingdom, and,
nally, specimens of their fruit trees of the best and most modern
arieties which had a universal reputation for excellence.
Sut, in order to have an idea of Alcobaça in its prime, we
ave to read Beckford. His *Recollections of an Excursion to the
Monasteries of Alcobaça and Batalha* was published in 1835 when
e was an old man, and by a curious coincidence in the year
ollowing that in which the monks in Portugal were expelled
rom their monasteries. It purports to have been written in 1794,
ut, like his *Letters from Spain and Italy*, it was, in reality, com-
osed by him more than forty years later, and reverting in old
ge to his golden youth we cannot be certain how much, in retro-
pect, his pen has gilded the monastic scene. His lodging was an
partment with painted and gilded ceilings, Persian rugs upon
he floor, silver jugs and saucers on the tables, and napkins
vorked with the needle-point. He mentions the kitchen with a
iver running through it, the fish tanks, the mountains of game,
ruit, and vegetables, mounds of white flour, and heaped-up
ugar cones. For his dinner he was given all kinds of rare and
hoice foods, excellent sausages and lampreys, and foods brought
rom Asia and Brazil—swallows' nest soup, and sharks' fins pre-
ared by a Chinese lay brother according to the latest fashions

from Macau. Beckford was clearly in his element. But the monk of Alcobaça had become a little too luxury loving, long siesta succeeded to exotic meals while financial ruin threatened, an after the French invasion it is remarkable that monkish rul should have lasted till as late as 1834.

Batalha, twelve miles away, and more splendid still in arch tecture, was never celebrated for high living. It seems always t have preserved something of Benedictine austerity, and all th luxury was in stone and marble. The monastery lies in a little di under the hills, so that coming from the North you do not see i till you are on top of it. Sad to relate, the same band of scrubber has wrought havoc at Batalha, doing their best with broom an chisel to expel poetry from the building. Its construction date from 1388, and it was built by Dom João I in commemoratio of the battle of Aljubarrota, where he defeated the armies c Castile and secured the independence of Portugal as a separat kingdom. It was Dom João I who started the alliance wit England and married Philippa of Lancaster, daughter of John c Gaunt.* It is thought that she caused English masons to be sen out to Portugal for the building, and it has even been suggeste that Henry Yevele, the master builder of Edward III, had a han in it, though none of his known work much resembles Batalha. Yet, at the same time, it does seem more English than French both in plan and detail, while it has certainly no Portugues antecedents. The church, proper, is built all of a piece, in on jet as it were, while it is perhaps not possible for an Englishma to walk round the exterior of Batalha, even including th Unfinished Chapels, and not feel how English it is in aspect an in feeling. Batalha is built of a warmer toned stone than the whit limestone of Alcobaça, and in the course of ages it has taken on honeyed colour. Even the ferocious scrubbing and chiselling o

* The Treaty of Westminster, 9 May 1386, had for its object the placing c John of Gaunt upon the throne of Castile. The marriage of his daughter Philipp of Lancaster to their king left a lasting impression upon the Portuguese Some of the bluest blood in Portugal bears the name Lencastre to this day. Th Conde de Lousã is head of one branch of the Lencastre family descended, I writ under correction, from the King Dom João II (1481-95).

† Batalha was begun in 1388. If, therefore, Philippa of Lancaster sent fo architects from England it was during the reign of her cousin, Richard II (d 1399). Henry Yevele died in 1400.

27   Batalha: the Cloister

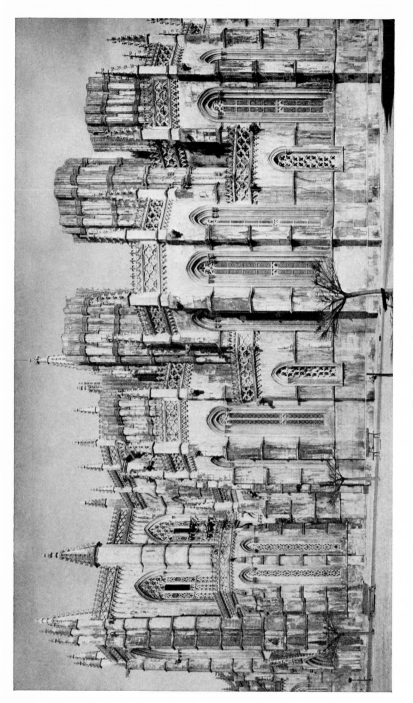

he restorer has not altogether removed this golden tone. As
ıll of spires and pinnacles as Milan Cathedral, Batalha is incom-
arably more beautiful, and it is but natural that in Portugal it
hould be extolled as the national symbol of their independence.

The Founder's Chapel is a square chamber with an octagonal
antern in its centre, borne by eight clustered columns. Here lie
)om João and Philippa of Lancaster, hand clasped in hand. The
Ling is dressed in a suit of heraldic armour, and the tomb is
overed with many devices, among them the insignia of the
)rder of the Garter, founded by Edward III, grandfather of
'hilippa of Lancaster, and with which Dom João was one of the
ırst foreign sovereigns to be invested. This double tomb is not
ıearly equal in conception or in execution to the tombs of Dom
'edro and Dona Inès de Castro at Alcobaça. But the octagonal
omb chamber is beautiful, and so is the eight-pointed star
aulting of the roof with its carved bosses and central rosace.
t has to be said of the church of Batalha as a whole that the
nortar lines show too much between the stones, giving an effect
vhich is tiring to the eyes.

But the true beauties of Batalha are still to come. There are
wo cloisters, the Claustro Real and the cloister of Dom Afonso
′. Out of the Claustro Real opens the chapter house, where
'ortugal has seen fit to bury her Unknown Soldier. It is easy to
ympathize with the sentiment, but in so doing they have ruined
ıne of the masterpieces of the Middle Ages. The entrance to the
hapter house through a beautiful arched doorway is flanked by
 pair of windows, and it is now difficult to stand in the middle
ıf the floor and look out, as was intended, to the Claustro Real.
"his chapter house, more than any other part of Batalha,
eems to show an English influence, as I think would be agreed
ıy anyone having the chapter houses of Wells or York cathedrals
ecently in mind.* The fact that at Batalha the scheme is carried

* This is certain, my instinct tells me, and on looking closer into the matter
find that Reynaldo dos Santos attributes the chapter house to Huguet or
)uguete (1402–38), a mysterious figure who may have been one of the masons
 r architects sent from England to Portugal by Henry Yevele, architect of
dward III, at the request of that King's granddaughter, Philippa of Lancaster.
 Ꮞy curious coincidence, however, one of the primitive Catalan painters was
alled Jaime Huguet, which adds confusion to the argument. *Cf. Henry Yevele*, by
ohn H. Harvey, London, B. T. Batsford & Co., 1944, p. 45. "The remarkable

out without a central shaft would seem to show how much
attention they attached to an unimpeded view, although, of
course, the marvellous window traceries of the Claustro Real are
of later date, for they were added in the reign of Dom Manoel
and count among the most original and startling conceptions of
the Manoelino. According to Reynaldo dos Santos these are due
to Boytac (d. 1525?), the Frenchman from Languedoc who was
architect of the cloister of the Jerónimos at Belém. If this be so
to Boytac are due the two most sensationally beautiful cloisters
in Europe.†

The stone grilles with which Boytac filled the windows are in
slight variation on two patterns, and are certainly inspired by the
moucharabiyés of Morocco and North Africa, while being formed
with wonderful ingenuity from vegetable shapes of artichoke,
cardoon, and poppy (20). This seems to be the correct interpretation of their design, but other authorities have seen in them
"an elaborate network of briar-branches, enclosing the armillary
spheres that formed the 'devise parlante' of Dom Manoel", in
the one pattern; and in the other, "a singular combination of
the double Cross of the Order of Christ with the stems and
blossoms of the lotus, evidently symbolizing the enterprises of
the Portuguese in the distant Orient." Nevertheless, the other
interpretation is the true one, and there is in the stone traceries
a lifelike imitation of the little scaled petals of cardoon and artichoke. They grow rather in the manner of the scales of an arma-
dillo. The well house or lavabo in the corner of the cloister is
unique in beauty, and one may take away with one from Batalha
the impression that this is the most beautiful architectural conception in the whole of Spain and Portugal. The three-storeyed
water basins, the highest of them far out of reach, are of marvel-
lously cooling effect and sound. Such water pavilions in the

founder's chapel at Batalha, on octagonal lantern enclosed in a square ambula-
tory, and a church with features reminiscent of the English friars' churches and
of Holy Trinity, Hull, shows that the tradition of English influence is not un-
founded. The aisle windows of the nave of Batalha have tracery so like that of
certain of the choir windows at Lichfield that one is led to wonder whether
'backward' designs were not exported of set purpose in order to preserve the
monopoly of the new English Perpendicular style."

† Boytac may, also, have designed the parish church, or Igreja Matriz of
Batalha. It has a fine Manoelino doorway.

corner of a cloister are at their most beautiful in Spain and Portugal, as witness that in Barcelona Cathedral where the sacred geese disport. It would seem that the whole conception of the cloister at Belém, and of this finishing touch of the stone grilles in the Claustro Real at Batalha, must argue some acquaintance on the part of Boytac with the Courts of Oranges at Seville and Córdoba, formerly the courts of ablution of the Moslems when both cathedrals were mosques. Through the cusped arches of the well house we look across to the Unfinished Chapels, the open sides beyond the water basin being filled with Manoelino traceries almost resembling a portable screen, and bearing a strong suggestion in their design that they are by the same hand responsible for the beautiful doorway to the sacristy at Alcobaça.

The Unfinished Chapels are based on a most elaborate ground plan in which the rounded central octagon would have had seven large chapels round it, excluding the side of the octagon occupied by the grand portal leading to it, while these chapels in their turn were to have six pentagonal chapels in their intervening spaces (28). The marvellous richness of this plan has to be appreciated, also, from the exterior, where you see the chapels with smaller chapels between them, and coming up above them all the unfinished buttresses that were to support the dome. These buttresses only have an elevation of about eight or ten feet above the empty, unroofed octagon below, but are, themselves, of most curious 'ingredient' for they seem to consist of bundles of some indeterminate vegetable form that has not yet taken shape, the secret of which would have been revealed had they been carried but a few feet higher. Reynaldo dos Santos, the only safe pilot through the shoals and mazes of the Manoelino, attributes the completion of the Unfinished Chapels, as far as they went, to Boytac. But the fantastic and huge portal leading to them is the work of another architect, Mateus Fernandes, in whom, as he says, there is definitely a Gothic hand, but carried to its ultimate fantasy of mediaeval richness. Mateus Fernandes is to be seen again in the vaulting of the chapels, in vegetable Gothic, but it is not in Boytac's taste; and the whole scheme for the Unfinished Chapels collapsed when Dom Manoel died in 1521, followed a year or two later by the death of Boytac (who is buried with his wife at Batalha). Mateus Fernandes died, earlier, in 1515, and it was then that Boytac was called away from Belén and set to work by Dom Manoel at Batalha. Mateus Fernandes, a Reynaldo dos Santos points out, is the most Gothic of the Manoelino architects, and in his great doorway to the Unfinished Chapels he attains to an Indian exuberance. It is, again, the same authority who points to the rose-coloured stone of the chapel vaulting, just referred to, which has taken on with age almost the hue of pink coral, worked, as it is, with the emblems of Dom Duarte and Queen Léonor.* It achieves a richness as of a sea grotto, and although in the language of the Gothic, lifts itself on to a transcendental level with the Manoelino. Such are the Unfinished Chapels of Batalha which do, indeed, leave a most extraordinary impression, and one far wilder and more exuberant, more Indian in poetical imagery than any of the fantasies of our own Perpendicular, even when expressed in the fan vaulting of King's College Chapel, Cambridge, or the Henry VII Chapel at Westminster Abbey. It is enough to take a last look at the great 'Indian' portal of Mateus Fernandes, or the vegetable *moucharabiyés* of the Claustro Real, and you may come away from Batalha convinced that there is no comparable architecture nearer than the temples of Angkor.

After visiting the two Abbeys it is a good plan to go for a change of scene to Nazaré, which is but eight or nine miles from Alcobaça. For they cannot but profoundly affect the memories of all who see them. Two other abbeys, five hundred miles away and near the Mediterranean coast, come into mind. They are the Cistercian abbeys of Poblet and Santas Creus, the former of them also ruined by restorers since I first remember it in 1929. But Poblet is tame and correct in comparison to Batalha, where, again, as at Belém the genius of a race of great explorers and navigators expressed itself in a generation or two, and was snuffed out. And on the way to Nazaré it was impossible not to think of so many wonders of monastic building all over Europe. The most touching and extraordinary collection of human beings

---

* This is confusing, and should be explained. João I began the building of Batalha in 1388. His son Duarte (Edward I), called after his English grandfather, began the building of the Unfinished Chapels. His successor, Afonso V, was too occupied with military campaigns to continue work at Batalha, but the chapels were carried further, though left uncompleted by Dom Manoel I (1495–1521).

of my experience were the Russian monks of Petropavlovsk, in the Danube Delta. What can have become of them now that they are under Russian rule again? But there are stories, just as pathetic, of the last surviving nuns in Portugal who outlived the suppression of the monastic orders in 1834 for sixty years or more, and were found half-starving in some nunnery near Buçaco.* But before there is time to think further we are at Nazaré.

Arriving at Nazaré you see a pilgrimage church upon a promontory, and perhaps notice that the loose sand of the dunes is kept together by the mesembryanthemums which, with their spiny lobes, form meshes as heavy as the fishing nets. They may or may not be in flower, but there is not a moment more, for without further warning we are among the white cubical houses of the little fishing town. And still no sign of the fishermen. Nazaré consists of three or four parallel streets, no more, but we are suddenly round the last corner and on the sea front, which is swarming with them. There is wild hurry and rush, and barefooted men are running up and down. They are hurrying like ants in an anthill, and all are wearing check shirts and trousers in bewildering colours. It is only when we think how many combinations can be worked out from the simple numbers and the letters of the alphabet on a telephone dial that we can cease to be surprised at the fishermen's checks of Nazaré. Soon one realizes that, in addition, the fishermen are peculiar looking. The young men have noses and foreheads in a straight line, and yet are more Semitic than classical of feature, while the old men are like satyrs if, that is to say, satyrs wore black stocking caps and whiskers. The women, too, are Oriental. When not busy mending nets, or salting fish, they are Oriental in their impassivity, especially when sitting in a circle on the sands, or on the stone steps. They are dressed in black and wear black shawls, and some of them wear curious black felt hats. They appear to be quite content, sitting motionless, hiding their faces with one hand pressed to their black shawls.

In Portugal it is a commonplace that the fisherfolk of Nazaré are of Phoenician descent, and it is arguable from their Semitic features that they are a race apart. It has even been seriously suggested that from their love of tartans they are of Scots descent!

* Probably it was at Lorvão (see p. 220).

(29, 32, 34).   Tyre and Sidon are, perhaps, not further from
Nazaré than the Hebrides, yet there is some reason in the Phoeni
cian argument. Cádiz, after all, had been a Phoenician settlement
and was the Phoenician Gadir ('castle' or 'fastness') founded
from Tyre about 1200 B.C., and mart for the silver of Tarshish and
the tin of the Cassiterides. Phoenician cities in Spain were
Abdera (Adra), Sexi (Almuñécar, near Motril), Malaca (Málaga)
Suel (Fuengirola), and Calpe, which is Gibraltar. Look on the
map at the configuration of Gibraltar, or of Cádiz, and then at
Cabo de Peniche, a little below Nazaré, and with its suspicious
Phoenician echoing name! We have to remember, too, that
Carthage, a colony of Tyre and Sidon, succeeded to the Phoe
nicians, and that there must still be Carthaginian blood in Spain
Was not Cartagena, with a configuration so much resembling
those of Gibraltar, Cádiz, and Peniche, founded by Hasdrubal
son-in-law of Hamilcar Barca, as the New Carthage, a history
that is still persistent in its name? There seems to be little reason
why Nazaré, not far from the great river Tagus, should no
contain living descendants from that Semitic stock.

The sardine boats of Nazaré have been in all probability more
often sketched and photographed than anything else in Portugal
They are, it is true, squat and blunt in design compared to the
sickle boats of Caparica, or the *esguichos* and *moliceiros* of Aveiro
But they are peculiarly adapted to the wide Atlantic swell; broad
in the beam and blunt of stem. The twenty-eight pair of oxen
who haul them out of the water lie like animal statues along the
sandy beach. What we are not told is the folklore of these
fishermen, or whether in their vocabulary there are any traces o
whence they came. They are imperturbable and undisturbed by
summer visitors. This village of fishermen is quite as curious as
the more famous Marken and Volendam in Holland; and we can
only hope that the same fate will not overtake them that befel
the fishermen of the Claddagh. This was the fishing quarter o
Galway, the largest Erse-speaking population in all Ireland
living in streets of low, thatched cottages, and of which it has
been well said that the dress of the Claddagh women, a blue
mantle, red gown and petticoat, and head bound round in a
handkerchief, "imparted a singularly foreign aspect to the Galway
streets and quays". But it did not save them; within the last

years all but two of the houses have been pulled down, and council houses of hideous uniformity put up instead. Nazaré, unlike the Claddagh, may probably remain unspoilt.

Some miles out to sea off Peniche lie the Berlengas Islands, of which curious tales are told. They can be seen in the distance, nearly always in a rough sea, but are reached in an hour or two by motor-boat. It is said that the fishermen living there are even more marked in type than those of Nazaré, and that they are called names like Ishmael and Samuel which, if true, would suggest again that, as in Trás-os-Montes, they are descendants of Sephardim refugees fleeing five centuries ago from the Inquisition. But a *pousada* is about to open on the Berlengas, so that it will no longer be difficult to investigate such stories. There are marvellous wild flowers in the spring, and every opportunity for deep sea fishing. Having long been curious concerning them it was interesting to leave Lisbon by sea and, getting up for no reason to look out of the porthole of the cabin, to see that we were passing within some half-mile of them and that they were clearly outlined against the sunset. A ruined fort or monastery was visible; there were, unhappily, no signs of houses or inhabitants, though fishing boats were on the torpid August waters, as we went on into the night.

Refreshed with sea air we now continue on the way to Tomar, which in fact lies further inland on about a level with Batalha but nearer to the Tagus, and some eighty miles from Lisbon. It could be said that if only one of the three Abbeys can be visited, Batalha is the most obvious, but Tomar is in reality the most characteristic and unique of them. Much damage was done to it by French soldiers during the Peninsular War, but it is sad to say that the Portuguese, themselves, are injuring it, insensately, still further. Why is it that at this late hour the authorities cannot learn to leave well alone? It would be no exaggeration to say that they have more than half-spoilt Alcobaça and Batalha, and have now taken Tomar firmly in their grasp. There will, then, be little of the artistic patrimony of Portugal left to destroy, which is an additional reason why pains are taken in this present book to draw attention to out of the way and forgotten monasteries and convents which public opinion, once aroused, might insist on sparing. They form the only reserves left to Portugal; and having said this we now state, categorically, how incomparably more beautiful was Tomar, untouched, before hammer, broom, and chisel came to it. Herein lay the history and poetry of this little country risen to greatness on the Atlantic wave, which wafted its sailors to Indian seas where they knew the long lacquered afternoons of Herman Melville and sailed for home not forgetting the coral atolls and the madrepores. Tomar, in its mingled solemnity and exuberance, is the extraordinary monument of their sea-faring, and it is something to have seen it for the first time while it was unspoilt, in 1926. Never can I forget as a spur to that excitement the execrable road leading from Leiria, through Vila Nova de Ourém, and getting to Tomar so shaken and exhausted that we had to lie down for an hour after luncheon, expectant, the while, of the fantastic architecture in the huge building upon the hill.

But it is necessary to tell a little of the history of Tomar. There was a castle here, built in the 12th Century by the Grand Master of the Knights Templar. Its ruins still stand beside the monastery. When the Order was suppressed all over Europe in 1314 Dom Diniz (Denis) founded a new Order of the Knights of Christ, to which he transferred the property in Portugal of the Knights Templar. Hence, the building of the monastery and the beginning of its wealth. This was still further increased when Prince Henry the Navigator, son of Dom João I and Philippa of Lancaster, was Grand Master. The Knights of Christ were given spiritual jurisdiction over all the conquests of Portugal, and when Dom Manoel I became Grand Master in 1481 (he was King of Portugal 1495–1521) their possessions in Africa and India made them the wealthiest Order in Christendom. But it was not to last for long. In 1523 they lost their status as military knights, the Order was changed from one of chivalry to one of monkhood, and the Grand Mastership became merged in the Crown. The town of Tomar had in the meantime become prosperous owing to the Knights, so that the Convent of Christ is not the only monument. Perhaps the most material sign of its past riches is that Tomar has a synagogue of the 15th Century, the best preserved of any in all Spain or Portugal after the two synagogues in Toledo.* But there is, also, the church of Santa

* Santa María la Blanca and El Tránsito are the two synagogues in Toledo.

29   Fisher Girls of Nazaré

30 Tomar: 'Sea Window' by Diogo de Arruda, architect

Iaria do Olival, the mother church of all those of the Order in
idia and Africa, where the Great Chapters of the Knights were
eld, and where many of the Knights were buried. Why here,
id not in the Convent of Christ, I have been unable to discover.
nd another church, as well, São João Baptista, with good late
othic doorway and a fidgety, if famous, Gothic pulpit. A
naller church, Santa Iria, is said to have a chapel, the entrance
ch of which is carved with heads of Brazilian Indians holding
velins, but on no fewer than three visits to Tomar I have not
en this. And an architectural masterpiece of another order of
xcellence we will keep till sated with the Manoeline exuberance.

But we are now half-way up the hill with the huge building
f the Convent of Christ and its eight cloisters lying before us.
ll along the roof-line of the church runs a pierced parapet
epeating with Oriental insistence, as of Buddhist prayer wheel
r the chanting of the name of Allah, the square cross of the
nights of Christ and the armillary sphere which was the symbol
f the Navigators. In effect this crenellation is not unlike a coral
ecklace. The entrance to the church, which is agreeably side-
ays, at an angle, is through an archway carved as richly as the
oors of Belém. This is the work of the previously much-vaunted
rchitect João de Castilho, now stripped of most of his honours
nd deprived of the credit of being inventor of the Manoelino.
Vithin is the primitive church of the Templars, sixteen-sided
vith a central octagon, and built on the early Byzantine or
yriac model like other churches of the Templars, copying in
ict the ground plan of the Mosque of Omar at Jerusalem. It is
he same plan that we see in Raphael's painting of the *Sposalizio*,
i the Brera Gallery at Milan, supposed to be that of the Temple
f Solomon, as classical a plan in Christian architecture as is the
lan of the Parthenon to the architecture of the Ancients. The
hurch of the Templars at Tomar is, in any case, the best pre-
erved and most perfect of all the churches of the Knights
emplar. It gives the solemnity to Tomar which is lacking in
he Manoelino.

There is in the Convent of Christ one of the finest classical
talian conceptions in the Peninsula. This is the cloister of Dom
oão III, the king who changed the Order from being one of
hivalry, and in monkish zeal needed further accommodation for

his friars. But it is, if anything, too Palladian, in two storeys, and the incessant shunting and recoupling of the pillars becomes nois and monotonous. This cloister is the work of Diogo de Torralva —looking at it we have to admit that Renaissance building of th degree of grammatical correctness did not reach England till th reign of Charles I!—and it was continued by the Italian Filipp Terzi when Philip III assumed the throne of Portugal. The othe cloisters of the convent are all beautiful in their way, and th long cruciform dormitory with a chapel at the intersection is a impressive relic of monkish rule, rather recalling the corridor of the Hospital Real at Santiago de Compostela. One end o this immense corridor looks out upon what used to be the privat garden of the Conde de Tomar, whose family bought parts of th convent more than a century ago when it was falling into ruin.

But the supreme curiosity of the Convent of Christ at Toma is the exterior of the Manoelino nave, and this is best seen from the upper storey of the Claustro Real. It appears to emerg there above that Palladian cloister as though coming up, dripping from the sea. This is beyond argument the most curious buildin in Portugal, and it could claim to be considered as among th oddest in the world. The architect was Diogo de Arruda (fl 1508–31) who came from Évora.† This nave contains the un finished sacristy, which later became the chapter house. Th interior is odd enough, with pilasters framing the window whic

* Diogo de Torralva (1500–66), who lived at Évora, designed the od Michael-Angelesque church of Graça in that town (see p. 143; and see alsc *passim*, p. 134).

† It was his younger brother Francisco de Arruda who built the Tower o Belém. Diogo de Torralva, architect of the Palladian cloister at Tomar married his daughter. The names are muddling. Let us remember that the othe geniuses of the Manoelino style are Boytac, a Frenchman from Languedoc wh built, it is conjectured, the pepper-pot church of São Braz at Évora, the churc of Jesus at Setúbal with the twisted columns, and the church and cloister o the Jerónimos at Belém. He, also, added the Manoelino window traceries t the cloister at Batalha, and worked, as well, upon the Unfinished Chapels there It was Mateus Fernandes, on the other hand, who designed the huge archwa leading to the Unfinished Chapels. These identifications are due to Reynald dos Santos, and even this eminent authority had thought previously that it wa João de Castilho who designed the famous windows of the chapter house a Tomar. It is possible that the 'coralline' door of the sacristy at Alcobaça is du to João de Castilho.

pear to be built up, section by section, like the madrepores of
coral reef. It cannot be said that this is successful, but here a
nily likeness comes in to his brother Francisco de Arruda's
wer of Belém.

The outside is a transcendental work of the imagination, a
nception in which no sign appears of Italy, and the architect
ems to have dispensed with lessons from any other architecture
d to be intent on inventing a marine style of his own. Not even
 much a sea architecture as one based upon a fantasy of sea
otion, for it has for its imagery, cords and ropes, corals and
adrepores. The same crenellation, like a necklace of coral,
rmed from Maltese crosses and armillary spheres, ornaments
e roof-line. But the weirdest feature is the pair of great
ttresses that flank the upper and the lower windows. They
ve great 'suction' bases half-way up, like the bodies of sea-
emones, one of them worked incongruously with the insignia
' the Garter tying it in before it writhes up again, covered with
rds and ropes and ending in a pinnacle. The lower window, of
ntastic composition, seems to wish that it could convince you
was made of ropes, which are knotted over and over again, and
en appear to be unknotting themselves as though by ghostly
nds. The figure of a sailor underneath this window is as though
varfed by the mighty winds. And in fact the round window
ove, taking the place of the conventional rose window, is
thing more nor less than a tie-sail, tied in with ropes and
llying in the wind (30).

The entire naturalism of this architecture is what astonishes.
 is as though Diogo de Arruda had an uncanny prescience, not
ly of the poetry of Góngora, who flourished in Spain a hundred
ars after him, but of all the theories of *l'Art Nouveau* and the
atalan buildings of Gaudí. If it is certainly true that this archi-
cture can be seen nowhere else but in Portugal, this could be
larged into stating that it is a peculiarity that only flourishes,
r is given its opportunity, in Portugal or Spain. Boytac, the
ther original genius of the Manoelino, we have compared to
an Güas (see p. 98). Probably a foreigner, like Boytac, Güas
as given free rein to his fantasy only in Spain. Boytac worked
 Portugal, Güas in Spain. They are close parallels to each other;
ut Diogo de Arruda is the most original of them all. It is almost

beyond comprehension that this extraordinary building in t
Convent of Christ should correspond in date to the reign of o
King Henry VIII, and we are left with a hopeless longing to
shown the architect's drawings. Diogo de Arruda seems to ha
done nothing further, and to have been exhausted by this o:
effort.* It at least puts him among the inquisitive and curio
minds of all time, and we would like to know from what poet
or from what persons he drew inspiration. However fantastic
may be, it is appropriate. This is not an Art Nouveau tea-roo
in Glasgow by Charles Rennie Mackintosh, or one of Gaud
apartment houses in Barcelona. It is the expression in a ne
maritime architecture of an Order of Military Knights who und
their King and Grand Master Dom Manoel had embarked upe
the age of exploration. There were Portuguese forts along tl
Gold Coast and in Mozambique, in Diu and Ormuz, in Malac
and in Malabar. Goa was the capital of this fantastic sea dominio
They were sending colonies to Brazil and to Macau, and had attaine
China and Japan. Once this is in our minds the Manoelino buil
ings in the Convent of Christ at Tomar are no more a mystery
   But one lovely experience is still to come. Half-way dov
the hill to the town of Tomar stands the little church of N.
da Conceição, and this could not be better described than in tl
words of a Portuguese author who says that entering it is lil
closing the visit to Tomar with a golden key. For it is in pu:
Italian style, and it could be compared, again, to hearing an ar
by Mozart incomparably sung in midst of a lot of local musi
however full of nationality and colour. There is no othe
building of such Italian line and purity in Portugal, and nor
in Spain.† Yet it is an anomaly, for it was built by Diog

*Reynaldo dos Santos attributes to him a pepper-pot church at Viano do Alen
ejo, between Évora and Beja. The Selective Traveller (p. 123) describes it: "Ma
of the local granite, the church has flying buttresses ending in pepper-p
turrets, while more pepper-pots stud the castellated balustrade round the who
exterior." He worked, also, on the Royal Palace of Lisbon, destroyed in tl
earthquake of 1 December 1755, see p. 87.

† This church would seem to be entirely Venetian in inspiration, and not
other critics would have it, 'Brunelleschian', which is to say, Tuscan. Tl
name of Sansovino, therefore, suggests itself, p. 137. The Palladian windows
the exterior suggest some church on the Venetian terra firma, for instance, tl
chapel at Villa Masèr.

31 Nazaré : A Bullock Team pulling
one of the Fishing Boats to land

32   Fishermen of Nazaré

33   Portuguese Water Dog
        from the Algarve

34   Fisher Girl of Nazaré

Torralva, architect of the Palladian cloister on the hill above.
ide all is harmony and exquisite of modulation. Corinthian
umns and entablatures of doors and windows are perfection.
s a breath of Greece and Italy, of the Mediterranean, but in
classical volutes you listen in vain for echoes of the coral seas.

V

SETÚBAL AND THE ALGARVE

Évora; Beja; Elvas

WHEN, if ever, the bridge over the Tagus is built ther⟨e⟩
every probability that the peninsula of Setúbal, wh⟨ich⟩
is the Southern bank immediately opposite Lisbon, ⟨will⟩
become overrun with holiday resorts. Perhaps that is inevitab⟨le⟩
but it will spoil a district of Portugal more beautiful, if ⟨less⟩
famous, than the mountain of Sintra. Setúbal and the Serra
Arrábida offer another change of climate, less lush and steami⟨ng⟩
more pertaining to the 'dew dropping South'. Sintra and ⟨its⟩
camellias are left behind and this is, if deviously, the road ⟨to⟩
Seville, most exciting of all roads in the Western world af⟨ter⟩
the road to Rome.

It is, indeed, the way to the whole of Southern Portugal, an⟨d⟩
is only the slight nuisance of taking the ferry from Lisbon to ⟨the⟩
nearest point across the river, which is Cacilhas, that ma⟨kes⟩
this seem more of an enterprise than the tame journey to Esto⟨ril⟩
The red earth and whitewashed houses, and the vineyards ⟨and⟩
olive trees, begin a mile or two from Cacilhas and continue m⟨ost⟩
of the way to Setúbal. The climate is Andalusian; and at the ⟨end⟩
of it, for this is a little enclave of its own, lies Setúbal. But ⟨not⟩
quite yet, for the road passes through Azeitão whence comes ⟨the⟩
delicious Faisca *vin rosé*, and with the palace of the doon⟨ed⟩
Tavora family set back from the main street. A little further ⟨on⟩
lies the famous Quinta de Bacalhoa, built at the end of the 1⟨5th⟩
Century and once lived in by Afonso de Albuquerque, son ⟨of⟩
the first Viceroy of the Indies and conqueror of Ormuz, of ⟨Goa⟩
and Malacca. This villa is a potent mixture of Orient and Occide⟨nt⟩
It has echoes of the early Renaissance villas of Florence. The⟨re⟩
were once medallions by della Robbia set in its walls. Sansov⟨ino⟩
(1460–1529) is known from Vasari to have spent six years ⟨in⟩
Portugal, where no other buildings are ascribed to him, a⟨nd⟩
perhaps the loggias at Bacalhoa betray his influence.* There ⟨are⟩

* Andrea Sansovino designed the Loggetta to the Campanile of St. Mar⟨k⟩
and also the Libreria Vecchia, one of the supreme masterpieces of the Ita⟨lian⟩

rdens of clipped box planted with orange and lemon trees, thus
r, Italian (35); but, also, pavilions with melon domes, and a
eat water tank and garden house with three pyramidal towers
d tiled rooms, much like the water tanks of the Aguedal at
arrakesh. The architect of those melon domes had surely been
Safi and to Mogador. A pair of beautiful azure-winged magpies
yanopica cyanus) nest in this garden, and are only found in the
eninsula of Setúbal, and thereabouts, and nowhere else in the
orld nearer than China. It is conjectured that the original blue
agpies were brought to Portugal from China by the early
yagers. The Quinta de Bacalhoa is a lovely half-caste of the
ast and West.

Setúbal wafts fish oil into the blue skies and, concurrently,
ould echo to the banging of sardine tins, except that the canning
carried out discreetly behind closed factory doors. It is a dusty
wn, and can be blinding in the heat and glare. Old and famous
r centuries for its harbour and fishing boats, there is one
riosity in Setúbal, the church of Jesus, with an interior which
an early work by Boytac, inventor and originator of the
anoelino style. Built to the order of Dom Manuel I, the vaulted
of is upheld by six columns, each formed of three stems of
one that enrol and wind round one another, giving a typical but
rious effect (37).† This is as 'natural' a local development of
e Gothic as the Perpendicular fan-vaulting of St. George's
hapel, Windsor, or the Henry VII chapel at Westminster Abbey,
hich are features peculiar to England, but, at the same time,
ke much else of the Manoelino, more in the spirit of the
roque than anyone seeing it for the first time would ever ex-
ct of a late 15th Century building. This interior of the church
Jesus, even if not great architecture, is one of the salient
emories of Portugal. Other churches are charming, and just
orth entering. The little fishermen's chapel of the Senhor de
omfim, in the Rococo of the curiosity shop, is full of votive

naissance. According to Vasari, he executed many works of sculpture and
chitecture for the King of Portugal, and when he departed in 1500 "he left
hind him one who could complete his unfinished works" (see p. 132). He
ilt for the King "a splendid palace with four towers".

†Boytac probably designed the church at Olivença, but put less of a twist
to the pillars.

paintings of naïf nature and is hung with enough internal orga
and limbs of wax to fill the dreariest and most horrible of anat
mical museums. Another church, Santa Maria de Graça, brig
with blue and white tiles and gilding, has a set of six lor
grisaille paintings of the Passion, "painted in the Chinese styl
with 18th Century Chinese figures", but they are, alas, di
appointing. It is not enough for an indifferent picture to I
painted in monochrome and called a *kakemono*.*

Setúbal lies at the neck of its own peninsula, and the road
Arrábida soon leads to what is one of the strangest and mo
beautiful parts of Europe, of much more interest, we say agai
than Sintra and its mountain. In this new climate, facing Sout
the vegetation is Mediterranean, or even African. In early sprir
it must be a paradise of wild flowers. Ilex and arbutus, hug
tree-heaths, bay trees and palms, are all here in high summe
and one must be left to imagine for oneself the pæonies and blu
bells in spring. The road climbs, while down below a stran;
promontory of golden sand with a sickle edge advances, ar
nearly reaches us, and dies away. This is the promontory
Tróia, of potent name, for it was a Roman settlement and ag
before had been Phoenician. Its peculiar and haunted spit of lar
is said in spring to be even more paradisal with wild flowers tha
this mainland. Tróia is, obviously, a site of great antiquity, ar
floating off it in a boat the walls of Roman villas can be se
under the water. It has only been superficially examined ar
interesting archaeological finds may lie hidden in the sands ar
shallow sea. An air of Grecian Italy, of Asiatic Greece, of Ty
and Sidon, attaches to Tróia; and after a few more turns of tl
road upon the high cliffs we look down and there is a whit
washed, flat-roofed monastery, the Convento Novo, which mo
strikingly recalls the Cappuccini at Amalfi, and could be in ar
one of the little towns between Sorrento and Salerno. It is con
pletely in that domed and whitewashed 'Greek island' sty
which perhaps started from Capri, with its Greek ancestry, ar
spread all through the peninsula of Sorrento. Coming down to tl

* The same authors, *The Selective Traveller in Portugal*, mention a painti
which could be more interesting, "an 18th Century canvas of St. Fran
Xavier, painted in the Chinese manner by a European". This in the villa
church of São Domingos de Rana, on a hill inland, half-way to Estoril.

35 Topiary Hedges in the *Quinta* of Bacalhoa near Setúbıl

36 Elvas: the octagonal
Chapel of Freiras
de São Domingos

37 Setúbal: the Church
of Jesus by Boytac

little fishing harbour of Sesimbra, which lies below, it is a surprise not to hear Neapolitan songs, and strains of the tarantella
and the mandoline. This part, or, indeed, most of the peninsula
including the Convento Novo, is the property of the Duke of
Palmela, whose palace of Calhariz (which I have not seen) lies
near by, with formal hedges and canals, reputed to be among the
most beautiful of Portuguese country houses, and evidently rather
earlier in date than most of them. Right at the far corner of the
peninsula, where also I have not penetrated, is the Cabo do
Espichel, with the pilgrimage shrine of Nossa Senhora do Cabo.
This much venerated image is brought yearly to Lisbon and taken
round the churches. At Belém we have already seen the *berlinda*
made to the order of Dom João V, in which it made its rounds.
Here, at the shrine, two arcaded wings of whitewashed lodgings
for the pilgrims were built by Dom José I in bucolic Rococo,
looking, in the photograph, like flimsy theatre scenery. But the
country round the shrine is wild and beautiful, in the spring
particularly, because this end of the Setúbal peninsula is one of
the habitats of the little hoop-petticoat daffodil, *N. bulbicodium*.
I have been to Caparica at the other, North-Western corner of
the peninsula, where, in summer, through a haze of heat far out
on the sands past rows of bathing tents you may descry the high
poops, and then the whole half-moon outline of the huge fishing
boats drawn up on the beach. There were twenty or thirty of
them, when I was there, at intervals over perhaps two miles of
sands. In this land of peculiar craft ancient in origin, of the sardine
boats of Nazaré, and the *esguichos* and *moliceiros* of Aveiro, the
sickle-shaped fishing boats of Caparica, riding like half-moons on
the water, or tilted on the sands, are not the least curious of all.

We are now set out and bound for the South, always an
exciting prospect, and take the road from Setúbal for Évora,
passing on the way Vendas Novas, where a dull building, now an
Artillery School, was built by Dom João V only in order to house
the Court for two nights on the occasion of the double marriage
of his daughter the Infanta Maria Josefa to Don Fernando, eldest
son of Philip V of Spain, while the Spanish Infanta Mariana
Vitória was married to his own son and heir, Dom José. The
palace may have been alive, then, with curious characters for two
nights and two days. Now, neither Vendas Novas, nor its palace

are to be recommended. But the town of Évora is another matter. After Lisbon and Oporto there are only two considerable towns in Portugal, Coimbra and Évora, and Évora, the smaller of the two, is the more interesting.* It is of quite another character from Coimbra, and is in fact a town entirely on its own, remarkable and interesting in many ways, with a different taste of Portugal from any other town. Évora has a Roman temple, the Temple of Diana; and the Hotel Alentejano was once the palace of the Inquisition. The dungeons are below the dining room. This 15th Century palace with its wooden ceilings, all things in proportion, has something of the semi-Moorish air of the Duke of Alba's palace of las Dueñas in Seville. It has had, it is true, a more terrifying history, part of which may be in connection with the story of a false Messiah!† A certain Solomon Molcho, a Marrano (converted Jew) born Diogo Pires, from Portugal, had been received in the Vatican by Clement VII, but ended his career by being burnt at the stake at Mantua: "And the Lord smelled the sweet savour, and took to Him the spotless soul." So said his followers. His prophet had been David Reubeni, a Jew from Central Arabia, perhaps from the Yemen, of black complexion, of dwarf stature and a hunchback, worn to a living skeleton by his fasting. David Reubeni, like a terrifying apparition of fanaticism, rode on a white horse to the Vatican, where the Pope received him. He was arrested and imprisoned with Solomon Molcho, the Messiah whom he preached. His fate is uncertain. But a Jew, 'from Arabia', after long imprisonment was burnt at Évora by the Inquisition, and it is conjectured that this was probably David Reubeni. There are long inscriptions scratched into the damp walls of the dungeons in this old palace at Évora, and perhaps one of them is by the hand of David Reubeni. All this is perhaps little to the point, but it gets you into the right atmosphere for Évora.

It is an extremely picturesque town with a wealth of old buildings, some of them exceedingly curious. How odd, for instance, the Palácio Cadaval, with its two towers topped with

* I find that Braga has a slightly larger population than Coimbra, but leave the remark unchallenged in order not to spoil my argument.

† For a history of false Messiahs, see my *Splendours and Miseries*, London Faber and Faber Ltd., 1943, pp. 125–42.

pyramids, where once lived the King Dom João II (1481–95), and which resembles a crypto-Arabic 'throw forward' to William Kent's twin lodges with pyramidal roofs for the Worcester Lodge at Badminton! Odder still, the extraordinary church of São Braz, which is attributed to Boytac, and, if so, is an early, immature work of his, for with its pepper-pot turrets it is like a toy fort! Then, so many of the houses at Évora have the remains of *sgraffiti* decorations upon their walls; there are so many arcaded streets, and white arches flung like buttresses across narrow lanes in case of earthquakes. There is yet another most peculiar building, the church of Graça. This is attributed to Diogo de Torralva, who married the daughter of one of the Arruda brothers, pioneers of the Manoelino, and on his death was made chief architect of the Alentejo, of which Évora is the most important town. He is supposed to have worked on the church of Graça with the French sculptor Chantarène, and on the strength of his obvious study of Italian Renaissance architecture this church is said by every authority to be an example of the Michael-Angelesque Baroque. It is of granite, with an under porch supported by four Corinthian pillars. Above is a pedimented window in the style of the rock tombs at Petra in Arabia, immense and disproportionate stone rosettes, four or five feet in diameter, which may have looked well on the drawing board but are distinctly amateurish in practice, and four strange and incongruous stone giants or atlantes sitting in pairs upon the pediment, below stone globes which represent flaming grenades. The interior of the Graça is in a state of ruin. This façade is extremely peculiar, but markedly provincial in style. In Spain, in a town like Salamanca or Valladolid, it would be little thought of. In Portugal it is remarkable. The Sé is sumptuous and dull, with a chancel and high altar by the German Ludwig who laid the load of Mafra upon the wooded plain.* There are rich objects in the sacristy. But, above all, Évora is the town of *azulejos*, and there is a superb collection of them in the former Jesuit College,

---

* The 12th Century lantern tower of the transept, of Perigourdine type with little turrets, much resembles the Torre del Gallo in the Old Cathedral at Salamanca, and the dome of the Cathedral at Zamora, of Oriental influence, that is to say. A fine altar piece from the Sé by the Flemish painter, Gerard David, is now in the museum.

lining the cloisters and staircases, together with a little 18th Century theatre reminiscent of the theatres for sacred dramas in the Franconian abbeys of Ottobeuren and Zwiefalten. Among the delights of Évora are the monasteries outside the town, chief of them the Cartuxa, a rarity in Portugal for there is only one other monastery of the white-robed monks, a church with a façade in correct, if dull Italian style, for Filippo Terzi was the architect, and the usual immense cloisters lined with pretty tiles. A mile or two further along the same road São Bento de Castris offers an identical mixture of delights, but with a Moorish touch thrown in. Both monasteries are beautiful on a spring evening.

The improvement of old roads and the making of new ones, which has transformed Portugal, has made it that many towns can now be visited in another order from that prevailing until a few years ago. We are now on our way to the South, and Beja was barely accessible before the War unless you went by way of Évora. Now, a road leads directly there from Setúbal. But it is better not to be fanciful, and keep to the order in which these towns were seen. The South begins somewhere between Évora and Beja. I have already in another book written my impressions of this town, and because those were written nearer in time I now resume them.* First, and most important of these impressions, is the approach to Beja. This is the South, for the Alentejo borders on Andalusia. For mile after mile there is a straight road across the plain. To either side of the road are rows of eucalyptus trees, which may have been Australian once, but here, with the nests of storks high in their branches, they are in sign of Barbary or Tartary. The white pallor of the landscape is extraordinary, this in March or April, but in summer it must be a golden plain of wheat and corn. It is not the white of snow or dust. The colour comes to it from its immensity. There is no shade at all except the rubbery leaves of the eucalyptus. Presently, far away, a white pyramid is seen with other, simple cubical shapes at its foot, on a hill in the very middle of the landscape. That is Beja. It has a white square, or praça. And far away, through a white archway, there is another town, a simple cube or pyramid in the distance, and the blue sky.

* In *Sacred and Profane Love*, London, Faber and Faber, Ltd., 1940, pp. 163, 164.

Here, in Beja, is the convent of Mariana Alcoforado, Sœur Marianne, or 'The Portuguese Nun,' known to the world for her intrigue, and her letters, with a Frenchman, the Chevalier de Chamilly. But did she, in fact, write the letters? For no one knows. She lived in the 17th Century, a nun of that name who was portress at the convent of the Conceição dying in 1723. But the first edition of the *Letters* came out in Paris in 1669. What had happened to Sœur Marianne during all that long time? The grille of her cell, suggesting in similes the spokes of her fan, has been taken out from the convent and put into the local museum. It was through this barred window that she spoke to the Chevalier de Chamilly. The chapel of the Conceição is one of the golden wonders of Portugal, not less glorious than that in the Convent of Jesus at Aveiro (see p. 216); and the chapter house of the nuns, Poor Clares, is a high, vaulted hall with lustred *azulejos* comparable to those lining the staircase in the Casa de Pilatos at Seville. And in Beja there is nothing else at all; unless, which is improbable, the same military band I heard still practises Spanish music through the hot afternoon in a room of the barracks, that was once another convent; music by Albéniz, and music of the Spanish *zarzuela*, *pasadobles*, quick marches slightly mocking the *toreros*, military fanfares, and again quick waltzes or *estudiantinas*, all looking towards Spain. It was tempting to wait until the evening, when they played in the garden underneath the acacia trees.

From Beja we drove due South to the Algarve, for long a separate part of the kingdom, indeed the kings of Portugal were kings of Portugal and the Algarve, ending a tiring day at Praia da Rocha, facing the Southern Atlantic, and with the best winter climate in all Europe. But it is, in fact, too much to the South in Portugal to be interesting. There is little architecture and few works of art, and only the climate and the wild flowers. Of the Moorish antecedents of the Algarve there is little sign. The peninsula of Setúbal is more beautiful. There is the tunny fishing town of Olhão, christened 'la ville cubiste', but the whitewashed roofs are no flatter than they are at Nazaré. The famous, pierced open-work chimneys of the Algarve are best seen inland, at Loulé, if, indeed, they are worth the trouble. Of greater interest is the rumoured old garden at Estoi, not far away, with clipped hedges, statues and fountains, and walks lined with azulejos, reported as a second Queluz, but up to this year it has not been photographed. At Faro there are many Sephardic Jews, with two synagogues; and at Lagos, with its magnificent bay and roadstead, there is the golden chapel of São Antonio, one of the five or six peerless chapels of its sort in Portugal. Sagres and Cape St. Vincent are a few miles further on; Sagres, where Prince Henry the Navigator had his headquarters in the fort, and Cape St. Vincent, celebrated for not one, but for two naval victories of the British Fleet. In general, and despite its Southern nature, I found the Algarve disappointing.*

On the way North again from Évora we made a detour in order to see the palace of the Braganças at Vila Viçosa. Here was their *tapada* or hunting park. The palace, in three storeys, is only marble fronted on one side; but in the interior are Flemish tapestries; a few rather insipid decorations by Quillard, a painter who had worked in Watteau's studio, but made poor use of that good fortune; many *azulejos* of proved Dutch, and not Portuguese origin; and a weird collection of late Victorian and Edwardian incongruities, inkpots, palm-stands, and photographs of Royal shooting parties. Many personal belongings of King Manoel and Queen Amélie fill the rooms, while the fortunes they so nobly left back to the country are largely laid out in agricultural and other schemes in the near neighbourhood. The tombs of the Braganças, depressing in black and white marble, are in the uninteresting church of the Agostinhos.

Borba and Estremoz are two towns on the road back to Lisbon; the first, a little place entirely glittering in whiteness, and where what is not whitewash is white marble. Here, and at Estremoz, it is not difficult to imagine a Moorish population, and at Estremoz there are churches that were once mosques. The town is built, too, of that scintillating marble, made more picturesque

* Among the curiosities of the Algarve are two breeds of dog which, so far as I know, have not been brought to England. The Cão d'Agua, the Portuguese Diving or Fishing Dog, was once common to the entire coast, but is now confined to the Southern shores of the Algarve. It retrieves lost tackle, broken nets, etc., and acts as courier between the fishing fleet and shore. Colours are black, black and tan, tan, tan and white, and browns. Coat, clipped poodle fashion, with a top-knot, and a lion-tuft on the tail-tip (33). The other race, still more restricted in number, is the Pêlo Encara Colado, more like a poodle.

still by the old fortifications which, in the diurnal moonlight created by so much whiteness, seem to echo with ghostly bugle-calls. Estremoz in its white marble is haunted by spectres of the barracoon. Unfortunately, both on this and on other visits to Portugal, I have missed seeing Elvas, which lies hardly ten miles further along the road to Spain. The town of sugar plums, according to report, is as light and fanciful as its name suggests. Badajoz is the first Spanish town across the frontier and its beggars are in contrast to this Arcadian plenty. Yet it is Spain; and though but fifteen miles away it had its painter, Luis Morales, 'el Divino' (d. 1586), author, in Beardsley's phrase, "of the egg-shaped Madonnas." In Portugal there are no painters. But, in Elvas, there are white houses and narrow whitewashed alleys, bugles sounding across the ramparts towards Spain, and several lively churches. One of them, the Freiras de São Domingos, is quite exceptional in that it is an octagon, supported on eight painted columns, and with tiles lining the walls up to the lantern. It is in effect a china octagon (36). Elvas, moreover, is in the centre of that part of the Alentejo where striped blankets are woven that give so gay an air to a few of the shops in Lisbon. They are in broad stripes of red and black and green and yellow, and some are a warm blue and crimson, with a wide repeat, and are among the prettiest things to be bought in Portugal. Near to the gate of Elvas is a *pousada* or Government inn built to accommodate travellers to or from Seville. All who have stayed there, and seen the china octagon of a church and the white houses, say that Elvas is a delightful welcome or farewell to Portugal.

VI

TRÁS-OS-MONTES

Santarém; Castelo Branco; Viseu; Lamego; Vila Mateus;
Bragança

IN contradiction to other lands where the warm South is the
attraction it was an excitement to leave Lisbon on an August
morning in 1953 for Trás-os-Montes, Bragança, and the unknown North. The road is a long bottle-neck beside the Tagus,
the only approach to the capital, jammed with lorries and slow-
plodding bullock carts, as far as where the new bridge is thrown
across the river just short of Vila Franca de Xira. Across the
bridge is a hotel, with an English owner, where a small private
bull-ring opens out of the dining room. For this is the Ribatejo,
the part of Portugal famous for black bulls and for its bull-fights.
Vila Franca de Xira is its centre; and in the spring on the day of
the *romaria* bulls are let loose in the main street, as at Pamplona.
Here is to be seen the *campino* of Portugal in his glory, in red
sleeveless waistcoat, a red sash round his waist, knee-breeches
with bright buttons and coloured garters, white stockings, and
a green stocking-cap, carrying a long lance or pronged trident.
His dress is pure 18th Century (16, 17).

Soon Santarém is reached, with churches, but nothing particularly interesting inside them, unless it be São João de Alparão,
now the museum, and easier to enquire for by that name, where
is the tomb of a nobleman, Dom Duarte de Menêses, so effectually
killed in a battle with the Moors that a single tooth is all that is
left of him, and there is nothing else but that inside his coffin.
Just before Abrantes, the castle of Almourol can be seen on its
island in the Tagus, a fortified castle built by the Knights Templars, to be rowed out to in a little boat called, prettily, an
abrangel. Abrantes is more interesting than Santarém; and so the
road continues towards Castelo Branco.*

* Two other towns, these are all small towns of from five to ten thousand
inhabitants, lie off this road which would lead eventually to Cáceres, in Spain.
They are Castelo de Vide and Portalegre, and I have not seen them. Castelo

We are now in the province of Beira Baixa and have crossed e lower end of the Serra da Estrêla. The mountain road goes and up till you look down on the roofs of the last village and e the plain with its vineyards and white villages lying into the stance. The Serra da Estrêla is a backbone of mountain running wn, not the centre of Portugal, but considerably to one side, that it cuts off the section of country along the Spanish frontier. is, understandably, one of the unaltered and least spoilt parts Portugal for the Estrêla range is extremely wild and has still it two roads across it. But Castelo Branco, where there is a od hotel, is still Southern in character; if not influenced by, for e two nations never understand each other's language, at least, a natural parallel of its own to Spain. We dined in a little staurant in Castelo Branco, where there were but two other bles, one of them occupied by a 'horsey character', clean aven, wearing a grey *sombrero*, loud in discussion of bulls and rses with his companions and interrupted every few moments one or other of his grooms, grizzled and sturdy old family tainers holding their hats in their hands, and who joined thoritatively in the talk of prices. He was a rich farmer or ndowner come into the town from some far off, whitewashed *inta*. At the other table, it was not far off midnight, sat an old riest with his two sisters. But for the language it could have en a market town in Andalusia. The olives in Castelo Branco e of peculiarly acrid kind; the peasants live off a handful of read and olives as the Arabs live on a handful of dates. A road ads from here to Spain, which is but sixty miles away; and but few miles over the frontier is the ruined castle of Alcántara on a ill above the Tagus, as historically famous and just as ruinous as ie Portuguese castles of Crato and of Aviz on their rocks far out n the plain.

In Castelo Branco there is nothing to see except a garden, ut it is one of the most elaborate and formal of old gardens in e Vide, the smaller of the two, is a hill town with white houses, old churches, id a few small palaces; a town of Roman origin, it has one fine church, the Conceição, the usual cloisters and *azulejos*, and among other palaces that of the onseca-Accioli, with china hunting scenes on the walls of the staircase, the ccioli being a branch of the old Florentine family of Acciaiuoli. An abbé of iis family comes into Beckford's *Letters*, and there are still Acciaiuolis in Iadeira and in Brazil.

Portugal, and built by the bishop (38, 39). The staircase w
statues of kings on pedestals is not the most beautiful feature
this garden, for they are wooden in effect and not in the traditi
of garden sculpture. But in that glaring heat the garden is
oasis of clipped box and stone and water. There is a complicat
box-parterre to one side, scrolls and embroideries of box, a
in the middle a stone basin of elaborate outline. On the t
terrace is the water tank with bearded masks, backed w
pebble landscapes. Below in a corner, taking advantage of
triangular piece of ground, is a clever garden fantasy unkno
elsewhere and of which this is, perhaps, the only example,
triangular pool with islands of stone in it, or, in fact, it is
parterre of stone, the stone arabesques taking the place of clipp
box, they are planted with flowers, and the stone arabesq
floats upon the water.

In what contrast to this Elysian garden must be the mounta
village of Monsanto, to which we never attained because
engine trouble which developed on the steep roads, a villa
recently 'discovered' and billed as "the most typical Portugue
village in the country", climbing, breakneck, up and down
stony hillside, and with handsome aquiline inhabitants who
some authorities identify as the descendants of Sephardim Je
fled in the late 15th Century to this remote fastness! There is e
dence of a Jewish strain in the population in much of this part
Portugal lying behind the Serra da Estrêla and along the Spani
border; at another village, Penamacor, at Belmonte, and in f
off Bragança. The traveller is to be pitied, stranded for the nig
in Monsanto or Penamacor! Many of the mountain hamlets off
a small pattern of Monsanto with their walls of cyclopean ston
roofs of stone slats, and the smoke coming out of the corners
the roofs instead of out of chimneys, a most curious effect unt
you know the reason.

Belmonte and its castle are in the plain. Here was born Ped
Álvares Cabral, the discoverer of Brazil, only less momentous
landfall than that of Columbus, and Cabral would find Belmon
not much altered from his time. Only ten or fifteen miles awa
and seen on a previous visit to Portugal, lies Guarda, the capit
of all this rocky country, three thousand feet up in the air, sta
cold at night, and with a cathedral of dour granite. Reynaldo d

tos ascribes the twisted pillars of the nave to Boytac, 'twister'
the columns in the church of Jesus at Setúbal, but even the
berant Boytac was a little subdued by grey Guarda. He may
e worked there during winter. Guarda is far removed from
cyon Portugal; and we plunge into the stony mountains of the
rêla climbing higher and higher through chestnut woods on a
ding, ever winding road, wondering if it is even possible to
mb higher, seeing another ridge above us, reaching that, and
n climbing higher still, until, at last, on the very summit
ong the boulders, we come to the Pousada São Lourenço, one
the Government inns, with a hot luncheon and a stupendous
w.

There is a beautiful, serpentine descent from here towards
ngualde, but before that is reached we come to the Hotel
geiriça, at Canas de Senhorim, a hotel under English owner-
p, to be mentioned here because it is the centre from which
e surrounding country can be explored in comfort. Not so long
o the hotel at Buçaco, remote as a dream, was the only means
visiting any of this part of Portugal, except for those persons
lling to endure real hardship. But Guarda, Coimbra, Viseu, and
mego are all near here; and were there time to wait for the
rmission we could also see the Casa da Insua, the house and
rdens of the Albuquerque family at Castendo, quite near
ngualde, where the patriarchal life is led as in former centuries.
geiriça lies in a lovely part of the country, not too high up,
d where heaths and mimosas scent the airs in spring. Basking
this oasis for a night we continued in the morning towards
seu, famed for its primitive paintings of the local school, by
sco Fernandes and other masters, but they are not great
ctures. No amount of argument will make them equal to the
emish painters. The cathedral of Viseu, even while we were
ere, was undergoing furious and noisy restoration. Men on
dders, armed with hammers, were knocking away, sparing
ither stone nor wood, an insensate example of how the Portu-
ese destroy their ancient monuments. It is the great vandalism
' our lifetimes, I myself having lived to see the great Abbeys of
talha and Alcobaça so much scrubbed and cleaned that, now,
ey are scarcely worth entering. The patina of ages was being
moved at Viseu, as elsewhere, and when it is gone the empty

vessels of the churches denuded of all ornament are made
look brand new. Once, the cathedral at Viseu must have be
delightful in its accumulation of the monuments and bric-à-b
of centuries. They were knocking down, as far as could be se
through the dust-cloud from their hammers, even the Manoeli
stone groining of the roof with its knotted cables. This cathedr
formerly gay and beautiful, will soon be bare as a hospital. N
content with that, they were knocking the tiles down from
walls of the double cloisters. Soon, no doubt, they will st
upon the sacristy.* There are more cloisters and staircases of
cathedral all in danger, and all to be regretted once they are go
for ever. In front of the cathedral there is the 18th Centu
façade in stucco and granite of the Misericórdia, most typi
with its twin towers, and over its windows the bat-wing volu
of Tuscan derivation, that are eloquent of Portugal. By
stretch of fancy could this building of the Misericórdia
Spanish, or anything else but Portuguese (see frontispiece).

São Pedro do Sul was the next stopping place, the only time
my life I have had persons come up and touch me while I h
luncheon in order to see if I were real. There is an oversm
chapel of the Misericórdia here, more suited to a doll's hou
with a little balcony, a hooded pediment, and ugly blue til
while the church of the Frades is difficult to get into, a
depressing once one is inside. Vouzela, down another road,
a creepily unpleasant Misericórdia, with horrid portraits of ea
19th Century benefactors, fly-blown objects, and mange a
ringworm in all around. These, however, seem only to be loc
conditions confined to one small area, for nothing could be mo
beautiful, or more happy and laughing, than the last few mil
to Lamego. It is one of the prettiest towns in the whole of Port
gal, and we are now entering the Northern region of go
architecture.

This is the remote province of Trás-os-Montes, or 'over tl

---

* The ceiling of this sacristy is much overpraised by the authors of *7
Selective Traveller in Portugal*. "Boars, apes and satyrs abound", but they a
incompetently drawn. The true example of "a sacristy to end all sacristies, ev
in Portugal", is to be admired for a few months longer at the Sé in Oport
for that, too, is scheduled for destruction (see p. 196). The ceiling at Vis
is earlier than it looks, and may date from 1580.

untains', though Lamego, properly speaking, pertains more
the Minho. It is a town, like Aix-en-Provence, like Lecce in
ulia, or Noto in Sicily, of lively and graceful buildings dating,
stly, from the 18th Century. I was reminded, too, of Taxco in
xico, which I had seen a few months before. What a lovely
sation to come down over the hills into the town and see the
rch towers of Lamego climbing up out of the valley! It is a
ticularly rich and fertile district of Portugal, not one of those
vns where you wonder how the inhabitants ever had the
rgy to erect such buildings, and the style is so much in the
nacular, as it could be said in the local speech of every day,
t the churches and palaces have little air of antiquity and look
ost new. It is as though they completely satisfied the needs of
population. Not a big town; perhaps with ten or twelve
usand inhabitants, and therefore its old buildings are in pro-
rtion. They occupy the centre and perimeter of the town, and
eyards come up almost to the houses. We drove into the
vn, not knowing the way; and enquired and were sent up the
l again, up and up through a wood in hairpin bends among the
es, coming out at last in front of the little *pousada*, a private
operty, this, belonging, I think, to the wine growers' associa-
n of Lamego. For this is a town famous for its wines, which
of many sorts. There are champagnes, including pink cham-
gne; and Lamego, as well, is celebrated for its hams that are
ly second in excellence to the hams of Chaves.

Climbing a little way into the wood behind the *pousada* the
in towers of the pilgrimage church come up out of the hill-top
th a Mexican profusion. They are the towers of N.S. dos
médios; and now a couple of Gitanos have come to the door
the hotel, each with a loudly yelling small pig held by a hind
, head down. There is a theory that the French aristocrats
uld never have been guillotined in such numbers during the
ench Revolution had they only protested more loudly about
and not suffered themselves out of pride to be led in silence
the slaughter. It is said that as soon as a few of them yelled
d screamed and made an outcry both the tribunal and the crowd
anged their mood; executions became fewer and before long
pped altogether. For the small pigs it was only a postponement
the evil hour, and they were led down, yelling, through the

trees. The pigs will have been bought cheap by the Gypsies
hawked from house to house. They feed on acorns in the wo
on high ground, and are not to be seen here rooting among
vines. Lamego is one of those little towns with a tempo of th
own. Let us think of others besides those named in an earl
sentence; Quimper in Brittany, Dinkelsbühl in Germany, and
the strength of twice driving through it in a motor-car, the lit
town of Sharon in Connecticut, with its wooden houses, whi
painted verandahs, chapels with porticos and wooden spires,
the houses facing directly on to the grass verge as though i
their communal property to be shared by all: bucolic towns w
their own measurement of time. Among such is Lamego, wh
you can be happy for a night, and feel ever afterwards that it
little part of your own life.*

These towns must each be in the centre of a rich agricultu
district; of Aix-en-Provence, while Cézanne lived there, it
said "it is surrounded by hills of abundant fertility, ami
almond groves and plantations of olives, furnishing the *sweet*
of Aix, the most esteemed in France"; Noto lies in the b
orange groves of Sicily; Taxco had its silver mine; Lamego
sweet wines and hams. By each contributing their mite,
inhabitants built over the years a beautiful monument to t
fertility, for N.S. dos Remédios is more than a pilgrimage chur
It takes a shape unknown except in Portugal, that of a sacr
garden (40). There is surely a literary origin for this, related,
instance, to the sacred dramas of the Jesuits. It is essentiall
conceit of the 17th Century, dear to the imagination of t
metaphysical poets. Indeed, neither Herbert nor Crashaw wou
have found it alien to their conceptions. But, in architecture,
is found nowhere but in Portugal, for it bears no relationship
for instance, the Sacro Monte di Varallo, in Piedmont, whe
there are chapels or oratories with life-size terracotta groups
Biblical figures from top to bottom of a hill, prototype of ma

* It would be interesting to go from Lamego about twenty-five miles to São J
de Tarouca where there is an old Cistercian monastery, and five miles bey
that the mountain village of Almofala with primitive customs, huts w
pointed roofs covered with turf, and a population still wearing mantles
cabuchos. It must be a little primitive enclave, like Miranda do Douro, o
smaller scale; or like Montalegre (see p. 164), or Castro Laboreiro (see p. 23

ier pilgrimage churches to be found all over Catholic Europe.*
was for the Portuguese to make the pilgrimage shrines into
rmal gardens.

N.S. dos Remédios at Lamego covers one whole side of a hill,
t is perhaps more impressive if you see it first from above, not
om below. The road leads up through the park, finding it
esistible at one moment to burrow under the formal staircase
th a tunnel, and ends with a flourish to the side of the church
ar to a postcard shop and the giant trunk of a dead tree. It is
om here that the church with its two towers is reminiscent
Taxco. The scheme consists of an immense double staircase
th nine landings, and below that a long ramp bordered with
ws of trees that leads down to the town. Cleverly, the space
.mediately in front of the church has been kept clear for the
ew, and it is only when you get to the balustrade that you look
own into the praça dos Reis, or Court of the Kings, which is
e top landing of the stair. This is a granite platform of octagonal
ape treated in scenic fashion as though by a theatrical scene
inter of the Bibiena school. Only it is a scene sculpture, not
ene painting. There are granite columns carrying statues, and
rings' made out of granite pillars and looking as though they
d just been moved into place. There is much play of squared
d round obelisks, not seen elsewhere. In the middle of this
:tagonal platform of granite is a fountain supporting an obelisk.
ie sculptures are not good. They are squat and clumsy; but
e architectural portion is so well designed and has so much of
ace and elegance that you do not notice the discrepancy. Some
the sculptures are of dwarf figures, but as the scale is wrong
ou do not know whether, or not, dwarfs are intended. Most
the carvings belong to the realm of pantomime kings, only it
curious to find what should have been carried out in papier
âché or cardboard carved out of hard granite. This is by far
e most decorated of the landings. The others have fountains
d octagonal pavilions with pyramidal roofs. Coming back up
e stairs again the praça dos Reis reappears in redoubled grace
d elegance, and there is a view of the front of the church as
ur head comes above the balustrade. It is graceful; but so
egantly empty in the interior that it is no more than a graceful

* The Sacro Monte di Varese, in Lombardy, is another example.

shell, and upon a magnified scale suggests a shell of chocola
waiting for a filling.

All this part of Northern Portugal must have been influenc
by the contemporary building activity at Santiago de Composte
We are to assume that regular pilgrimages went over the fronti
into Spain. And yet there could be no greater distinction th
between the Spanish Baroque of Santiago and this sacred gard
at Lamego which is entirely eloquent of Portugal. The me
shape of the pavilions, which are of course chapels, up and do
the staircase at N.S. dos Remédios, is completely Portugues
and reminiscent even of the corner towers at the palace of t
Meninos de Palhavã at Lisbon. How beautiful the view down in
Lamego from the balustrade! The clipped trees at the foot
the hill carry further the suggestion of good architecture, a
make you wonder if there is not a square down there equivale
to the Place Stanislas at Nancy. This is not so. But there a
plenty of delightful buildings, including the Bishop's pala
carried out in the granite and whitewash that is the vernacular
Northern Portugal. An Italian, Nicolò Nasoni, had a hand in t
cathedral. He was a Tuscan from San Giovanni in Val d'Ar
and came from Florence to Oporto.* At Lamego he 'regularize
the interior of the cathedral and must have been told to do l
best to make it look Italian. The cloister, however, is typical
Portugal. But Lamego is a town where there is some pret
building round every corner, and the only pity is that you a
out of the town after walking for five minutes. Particularly i
triguing is an enormous palace with long flights of window
What does it contain? Painted rooms, a fine staircase, a gard
at the back with fountains and clipped hedges? For Lamego

* Nicolò Nasoni lived for forty years in Oporto, 1732–73. He designed t
villas of Prelada and of Freixo, near Oporto; but his chief work there is t
church and tower of the Clérigos. It is surely a little fanciful to suggest th
the façade of this church "shows contacts with the South Italian Baroque
Lecce, in particular with the ornament of Giuseppe Cino's late 17th Centu
church of Santa Chiara, while the tower of the Clérigos seems to derive fro
the campanile of the cathedral at Lecce by Giuseppe Zimbalo (1659–70)", (
an article, 'The Arts in Brazil (i) Baroque Architecture', by Robert C. Smit
in *Portugal and Brazil*, edited by H. J. Livermore, Oxford, The Clarendon Pre
1953, pp. 378, 379. Why should an Italian, and above all a Tuscan, choose
copy the buildings of Lecce, in far off Apulia?

38, 39   Castelo Branco:
the Bishop's Garden

40   Lamego: Pilgrimage Church of N.S. dos Remédios

41   Vila Mateus, near Vila Real

emote and far away from the 'norm' of palaces in Italy or Spain. A middle-aged lady in black came out, shutting the gate behind her, of determined walk and mien. She must be the Baronessa, the owner of the palace. Walking by, she looked at me as one ghost recognizing another, and passed on.

It is all important not to stay in towns like Lamego for too long, and soon after mid-day we were on our way to Vila Real. When we arrived there it was half-past one, and hotter still. A memory of a small town in blazing heat, and walking in the streets looking for a place for luncheon; hearing the sound of music, and in a few moments eating slices of iced melon and drinking one of the delicious white country wines of the district. The 'lion' of Vila Real is the façade of the Capela Nova or Clérigos, 'waiting' down the next street and inviting a determined attack upon it through the barrage of sun. So hot was it that your hand was scorched if you but touched the plaster of the wall. The façade of the Capela Nova is an instance of the Portuguese cleverness in dealing with the 'wing' between two streets radiating apart in front of you. Coming towards it, that is to say, it is at the angle where the two streets meet in an arrowhead; and in Portugal they seem to have appreciated this opportunity of cleverness. The Capela Nova is of a greener granite than that used in the Minho and further to the West in Portugal, indeed it more nearly resembles the greenish-black 'tufa' of the Uffizi and other Florentine buildings. The ornament of the window over the door looks, too, to be Florentine in influence. It is a good picturesque bit of scenic invention; but in the interior, after painfully lifting the hot leather curtain, there is nothing at all. And in Vila Real there is little else; a town hall with 18th Century statues on the skyline, in a square which is somehow reminiscent of Astorga in Spain, whence come the Maragatos; and when it says in the *Guide Bleu* that Don Carlos, the 'original and genuine' Don Carlos of the Carlist Wars, driven from his country and living for some months in Vila Real, would retire to a place behind the town, "aimant rester des heures entières dans ce site grandiose", admiring the view in the direction of Spain, we may think that we share and condone his feeling. But, unfortunately, there are other reasons in plenty for mistrusting his sensibility!

A mile or two out of the town lies Vila Mateus in a halcyon
setting. It is, at once, the most typical and the most fantastic
country house in Portugal. The Vila Mateus advances toward
you, lobster-like, pushing two long tentacles or claws in front of
it; it has two long fronts looking inwards on each other, with
an outer 'attack' of but two windows each, whereas there are
six windows on the sides. But first, and set back on a level with
the main body of the Vila Mateus, is the chapel, with rich and
complicated frontispiece in full-blown Baroque, and a nice shell
inside of it, but nothing else. The villa is of the usual granite and
whitewash, and apart from the 'Italian' balconies on the outer
windows in the two long wings, its emphasis comes from the
extraordinary, high stone ornaments at every corner of its roof
line. The main body, richer still in effect, has a double stair
leading up to the door on the first floor, and this long enclosed
court of the Vila Mateus cannot fail in effect as you look up over
the doorway at the huge coat-of-arms (41). Another good effect
of peculiarity and of importance is the porch in the long side front
beside the church. It conveys a wonderful effect of the arrival of
fantastic personages in long periwigs. You walk right through
the main body of the building to the garden behind, which has a
beautiful box-parterre of the early 18th Century and an idyllic
landscape to back it. There are few more beautiful gardens in
Italy than this.

But the supreme fascination at Vila Mateus is the inside of the
house. Here, at last, is an interior which is not a disappointment.
The rooms have high coved ceilings of wood, superbly carved
of a Portuguese character to be known at once from its relationship to the mahogany vestment presses in the sacristies of their
churches, and from the four-poster beds with tapering, cork-
screw pillars that were made by Portuguese colonists in Brazil.
But this particular type of carved ceiling is probably peculiar to
Northern Portugal. There is a long enfilade of rooms, and in
one of them a set of those curious paintings in which a woman's
portrait is seen on nearer inspection to be formed entirely out
of fruits and flowers and vegetables. The painted ladies are so
many portraits of Ceres, and with Dalí-like ingenuity each in
turn resolves into so many components of Flora and Pomona.
Who was the painter? These allegories, so dear to the heart of

ie Emperor Rudolph II (1552–1612), would seem to place the
ainter in Prague or in Vienna, except that from internal evidence
iey are later in date and could be described as Louis XIV in
eriod. There are, as well, at Vila Mateus Royal portraits of a
scinating degree of badness, especially one of a king of Portugal
–the infant Dom José I?—about five or six years old, wearing a
eriwig so gigantic in proportion that it should have been worn
y Peter the Great or Augustus the Strong. These old portraits
ve to Vila Mateus an air of faded grandeur; and thinking of
iem, it was not without interest to look in the visitors' book
id find the signature of Dom Duarte Nuno, descendant of Dom
Iiguel and present claimant to the throne of Portugal. But the
me of Vila Mateus comes, now, from its wine. There are red,
hite, and *rosé* wines of Mateus, all in flagons that carry a
iarming label of Vila Mateus upon their sides; and having been
ild of this *vin rosé*, the best in Portugal and coming from the far
rovince of Trás-os-Montes, some years before in Spain, it was a
elight to arrive at last at this fabulous villa and see it and its
vely garden in this Arcadian setting.*

When drawing up plans for visiting Bragança, a town which
es in so remote a corner of Portugal that there are still con-
derable difficulties in getting there, it resolves itself into a prob-
m more than all else of where to stay. There are inns, of
iurse, but a sense of caution advises that it is better to avoid
iem. Soon it becomes evident that it is wiser to 'raid' Bragança
om one end or other, pass through it and sleep the other side.
he execution of this plan of campaign requires some time in
lanning, but eventually we decided to get to Bragança from the
orth, and it was in pursuit of this scheme that we went first to
amego, spent a night there, and came on to Vila Real. The next
age of the journey, a short one, took us on to Vidago, where
iere is a hotel of hallucinatory size in a village of not more than
dozen or two houses. This is because Vidago is a spa and
atering-place. The mineral water of Vidago is the best in
ortugal. But the hotel is only open during the season, which is
om May or June until September. It is a huge 'Edwardian'

* A *quinta* resembling Vila Mateus is at São João da Pesqueira, about twelve
iles from Tua, on the Douro. This could be visited from Alijo (see p. 168). It
may be by the same architect; balcony, with coat-of-arms over door, etc.

hotel, exactly resembling those to be seen on old engraved hotel writing-paper, and built in about 1905 during the reign of the King Dom Carlos, whose bedroom can still be seen with its furniture of the period. It is impossible not to conjure up visions of him arriving here, at the small station, in the Royal train. There are portentous menus of dinners in those far off days. The food must have been good, then; and it is still. Very characteristic are the bronze statues of ladies at the foot of the grand stair! What a strange place it must be, empty all the winter long. The hotel has a small park in front of it, and the flower beds on the terrace have come down unaltered from that time. But the medicinal waters are excellent, every room is full during the season, and there is absolutely nothing for the visitors to do, there being hardly so much as a shop to buy postcards in the village.

The inactivity weighs wearily, and we decided to go on and spend an hour in Chaves, coming back to Vidago in time for dinner. However, even in Vidago, the lure of remote Bragança is in the air. For it is a corner of Portugal unknown even to the Portuguese, so remote the other side of the mountains that it is almost like another kingdom. It is to Portugal, perhaps, what Friesland is to Holland. And, indeed, some districts of Bragança are the only part of Portugal where a dialect is spoken almost amounting to a separate tongue. Friesland is across the Zuyder Zee, while Bragança is the true Trás-os-Montes, across the hills. What is needed is someone who can speak of its strange villages and towns; and by good fortune there was exactly that individual, a person owning a café and small pension in another part of the village of Vidago, lying a few hundred yards down the road. What he could tell us was of the deepest interest.

Bragança must be the most untouched part of the country. His knowledge, he explained, was confined to Bragança, and he knew little of the Douro and Minho. He could tell us nothing of the curious festivals at Amarante (see p. 170); that was too far away. So remote was this conversation, which had, of course, to be interpreted to me, that I was reminded of the occasion when I had arrived late in the evening, tired out, in Leeuwarden, which is the capital of Friesland, and Mijnheer van Buijtenen, a young man attached as librarian to the State Archives, came up to our

afé table and struck a pleasant note of an old and vanished world
y proposing to speak Latin to me! Our talk on this occasion was,
.o less, of old and far off things. My new friend spoke of the
xtraordinary superstitions of the peasants and of how they
till believed in witches. He spoke, too, of the Jewish strain in
illages round Bragança where there are crypto-Jews, descen-
lants of those who fled here during the time of the Inquisition,
.nd who still observe certain Jewish rites without being aware
.f their significance.*

It is round Bragança that the curious Dança dos Pauliteiros is
»erformed, an ancient dance of pagan origin, by men dressed
.s women, dancing with crossed sticks, obviously related to the
Maid Marian of our Morris dances, and probably the relic of
ome fertility rite. He spoke, too, of Miranda do Douro, fifty
niles South-East of Bragança, and but a mile or two from Spain.
Iere, where a special *patois* (mirandês) is spoken, hardly intelli-
;ible to other Portuguese, there are extraordinary old customs;
he bride is still carried off from her father's house with a
>retence of force; and the greatest festivals are the funeral
·easts. The *capa de honras* is worn, a cloak made of strips of felt
.ewn together, with a hood and a huge collar that comes half-way
lown the back. Both men and women wear the old costumes; and
iere, particularly, the *Dança dos Paulitos* (stick dance) is per-
·ormed. How long were we staying in Vidago? If we could give
tim but two days' notice he would take us into the country,
where we could stay with two or three rich farmers who were
·riends of his. He would get up a dance for us, in fact, the *Dança*
los Pauliteiros. It took but a day to collect the dancers. Some of
:hem had been to London, to the Folk Dance Festival, and had
lanced in the Albert Hall. He spoke of the dress of the Pauli-
:eiros; white skirts and petticoats with zigzag stockings, and hats
with garlands of false flowers round the crown. He promised us
local dishes, some of which took several days to prepare, and
wines of the region. At night there would be stories of old

* According to Dr. Cecil Roth, who discovered these crypto-Jews, they are
·ound in Trás-os-Montes, and particularly towards Bragança, also, in the province of Beira-Baixa. Castelo Branco and Guarda have the crypto-Jews; Pinhel,
Vilarinho, Idanha, and Penamacor and Monsanto, he says, "seem full of
:hem".

customs to listen to, more especially when we were staying wit
him near Miranda do Douro, and he told us of the big, old farm
houses and of the famous breed of wide-horned cattle of th
district. No doubt this would have been an unique chance to g
knowledge of this curious and forgotten corner of Portugal s
near Spain. It would be impossible to go there under bette
auspices, with someone who knew all the local characters an
had the intelligence to know what was interesting. But tim
prevented it. What a wonderful experience it might hav
been to find ourselves for a few days in that strange wil
country!

So bidding him good-bye we went on to Chaves, a name whic
means, quite simply, 'Keys'; the town is near the Spanis
frontier commanding the road into Portugal, and is pronounce
as though it is written 'Chuvvs'. It is from the oak and chestnu
forests in its neighbourhood that come the famous smoked hams
the best in Portugal and perhaps in the world, to be eaten cu
very thin and with a slice of melon. The Spanish frontier is bu
six or seven miles away and Chaves is the 'key' to Portugal,
small country town with a history going back to Roman times
It has a Roman bridge of many arches, built in the reign o
Trajan, a relic of the Roman road from Braga to Astorga. Jus
before getting to the bridge there is the picturesque octagona
church of São João de Jesus, hidden behind other buildings, wit
nothing whatever of interest in the interior, and it is better t
walk a little further down to the river and look at the line
spread out in the sun to dry, and at the sandbanks and th
clumps of reeds. The churches of Chaves are disappointing. The
contain nothing worth seeing, except the parish church with
gilded organ in its darkest corner, upheld by a pair of hydro
cephaloid (big head) dwarfs, and a satyr's mask between. Eve
this organ is lacking in the grace and beauty of so many othe
organs in Northern Portugal. It is a rather creepy example o
what in Italy would be called 'bruto seicento' style, only, being
in Trás-os-Montes, it is a hundred to a hundred and fifty year
later in date.

A country road goes for some thirty-five miles from Chaves t
another small town, Montalegre, which must be as remote a
Miranda do Douro, in the other direction beyond Bragança. It i

the middle of the wild district called the Terras de Barroso,
where the winters are cold and there is deep snow. The shep-
erds, sometimes to be seen in the streets of Chaves, wear straw
raincoats which rustle as they walk and give them the look of
oilers in a paddyfield from off a lacquer cabinet. Men and
women, alike, wear birchwood sabots of huge size. On the
pastures are bred the race of cattle called Barrosã, with quite
enormous horns, to be seen all over the Minho, where they are
draught oxen and part of the pastoral beauty of that idyllic land.
This district of Montalegre may be not less interesting than
Miranda do Douro and this, too, we could have seen with our
new friend. Coming back to Vidago in time for dinner we found
he had sent round two bottles of a famous local wine for us to
try, and form another inducement to go with him into the deep
countryside.

Next morning we were up early and on the road, for it was an
immense drive that lay before us all the way to Bragança, and
beyond, as far as the *pousada* at Alijo, where we were to stay the
night. From Vidago to Bragança may be no more than seventy
miles, but it is over one of the worst and wildest roads in Europe,
and one of the most beautiful! Not more than two or three
hamlets of a few granite houses are passed on the way. The dust
in the road, inches deep, is of the consistency of face powder, of
a yellow colour, as that might be conditioned for the use of
Chinese ladies or film actors, and within a few minutes it covers
everything in the car, and even seeps inside the luggage. If you
stop the car for a moment and get out to stretch your legs it
covers your shoes so thickly that nothing will shake it off and
traces of it can be seen for days. This is the only landscape in
Portugal to resemble in immensity the landscapes along most of
the roads in Spain. For the character of Portugal is not its drama,
but its bucolic and Arcadian beauties. This road, though, running
along so close and parallel to the Spanish frontier, not more than
twelve or fifteen miles away, has all of the Spanish melancholy
and grandeur. There are oak and chestnut woods with trees
standing far apart, and a hamlet at half an hour's distance in each
direction, and the road winds with no parapet and many hairpin
ends above a river gorge. This is the climax of the drive and at
its summit must be the watershed. More and more remote we

feel, and the only thing lacking are eagles patrolling the air as the
do among the mountains of Spain.

Then, at the far end of this wind-swept wilderness where yc
would not have thought it possible there could be any buildir
but a hut of granite, Vinhais is reached with its double churcl
the explanation being that Vinhais is nothing extraordinary whe
you consider that, going the other way round, it is but twen
miles to the ancient and historic town of Bragança. It is, hov
ever, easy to exaggerate the wonders of Vinhais, though it is
curious effect because the façade is below the highroad. The
are two churches in the façade, side by side, or rather, one is
little below the other, and what is pleasing about them are tl
lovely and graceful pelmets to the side altars and the window
These are no less than a speciality of the churches in Northe
Portugal, and it would be well worth while to make a book
drawings of them. We shall find better and better examples
this minor art on our way through the Minho and the Dou
districts. There are pelmets with the grace and line of a Beardsl
drawing, as deserving of collection into a book as the gargoyle
bench ends, or brasses of an earlier age. The other things wortl
of this treatment, as we shall see, are the church organs of tl
early 18th Century. Here, at Vinhais, the pelmets are gilded,
have a touch of green or scarlet, and there are embroidered alt
fronts of much beauty, worked with flowers. Vinhais, now
seminary, was perhaps a convent of nuns, and the embroideri
were their handiwork.* But the ceiling paintings in both churche
as usual, are insignificant. If, as has been suggested, "this
probably the finest painted ceiling in Portugal", then, judg
by any standard, it is poor stuff.

After Vinhais the rigours of the road are somewhat lessene
though Bragança contrives to hide itself until you are right
top of it. On arrival, I must admit to feeling more certain tha
ever that Dom Miguel de Lima Barreto e Menêses, one tin
Bishop of Bragança, whose elegant cabriolet we saw at Belér
had never been here. What impression could the 12th Centu
town hall have made upon him! This is by far the most inte
esting thing in Bragança, and conveys a very extraordinary ir
pression of antiquity and early life. Its odd shape, alone, mak

* Bragança was made a bishopric in 1764, but the bishop resided at Vinha

convincing, not being four-square, but built out at one corner.
is built over a well or water-cistern, so that you enter it up
one steps, and underneath each one of its round arched windows
t an elder, bearded, we may be certain, and muffled in a cloak,
ut carrying no cushion. Round arches apart, the town hall looks
uch older than the 12th Century and gives a picture of life back
to the pre-Christian era. The little windows frame the green
ndscape, and we can think of the elders in their woollen gar-
ents, and with their wealth of horned cattle of the same race
those upon the roads today. There are few other buildings as
nmistakably ancient as this 12th Century town hall. How much
lder it looks than a Greek temple, and how much nearer to
tonehenge! It is quite a sensation to walk from the town hall to
hotel, and discover there a small sitting room—which is nearly,
not quite, a 'museum piece' of 1890. There were fresh trout
om a mountain stream, but it is the shades of night descending
at bring a touch of horror to the hotels in small country towns!
here are several churches in Bragança, of which we entered
wo or three; the best of them being São Bento with a wooden
arrel-ceiling painted all over by an indifferent hand. The effect
dark and very gloomy. Bragança is for the folklorist and
aturalist, not the art lover.

It is some sixty miles to Murça and time to go. A better road
rough an empty, desolate country with no shade. At an
ccasional fountain by the roadside the stone walls were too hot
touch. There are mountains with huge rocks perched upon
eir slopes, ready to roll down, and an occasional pine tree or
n olive grove. The distance reaches out into immensity as on
e roads in Spain. Murça has one curiosity, the granite 'pig of
Murça', now put in a public garden where it is difficult to see.
he sculpture is of the Iron Age, three or four hundred years
.c., unmistakably boar-like, that is to say, the pig is still rooting
bout, and not after an instant's glance to be mistaken for a bull.
here are these granite boars all over the Iberian peninsula,
otably at Avila, but this 'pig of Murça', more than most,
vokes modern sculpture and the hammer and chisel of Henry
Moore. In Murça there is, also, a Misericórdia chapel of miniature
roportions, with Salomonic granite pillars carved with grapes
nd vines, and so primitive an interior that it suggests a 'mission'

167

in New Mexico. The painting behind the altar is as odd and
curious as that, and so are many of the broken bits and pieces
This could be a chapel of pueblo Indians; and the landscape is
bare and clear and quivering with heat. It grew hotter and hotter
the hottest time of the day being between five and six o'clock in
the evening, and it had become as hot as the Sahara when we
arrived at Alijo, to find a fair in progress with merry-go-rounds
steam organs playing Mexican and Brazilian dance tunes, and a
'voice' on a loud speaker drowning all. This continued till mid
night, making sleep difficult in the otherwise comfortable, if
oddly named Pousada Barão Forrester.

VII

MINHO

marante; Guimarães; Barcelos; Braga; Ponte de Lima;
Viana do Castelo

E come now to what is beyond argument the most
beautiful province of Portugal. So far as circumstances
will permit on this earth it is an Elysian setting. The
 rtuguese are aware of this, themselves, and talk of it as the
 veliest part of their country, though it is only the natives of
 inho and inhabitants of Oporto who know it well. This is
 cause it is so far to the North and Portuguese, even now, have
 t the habit of travel in their own country. Still less do foreigners
 ouble themselves to go up North between Oporto and the
 anish frontier.

The Minho has long had this character of fertility. The Roman
 ldiers stationed at Ponte de Lima called the district the
 ysian Fields and were reluctant to leave here when their legion
 as moved on. But not only is it the most fertile part of Portu-
 l, it is the richest in old buildings. The most interesting early
 urches are in the Minho, including São Frutuoso, near Braga,
 Byzantine style, which carries in its name more than a hint of
 e surrounding bucolic plenty. So beautiful and fertile is this
 hole countryside that it is not surprising to learn that in several
 aces remains of an old pre-Christian fertility rite still persist, as
 e shall discover shortly when we arrive at Amarante. Finally,
 iring the 18th Century, the whole of this part of Portugal had
 s own flowering of Arcadian Rococo.

Leaving Alijo, and passing once more through Vila Real, the
 ad climbs to dizzy heights upon the mountains crossing the
 rra do Marão, and at the very top it is irresistible to stop for a
 w moments at the Pousada São Lourenço, one of the most
 arming of the Government inns, three thousand feet in the
 r, but it seems higher, a horseshoe-shaped building with a
 upendous view. In a wood beginning a few hundred feet away
 ere are wolves, and some wild-looking dogs tied up at the

door had, we were told, wolf blood in them.* Then, the descen
begins, and down in the valley there is a trout-breeding estab
lishment, State owned, and with its tanks formally laid out an
their banks planted with white and pink oleanders. We are no
entering into this Elysian country, at a corner which I place fo
convenience in the Minho although it lies, in fact, in Beira Alt
The road follows a river famous for its trout-fishing; vineyard
begin, there are primitive haystacks formed by hanging the stra
from the branch of a tree, cypresses and orchards appear, th
fertility thickens, all is bunched and heavy with ripeness, and w
arrive at Amarante.

This is a wholly delightful small town of not more than thre
or four thousand inhabitants, entered from this direction alon
a narrow street of houses, some of which are restaurants wi
terraces that overhang the river Tâmega. We chose a restaurar
which was also a confectioner's and looked at the cakes in th
windows labelled, correctly, *lerias, galhofas, papos de freira*, name
that are given in the guide books as specialities of Amarante. O
the way through the shop to the restaurant we asked for th
special cakes made for the *romaria*, and it is sad to have to say th
even the name of São Gonçalo aroused no response, and entir
ignorance was affected of all or anything concerning him. Bu
this is not to say that it was not a pretence on their part and tha
they were not concealing their knowledge from us. Also, it ma
well have been one of the situations known to all travellers whe
something is so well known that it is obvious, and the loc
inhabitants cannot bring themselves to believe that one is askin
about a thing that is plainly evident and always before their eye
Ask for St. Peter's at the main door of San Pietro in Vaticano
and it is more than likely that you will be misdirected and sen
away again! For the subject under discussion is nothing other tha
the famous and notorious festa of São Gonçalo, the patron sain
of Amarante, and we can do no better than quote a well-know
passage from the *Guide Bleu*: "En juin et janvier, la *romaria* (par
don) de São Gonçalo, patron de la ville et protecteur de
mariages, attire à Amarante une affluence considérable. A cett
occasion on fabrique des gâteaux en forme de phallus que le
jeunes hommes et les jeunes femmes ne se gênent pas de s

* Sheepdogs of the Serra da Estrêla are the most popular breed in Portuga

170

42   Mafra: the Palace, by Frederico Ludwig or Ludovice

43   Amarante: Church of São Gonçalo and bridge over the Tâmega

44   Solar da Gloria, near Ponte de Lima

45   Guimarães: the Palace of Lôbos-Machados

demander et de s'offrir mutuellement. Il s'agit ici, très probable-
ment, de la survivance d'un culte phallique très ancien." São
Gonçalo, in fact, is the patron saint of marriages, and every
confectioner in Amarante sells special cakes baked in the form of
a phallus which the young men and women give as presents to
each other. Knowing this, it is possible to read an ulterior
meaning into the very syllables of the name Amarante. It must
be the most strange survival of pagan times in all Europe,* yet
little or nothing is known of it, or what little is known is kept
secret. It would be of great interest to know more of the folklore
of this whole region.

The town of Amarante, it has been stated, is quite charming.
Delightful to eat luncheon on the terrace, to drink the white
wine of Amarante, and look down the river at the laundry spread
out on the sandy islands and over to the church of São Gonçalo at
the far end of the town! To finish the repast there are the famous
peaches of Amarante, perhaps the same as those we found later
at Oporto and thought to be even superior to the peaches of
Alcobaça. The town of Amarante has a conspicuous neatness in
its arrangement. You go to the end of the street, and in front of
you there is the bridge over the Tâmega with a pair of obelisks
at either end, built by Queen Maria I in 1790 (43). Across
the bridge rises the church of São Gonçalo, and on the cliff
above it, to the right, the little round church of São Domingos.
São Gonçalo has a fine Italianate façade, a façade worthy of Italy,
in granite of a golden tone, in three storeys of architecture, with
a cupola of blue and yellow tiles (43). The church has a pair of
good cloisters, but its most splendid feature is the organ. This
is among the most decorative of the organs in Portugal. In this
land of so few good paintings or sculptures, where the accent is
on the pelmets (see p. 166) and the *azulejos*, a particular beauty
attaches to the church organs. In Lisbon there is a superb organ

* Puck Fair, held every August at Killorglin, in Co. Kerry, and the crowning
of the goat, 'Ireland's only King', is of the same import. São Gonçalo, who is
buried at Amarante, died in 1262, so the *romaria* is obviously a pagan festival
continued in his name. Compare, also, the white cocks and hens of Santo
Domingo de la Calzada, in Aragon. Cf. *Truffle Hunt*, London, Robert Hale Ltd.,
1953, pp. 298, 299. At the festa, which is on the saint's day, new cocks and
hens are put into the cage in the cathedral, the old 'rooster' is killed, and there
is a big bull-fight in the evening.

in the church of the Paulistas, but it is of a different school from
the organs of Northern Portugal, which are beautiful enough to
deserve a study to themselves. There must have been, in all
probability, one family of craftsmen who made these organs, and
perhaps their headquarters were in Braga. This is a question that
no doubt, will be solved in time. The organ in São Gonçalo at
Amarante is upheld by a pair of tritons, and between them is a
merman with two forked black tails. This is, there can be little
doubt, by the maker of the tremendous organ case at Braga, and
who made various other organs betraying the same hand of orna
ment in monasteries and churches all over Northern Portugal
The high altar in São Gonçalo is one of the 'stepped altars'
peculiar to Portuguese churches, receding in diminishing steps or
shelves and culminating in a throne that has been given a shape
like the poop of a galley, in a setting, as always, of twisting
Salomonic pillars in Bibiena style, 'realized', that is to say, as
though from a drawing by some theatrical draughtsman. The
little round church of São Domingos, on the cliff above, which
throws down a welcome shadow on hot days in August, is
exceedingly pretty with its gilded woodwork and its little organ
set in a corner and supported by a pair of tritons. Another church
further up the hill, São Pedro, resisted all attempts at entry, and
it was so hot that one fell a ready victim to the refusal and went
on to Guimarães in a swoon of heat.*

Guimarães, with some ten or twelve thousand inhabitants, is a
town of Rococo churches and palaces marred by the awful
poverty of some of its population. In Guimarães, just as, long ago
in Spain, before they were exterminated during the horrors of
the Civil War, you will be followed round by beggars. Among

* Another of the wonderful old monasteries of Portugal that we missed
maddeningly, in ignorance, though it is only four kilometres off the road from
Amarante to Guimarães, is Travanca. The country lane branches off to it from
Vila Cova da Lixa. Travanca lies deep down in a wooded valley. It is a three
aisled church of Benedictine monks dating from the 12th Century. In the sacristy
the chests of drawers for the vestments are painted in green and gold with
chinoiseries of 'scènes champêtres et familiales' of about 1750. They should be very
pretty. Reynaldo dos Santos thinks that the monasteries of Travanca, Santo
Tirso, and Tibães (see pp. 177, 186) may all be due to João Turriano (1610–79)
a Benedictine monk, and son of the Italian, Leonardo Torriani (see p. 205)
A pleasant thought of a life spent on three romantic convents!

he most terrible of them are the children. There was a small
ɔoy who would reappear at intervals of a few minutes and unbare
ɨis chest, which bore the marks of terrible burnings. In a café
n the praça, adorned with ancient Egyptian carved figures of
ɩwful ugliness, like the evil dream of a designer of Egyptian
:igarette-box labels, it was difficult even to drink mineral water
ɔecause of the proximity of the horde of beggars, who evidently
ɔoked on this café as their rallying point. The castle of the Dukes
ɔf Bragança on a hill above the town was, once, of the 12th
Century but nonsense of that sort has been effectually knocked
ɔut of it by the restorers. It is said to contain copies of the famous
apestries of Pastrana. Many years ago I saw those tapestries in the
village church of Pastrana, in Spain, rolled up in the sacristy so
hat you could not examine them without treading on them.
They had been left to the church by the Duchess of Eboli, the
ïavourite of Philip II of Spain, but they are of historical interest
o Portugal because they depict the siege and capture of Arzila
n Morocco by Afonso V of Portugal in 1471; and because
Reynaldo dos Santos, although they are of Tournai manufacture,
ïees in certain lines of their composition, in the style of the
ɔortraits and in such details as the shapes and handles of the
ïwords, traces that the cartoons may have been drawn and
designed by the hand of Nuno Gonçalves, who painted the
wonderful triptych in the Janelas Verdes at Lisbon, and who is
he old master of the school of Portugal.* The castle of Guima-
ães was, however, hermetically closed and sealed, and so we
ɩad recourse to its churches.

The principal church, or Colegiada, has a detached shrine like
ɩ Gothic porch in front of it standing on the spot where Wanda,
King of the Goths, refused election unless the olive branch he
ɩeld in his hand would sprout immediately into leaves if it was
ɔut into the ground. If only the church restorers in Portugal
would approach the ancient monuments under their charge in
he same peaceful, non-aggressive mood, instead of flying at them
ɩammer and chisel in hand on the warpath, in emulation of the
ɩncient Goths and Vandals! Even more picturesque than this
ïhrine is the little town hall across the square, most Portuguese
n effect, but something of a puzzle. For the ground floor is

* *L'Art Portugais*, by Reynaldo dos Santos, Paris, Librairie Plon, 1953, p. 64.

vaulted so that you can walk straight through the town hall to the other side, and no doubt its mediaeval arcades were a meeting place on rainy days; it has a flight of five pedimented Palladian windows on the first floor, a battlemented roof line, and crowning that a statue of a king in armour and buskins wearing a plumed helmet, like the statue of Dom José I in the square in Lisbon, while the whole affair is described, nonchalantly, in the guide books as 'Manoelino'. The Colegiada, its proper name is Nossa Senhora da Oliveira,* has been furiously restored, in spite of which it is so dark that nothing can be seen except a lovely tomb in a grilled chapel by the door. There is said to be a splendid treasure of mediaeval vessels in this church but on that August afternoon no one had the key.

We saw two other churches in Guimarães; one of them with a late Adam interior in English dining room style as though decorated in agreement with the designer of the Assembly Rooms in some English county town. This church has a sacristy with looking-glasses in Adam style, and vestments and relics apart could well be the ladies' dressing room of the Assembly Rooms. Another, convent church, in contrast, is exuberantly Portuguese in style, now the chapel of a hospital and of nauseating approach, but, once entered, grand and golden in effect with great panels of blue and white *azulejos*. The pelmets in this church are among the best in Portugal, including the triple pelmet framing the nuns' raised choir. Once again, one cannot but think what an opportunity for good draughtsmanship of the ornamental order is offered by the pelmets, the organ cases, the gilded proscenium arches of these churches in Northern Portugal! There is more, besides, in Guimarães, in spite of the disappointing Casa dos Linhos in the chief square, where one had been led to expect printed cottons and linens of the Alcobaça sort (see p. 110), and only found drawn linen work instead, that being the local industry. But there are one or two fine palaces, and in particular the Lobos-Machados, standing in a narrow street, and specially designed to be effective from that point of view (45). This is a small town palace in 'Braga style', and like the façade of the

* Built by the King Dom João I in memory of the battle of Aljubarrota (1385). His architect was the Spaniard Juan Garcia of Toledo; and, indeed, this church is, perhaps, less like Portugal than Spain.

hapel we shall see before long in Viana do Castelo it is a thing
eculiar to Portugal, and which is unexcelled elsewhere. It is of
ark granite and whitewash, the body of the palace being only
ve windows in length, though another storey must have been
dded by the architect almost at the same time. All the ornament
f the façade is on the first floor; the over windows are deeply
ut so as to be visible in detail, sideways, from up or down the
treet; the central window over the door has a richly carved
oat-of-arms above it; and the whole of this frontispiece, which
s bound in by the pilasters at either end, has a waving cornice
which rises up in graceful curves to a climax and subsides again.

The poverty which is the unhappy feature of Guimarães is in
ontradiction to the Elysian fertility of all around and must come
rom the tendency of countrymen to flock into the towns. All
ound Guimarães there are farms and small quintas, and Rococo
onvents upon the sides of the hills above the vineyards.* For
ere the vines are trained on granite pillars and allowed to grow
o that they form festoons from tree to tree. They climb twenty-
eet high, and form tents or tunnels as in the appropriately named
ampagna felice or plain of Naples. It is, indeed, idyllic along these
oads of the Minho on a summer evening. Nowhere are there
uch long-horned oxen, or such beautifully carved wooden yokes.
hese are the oxen of the Terras de Barroso (see p. 165), with
yre-shaped horns often a yard across, led slowly along by the
traw-hatted women. Also, in few places in the world, and
ertainly nowhere else in Europe, will you see so many women
long the roads carrying heavy bundles on their heads, sometimes
s many as fifteen or twenty in sight at the same moment. Some
re carrying amphoras of classical shape; others, more prosaically,
re taking home their husbands' luncheon baskets, for the
easants in Portugal are inveterate picnickers, and often the

* Santo Tirso, a Benedictine abbey, is half-way from Guimarães to Oporto,
nd stands in the middle of a little town. The church has fine gilded Rococo
elmets to the chancel arch and all the windows. Pombeiro, another Benedic-
ine abbey, at the bottom of a wooded valley, is near Felgueiras, also on the road
rom Amarante to Guimarães, and like Travanca (see footnote p. 174), missed
n combined ignorance and innocence. At Pombeiro there is fine Rococo wood-
vork and more golden pelmets. Few foreigners have been to these old monas-
eries, and still fewer Portuguese. It is still not known what treasures they
ontain.

whole family take their midday meal together under the vines
Along one particular stretch of road between Braga and Guima
rães we met women carrying bundles of some kind of striped
handwoven material upon their heads, the spindle being on top
of the bundle, though no one, that day or the next, could tell u
who they were, or whence they came. The women under thei
heavy loads are ant-like in industry; while the whole landscape
with its tunnels of vines, the tufted hills, the magnolias and
camellias in every roadside garden, the brown wide-horned oxen
and fresh wines or *vinhos verdes* for which this country is re
nowned, make the hours go past as in an Elysian dream.

Not only are there Rococo convents, and *quintas*, there are
also Romanesque churches of an engaging simplicity. There are
several in the neighbourhood of Fafe, a little town lying abou
fifteen miles to the east of Guimarães, among them São Gen
with a 12th Century portal, and Font' Arcada with a beautifu
bas-relief above the doorway. This latter is beyond the pilgrimage
church of Nossa Senhora do Porto de Ave, a domed octagon with
formal terraces above it, and according to the authors of the
Selective Traveller, "a vast series of granite stairways, the parapet
set with huge granite flambeaux", fountains and statues, making
it sound as though this is an earlier attempt at the sacred gardens
of Bom Jesus and Lamego. The same authors mention "twir
organs in red and gold supported by merman and centaurs", or
the same makers, obviously, as other church organs mentioned
previously and worth a visit by the specialist.* There is a beautifu
purity and simplicity about the Romanesque churches in Portuga
as we shall see when we arrive at São Frutuoso (see p. 186), ever
if that is more Byzantine in style. They are churches, so to speak
of the bearded elders of the town hall at Bragança.

But we had seen enough for one day, and not pausing at Braga
nor even at Barcelos, for we were to visit both on the next day
we continued towards the sea, not having had a sight of the

* Another huge old convent lost in this countryside, and almost impossible to
identify on the map, is São Miguel de Refóios, near Cabaceiras de Basto, which
lies twenty miles east of Fafe. This is reported, "par l'élégance du dessin, par l
maîtrise de la mise en œuvre et par l'harmonie et la noblesse des proportions",
to be one of the most admirable specimens of the Rococo style. There are many
wood carvings in the "style contorsionné de l'époque", and it should be a
paradise for the pelmet-hunter and the amateur of golden organs.

Atlantic since we left Lisbon, and coming suddenly out of the foothills left the region of great heat, and entered an intermediate country of sea mists. The change of climate was most sensational. A land hardly above sea level, with brackish lagoons and a long sandy shore, and woods of pine trees; and in the midst of it, at Fão, a hotel of ultra-modern design with bedrooms that were like cabins on board ship, with built-in cupboards, and a little terrace to each room facing on the sea. There were persons staying in the hotel who had come all the way here from Lisbon in order to escape the heat. Certainly, the nights were cool, and even verging on cold, with the perpetual sound of the waves breaking which made sleep easier. But even this stretch of sandy coast is not lacking in things strange and peculiar. The fishing town of Apúlia, two or three miles further down the coast, is famed for its fishermen, or rather, seaweed gatherers, who have evolved for themselves a particular form of dress. Their work is to scramble over the rocks at low tide collecting the seaweed with their rakes or tridents, and the purpose of this costume is to keep dry in the spray of the Atlantic waves. What they have invented for themselves is a helmet and long tunic of white mackintosh, with a broad leather belt, exactly resembling those worn by the Roman legionaries (6), so suspicious a resemblance, indeed, upon this Atlantic coast, with its buried town of Tróia, its promontory of Peniche (Phoenicia?), and its fishermen of Nazaré of reputed origin, that one is tempted to attach a, per-haps, undue importance to the name Apúlia with its Roman echoes. How long this Roman dress of Apúlia has been worn, no one seems to know. It may be of very ancient origin, or it could be one of the last and latest inventions of all European folklore.*
But the fishermen of Apúlia are now famous, and a delegation of them had taken part in the *romaria* of Viana do Castelo a day or

* Peasant costume, generally speaking, is later in invention than might be supposed. Perhaps the latest instance of all is provided by the 'winged' women of Axel, a little town in Zeeuwsch-Vlanderen, the part of Holland south of the Scheldt and but a mile or two from the Belgian border. The women wear peaked shoulders that are like a pair of wings, but no photograph or drawing of this most mediaeval in appearance of all peasant dresses can be found before 1880, and it is the invention of the last decade or so of the 19th Century. I suspect that the weed gatherers of Apúlia invented their Roman costume at the same time. Cf. *The Netherlands*, London, B. T. Batsford, Ltd., 1948, pp. 148, 160-1.

two before. Certain rocks, not far out from the sandy shore at Fão, were one of their working grounds, and in the evening light we could see in the distance figures standing on the rocks and outlined against the sky, but it was too far to know whether, or not, they were the white-clad seaweed gatherers of Apúlia.

In the morning we started early for Barcelos, one of the prettiest little towns in Portugal, though with a population no larger than that of a big village. Barcelos lies on the top of a long hill above the river Cavado, which has to be crossed by a bridge, at the near end of which there stands a chapel with its foundations in the water. The chapel is the shape of a toll-keeper's lodge, with a porch all round it and a pyramidal roof, and under it there is a tank for lampreys, where they are kept fresh until they go to market. Whether these lampreys are as good as those of the Severn one could not tell, for their season is in the early spring. But the whole of the Minho is famous for lampreys, and there are gourmets who go specially further North to Monçao, on the Spanish border, for the sake of the lampreys and the local wine. If lampreys are counted as a folk dish, then, too, Barcelos has a double fame, for it is here that the gaily painted pottery roosters or cockerels are made. One of them, a foot or more in height, and tinted in garish colours, is among the grand effects of folk art in Portugal. They can be bought, inexpensively, in Lisbon. Barcelos, for its size, is full of good buildings, but best of all is the church of the Senhor da Cruz, an octagonal domed building which, for once, is as good inside as out. The furniture in the church is of superb quality; chairs and settees and chests of drawers of jacaranda (?) wood, the work of first-rate craftsmen. Outside, there are formal terraces which are part of the design, and an amusing contrast, as at Lamego, of round and squared obelisks. The Senhor de Cruz, which is of very early 18th Century date, and Baroque, not Rococo, is among the best buildings of its date in Portugal, by a more imaginative hand than the more vaunted palace of Mafra, and giving a rare distinction to Barcelos.*

* Attributed to João Antunes (1683–1734), architect to Dom Pedro II, but working mostly in the North of Portugal. Reynaldo dos Santos suggests his name for the unusual, octagonal chapel of the Senhor das Barrocas, at Aveiro. João Antunes was the leading Portuguese architect of his generation.

46 Braga: the view from Bom Jesus

47   Braga: the Cathedral Organ

It is but a few miles to Braga; and Braga, more than Oporto, is the artistic capital of Northern Portugal. It is the one town in the whole country which can compare in the number of its monuments with an Italian town. During two visits to Braga there was not time to see them all. Coming in from the direction of Barcelos you pass the palace of the Biscainhas, nearly at the corner of the market place. The beauty of this palace is its garden of clipped hedges with fountains and pavilions, though the palace itself, in belated *bruto Seicento* style, dwarf statues, and so forth, is a little reminiscent of the palaces along the Strada de Tribunali at Naples, where monstrous statues stand like post-boxes at foot of the stairs.* There is said to be a room in this palace with painted linen landscapes upon the walls. It was like venturing into a furnace to walk out into the market; a wonderful scene with bugles blowing from the near-by barracks, and every conceivable class of merchandise laid out for sale in stalls, or more simply, on the ground. The pottery, alone, is a revelation in these markets of Portugal; and there were whole regiments of the painted roosters of Barcelos.

The Archbishop of Braga is Primate of all Portugal, but you can look through all the guide-books and find no mention of the organ cases which are the beauty of the cathedral and that, somehow or other, have escaped the hand of the restorer. They are twin organs, and their carved and painted cases occupy all the height and the entire interior walls of a tower; or, at least, they have been shaped to form a tower. Seen from the floor of the cathedral they are an astonishing golden riot of tritons, dolphins, mermen, and satyrs or devils (47); and they can be admired again from higher up in the *coro alto*, where are the carved choir stalls and huge lectern. These organs, the most elaborate of any in Portugal, have an additional interest because by their date (1733–37) they were certainly played on by Carlos de Seixas (1704–42), the organist of Braga Cathedral, a pupil of Domenico Scarlatti, and composer of some nine hundred *toccatas* (or pieces for the keyboard) practically all of which are still unpublished. The whole of this West end of Braga Cathedral, organ cases and *coro alto*, are like an astonishing golden cavern. Hardly less grand

* Palazzo Roccella, with doorway upheld by faun caryatides, a pair of stone monsters standing on either side, and a further pair at foot of the stairs.

and sumptuous is the sacristy with its innumerable busts, man
of them wearing mitres, and all enclosing relics. In fact, th
relics are as the Theban Legion in number, and there are embroi
dered vestments and inlaid chests of drawers. More interestin
still is a Moorish ivory casket made at Córdoba in the 11t
Century, and only matched by those in the cathedral at Pamplon
and in the Victoria and Albert Museum.* The golden grotto o
cavern of Braga Cathedral is reminiscent of Spain, of the *coro* o
the *mezquita* at Córdoba, of churches at Valencia and Salamanca
but nowhere is there such golden stalactitic richness; while it i
only true to say that the porch of Braga with its iron railings c
reja type, and the floreated corbellings and crenellations of th
apse, recall the richness of late Gothic work at Burgos Cathedra
and at the Cartuja de Miraflores. Would it be unreasonable, too
to say that there is the hint or the taste of Spain in two cere
monies at Braga of unique character; the blessing of the grape
on 6 August, which is the Transfiguration, and the feast of St
John (São João), on 24 June, when during the course of pro
cessions down the streets David dances before the Ark, and th
rôle of David is always taken by a member of the same family
Something of an air of Spain clings, also, to the Capela do
Coimbras, a little chapel in a square near the cathedral, with
porch which, again, for railing has a Spanish *reja* of authenti
type, the chapel itself looking more like a truncated tower, richl
crenellated, while in the interior there is a *retablo* or altar wit
polychrome sculptures which are purely Spanish in feeling.

In point of architecture there is every temptation to wal
about the streets of Braga. An acquaintance, at long interva
of absence, but lasting half a lifetime, has not diminished th
beauty and fantasy of the *Palácio do Mexicano*, perhaps the mos
typical of buildings in the Braga style.† This has the sam

* By an extraordinary coincidence the Moorish ivory caskets at Braga an
at Pamplona are proved by inscriptions to have been made for the same perso
a minister of the Caliph Hisham II, under the direction of his Chief Eunuc
These ivory caskets are completely covered with carvings in relief, with leav
and flowers, and cusped medallions containing figures of men seated Moorisl
fashion upon the ground, hawking, or fighting with wild beasts, and with othe
single figures of lions, stags, or other animals.

† Known also as the Solar do Visconde de São Lázaro. This palace w
illustrated in *Southern Baroque Art*, 1924.

'binding in' of the composition at both ends as at the Lobos-Machados palace at Guimarães. A flight of seven windows with hooded pediments, an elaborate scheme for the doorway reaching through both floors to the roof-line, and the roof itself crowned with flaming urns. The Palácio do Mexicano is not granite and whitewash in the local idiom but, by way of variety, it is of granite and *azulejo*. There are other palaces in Braga little inferior to this; and a church built on the lines of the Gesù at Rome (N.S. do Populo), but with as many figures in blue *azulejos* reaching up to the ceiling as there are 'supers' in a film epic.* Most travellers, however, have little time for Braga but make haste for Bom Jesus, a pilgrimage church and sacred garden a mile or two outside the town, where, too, it is pleasanter to stay than below in the tram-loud town. The terraced staircase at Bom Jesus, with chapels on its landings and mosaic pavements, is due to Cruz Amarante (46, 48). But it would be idle to pretend that N.S. dos Remédios at Lamego is not more beautiful. There is no architectural climax at Braga as there is at Lamego in the obelisks and columns of the Court of the Kings; while, at Bom Jesus, the church is entirely negligible and not worth entering.†

Picturesque and fascinating buildings abound in this neighbourhood. Just outside the town is the Capela da Falperra, a little masterpiece of gracefulness in whitewashed surfaces and granite, and once again, though so typical of Portugal, of remote Tuscan origin, in that sub-style of the '*bruto Seicento*' which we may derive, fancifully, from Callot and from a study of bats.‡ The central feature of this chapel, forming the door and the window above that, and reaching in another storey up to the roof, has these bat-wing volutes in exceptional prominence. In another direction from Braga is the Quinta da Palmeira, built

*Another church, according to the authors of *The Selective Traveller*, that of São Vicente, has a white and gold organ loft upheld by four tritons.

† Cruz Amarante (1748–1810) is surprisingly late in date, affording yet another comparison with the Brazilian Aleijadinho (António Francisco Lisboa, whose dates are 1730–1814). Bom Jesus is prototype for his sacred garden at Congonhas do Campo, in the gold-mining state of Minas Gerais. Cf. also p. 23 of Introduction.

‡ It seems to have been the invention of Bern. Buontalenti (1536–1608), who experimented with it at the Palazzo Uffizi. This must have been an importation from Florence into Northern Portugal by Nicolò Nasoni (see p. 205).

by one of the Meninos de Palhavã (see p. 90). It is in small *quintas* and large old convents that this vine-clad landscape is abundant. What could be more promising than São Frutuoso? This early Byzantine church of the 7th Century is on the road to Ponte de Lima, built in the form of a Greek cross, and as Reynaldo dos Santos remarks, recalling the exterior of the mausoleum of Galla Placidia at Ravenna. It must be, as the same authority says, Visigothic in date and Byzantine in style; more Byzantine, it is certain, than the early churches of Santa María de Naranco and San Miguel de Lino, near Oviedo, in Spain, which belong to the 9th Century. The interior of São Frutuoso is in entire Ravenna style, so much so that this little chapel should not be omitted from any history of Byzantine art. It is of a beautiful simplicity, but speaks of early kings and queens, and not of pastoral elders as do the few other early churches in Portugal, in respect of which it should be noted that São Frutuoso (656–665), who was Bishop of Braga, had probably been at least once in his life to Rome. The huge convent church is next door, with golden pelmets and a raised choir (*coro alto*) with choir stalls surmounted by cherubs holding chains of flowers. It is a good and picturesque specimen of a large, old convent, and had we but continued a little further, rejoining the main road and branching off again, we would have reached Tibães, once the chief monastery of the Benedictine Order in Portugal, with no fewer than four cloisters, one of them with *azulejo* panels of the life of the founder of the Order, and a church with elegant pelmets and golden proscenium arch. The authors of *The Selective Traveller* mention a garden with miniature flights of steps and fountains, and say those of Bom Jesus were copied from Tibães.

Another huge old church is that of the former Cistercian monastery of Bouro, to the East of Braga and on the road to Caldos do Gerez. This is notable because of the life-size statues of kings of Portugal in plumed helms on the façade of the monastery, like those formerly adorning the church of Alcobaça, but long ago relegated by humourless authorities to the dustbin. Bouro, now private property, is half in ruins; though its former beauty is brought even a little further forward in imagination by the laconic remark, "oranges appréciées", in the guide book. We had time, alas! for neither Bouro nor Tibães, but went on

48   Braga: octagonal Chapel on the staircase at Bom Jesus

49 Monastery of Refóios
de Lima

50 Viana do Castelo:
Capela dos Malheiros
Reimões

ur way to Ponte de Lima, through one of the most fertile and
eautiful regions of all Portugal. So idyllic is it that the action of
assing through it induces a mood akin to that of being in a
ance, and for mile after mile one could imagine that it is stage
cenery for some old opera or ballet. This sensation is in no way
iminished where the road is being mended and the work all done
y hand. Dozens and dozens of men and women on their hands
d knees are hammering in little pieces of stone as though
rming a mosaic, but through a smoke as of the infernal regions.
ever before has one seen a hand-made road. Tar is being sprayed
om a primitive machine, and the Tartarean foremen and over-
ers shout their orders to stand aside and let the car pass by.
here cannot have been fewer than sixty or seventy women and
ildren working on this highway, and, like all else that is made
hand, these roads last for a long time and are easily repaired
long as labour is so cheap. Meanwhile the vines, if anything,
ow higher still, there are small *quintas* to every side, and it is
rough an indescribable, tufted richness of the quality only to
admired in old-fashioned scene painting that, at last, we reach
nte de Lima, a pretty town with some undoubted Manoelino
orways and a chapel at the far end of the bridge over the Lima,
hich has an onion-shaped belfry. Ponte de Lima is pleasant to
alk about in but there is little to see.

Beyond the bridge, however, and a few miles away to the
ght, is the convent of Refóios de Lima (49), of which we would
scribe the interior, in a phrase, as a notable pelmet centre.
hey are, in fact, enlarged specimens more deserving to be called
oscenium arches, for one single gilded pelmet is made to do
uble duty, framing two chapels to each side. From here we
rned back and took the road running along the right bank of
e river to Viana do Castelo. This is the classical region for old
anor houses (41, 44), of which one beautiful specimen is
ssed about half-way along the road. But there is, also, a whole
ction of country lying North of this as far as the Spanish frontier,
hich it would be intriguing to explore. Having reached that at
alença do Minho and turning right again along the river to
onção, where the good wine and the lampreys have been
ready mentioned, the temptation comes to go a little further
where there is a district as little known as the wildest parts of

Trás-os-Montes. This is higher up the Minho to Melgaço, famo
like Chaves for its hams; and then inland ten miles to Cast
Laboreiro, of which we are told that it is a small town on
rocky hill, with houses roofed with turf, that the populati
"aux mœurs archaïques" still wear hooded cloaks of heavy f
and great wooden sabots made of willow, and that a particu
breed of sheepdog, again a stranger to the show benches
Cruft's, inhabits the region. Spain is but a mile or two awa
and it would be interesting to visit that isolated, forgott
countryside (see p. 235).

Viana do Castelo is prosperous looking, and when we we
there was just recovering from the tremendous *romaria* of No
Senhora da Agonia, the date of which is 18 to 20 August. Triu
phal arches of wood and paper, brightly painted, spanned t
streets, and the many bandstands were pricked out with elect
lights. The lion of Viana do Castelo is the Misericórdia, wi
three storeys, of which two are open *loggias* with granite cary
tides. Nevertheless, it is a heavy, muddled building. In front the
is a pretty fountain of the Renaissance. But there is one piece
architecture in Viana of a notable grace and elegance, and of
kind not to be found outside Portugal, and that is the façade
the Malheiros Reimões chapel, fronting down a street (5o
This is, as it were, an enriched version of the Clérigos or Cape
Nova at Vila Real, where the purpose is the same, that of formi
an arrowhead to point down a street.* It is, therefore, built
an angle, and we are to observe the elegance of its side wing
but, more than all else, the rich and satisfying composition
door and window above it. The window is like a Rococo windo
frame, the pilasters framing the whole are just of the right pr
portion, while the granite jambs of the doorway of themselv
assume a 'sea' or 'fishing shape', and in any case have seashe
carved upon their lower portions, there being, as well, seash
motifs upon the cornice. This little chapel facing down the stree
the interior of which is not worth entering, is charming eve

* The Casa de Corso at Tondela, near Viseu, "built with its two wir
meeting in a blunt angle, where the chapel stands, one of the most beauti
Baroque doorways in the world", as described by the authors of *The Select
Traveller*, p. 185, should be another instance of this architectural speciality
Portugal.

time one passes and looks towards it, and to an unbiased mind it will be the chief ornament of Viana do Castelo. The town is full of shops selling the peasant dresses for which Viana is famous. The costume here is prettier than anywhere in Portugal. There are the curious black marriage dresses of the region; but, in general, the dresses of this district are scarlet and white, the scarlet predominating, though there is one particular village where the dresses are blue, instead of scarlet. There are, also, very charming dresses of black and green; and all of them, whether scarlet, blue, or green, glitter with tinsel and sequins. The costume of Viana has become, in fact, the typical peasant dress of Portugal. But it was now late in the evening; and so back for the night to Fão, which should be pronounced with as Cockney an accent as possible, 'Faow'.

VIII

OPORTO, AVEIRO, COIMBRA

OPORTO is the only place except Lisbon in the whole of Portugal where there is the sensation of being in a town of half a million Portuguese. Of course the quick way to realize this is to stand in the praça da Liberdade, the chief square, and listen to the noise. In the middle of it there is an equestrian statue of the King Dom Pedro IV the 'Liberator', but it is idle to pretend that he is a familiar historical figure to foreigners and his statue only adds mystery and confusion to the scene. It is better, therefore, not to find yourself in Oporto but to arrive there, as we did, passing through Povoa de Varzim, birthplace of the novelist Eça de Queiroz, with its huge suburb of fishermen, and by way of Vila do Conde, where the immense convent of Santa Clara has been practically ruined by the restorers.* In this way you come into Oporto along the river bank, and can admire this superb entrance into the town which enabled large sailing vessels in the past to tie up near to the churches, though, now, ships of any size have to dock at Leixões, several miles away. Suddenly, the huge iron bridge over the Douro comes into view and beneath it, painted on the sides of buildings, the bewildering variety of names of all the port wine lodges.

But an even better and subtler way of appreciating Oporto is to go up to the Sé, walk to the edge of its terrace, lean on the parapet and look down over the old houses of the town. Nearly

---

* Reynaldo dos Santos mentions the golden organ at Santa Clara, in Vila do Conde, as among the most beautiful in Portugal (53), though not having entered the church since a previous visit I have to confess I have forgotten it. Among other tombs is that of Dom Fernando de Menêses and his wife (late 15th Century), and it would be curious to know whether the heraldic ring of the Menêses, interlaced with phylacteries (and devices expressing the constant love of the husband for his wife Brites de Andrade), is of significance as to a Sephardic ancestry for this family. For the name Menêses, see p. 93, Dom Miguel de Lima Barreto y Menêses, Bishop of Bragança; and see p. 94, for Dom Pedro de Alcântara de Menêses, Marquês de Marialva, the friend of Beckford. Some of the greatest families in Portugal, as in Spain, had blood of the Sephardim in their veins.

wenty years ago I had spent long moments doing this until the mage of these old houses immediately below had become an neffaceable memory, and now so many years later they had not hanged, and the same old woman, it seemed to me, but it could ot in fact be the same old crone, hobbled to her attic window nder the tiles, nearly upsetting the flower pots on her balcony, nd put a little bowl of water in the small bird-cage hanging here. The same little children played in their attic at an incredble height above the winding street. The attic windows took up he whole width of one wall so that these were rooms with one ide open to the street. How narrow and rickety must be their lights of stairs; and now I noticed again, which I had forgotten, hat the stair wells in the old houses end in a glass lantern and hat there are dozens of these glass lanterns in the houses below oming up out of the tiled roofs like the stoppers of glass bottles r the conning-towers of submarines! All the roofs, too, have slight tilt to their eaves, giving them the look of old houses in ome town in China. They are not so much attic rooms as erraces. But life there must be still more curious when it rains. hen they would have to shut the windows, and must be walled n by their own noises which would be thrown back on them, nd in imagination one heard the torrential splashing of the rain. 'erhaps a whole day of rain, with water running down the gutters n the cobbled street, the bird-cage hung to a rafter, and the ousehold cat sitting, disconsolate, no longer able to sun itself pon the balcony!

How many more years will it be before the old houses below he Sé at Oporto are condemned and swept away? It will be a ity, because they have character, and we may be sure the umble families who live there are attached to them. They have hat slight hint of China from the tilt of the roofs, as much as a erson can look Oriental from having slanting eyes. Mariners ad sailed from this river to Goa and Macau; and one could not rget that, nor fail, on looking down at them again, to be eminded of the red roofs of Whitby and of how Captain Cook ad sailed from there for the South Seas. The roofs of the old wn of Whitby, under the cliff with the smoke rising stiff from hem into the Northern air, were only spared by authority after uch persuasion, and it is to be hoped that the destroying hand

at Oporto will be as merciful. So many lesser things that are no
merely historical give antiquity and beauty to a town. Oporto i
as much a city of steep hills as Lisbon. And soon enough, in orde
to get the atmosphere of Oporto, you will find yourself whirlin
down one hill and up another and passing the fronts of tw
churches of the Carmelite nuns, standing side by side, the whol
façade of one of them covered by an immense panel in blue an
white china tiles of nuns taking the veil. This is Portugal an
could be nowhere else in the world, unless it be Brazil! But hov
sorry one is to have missed the church of Sobreiro, near Aveiro
reported in *The Selective Traveller* to have "a façade entirel
covered with Edwardian tiled pictures of moustachio'd benefac
tors and saints!"

There is a narrow street at Oporto full of goldsmiths' shops
where may be bought the heavy golden earrings and tripl
necklaces of Gondomar, that being the beautiful name of th
suburb where is made the jewellery worn by peasant women a
the neighbouring *romarias*. And another sensation of Oporto i
to watch the coal barges on the Douro; and more particularl
the *ribeiros*, river boats with large sails, and a cabin amidships
and a gigantic rudder, which bring down the wine to Oporto fron
the vineyards up the Douro. That models of these *ribeiros* shoul
stand in the windows of many wine merchants in England doe
nothing to abate the beauty of these river boats. There are n
museums in Oporto worth bothering about, and all the interes
is in the streets. Oporto is one of those towns, like Naples o
Valencia, that have a Southern character, though of a temperat
nature, not suffocatingly hot, and with a climate perhaps bes
described by drawing attention to the unrivalled beauty of it
camellias. Many of these must have been brought out a hundre
or more years ago by Englishmen engaged in the port win
trade, and planted in their *quintas*. Liszt, writing to Mm
d'Agoult in 1842, says that he would like to send her "som
cartloads of camellias from Oporto", and bunches of them ar
certainly the characteristic flower of the town.

The British Factory stands in the lowlying part of Oporto
built in 1785 by the Consul, William Whitehead, and presentin
so perfect an illusion of the Englishman's club that it would b
a delight to get an invitation to it for the heroes of Jules Verne'

ound the World in Sixty Days. It will be remembered that they
egin their adventure after a substantial breakfast in a club in
all Mall. The illusion is complete and entire except that smoking
permitted during the sacred rites while the port is handed
ound, and that it is drunk chilled, rather as *vin rosé* is drunk in
rance. There are many portraits and much old furniture, and
ere are services of green Rockingham china and chandeliers.
ittle or nothing has altered, and the officers of Wellington's
rmy could walk in, hang up their swordbelts and shakos, and
xpress surprise at not being recognized. In short, it is as
nglish as New York's Chinatown is Chinese. More curious still,
e British Factory is not, after all, a club, but it is the property
f members of the dozen or fifteen different wine lodges, some
milies among which, such as the Warres, have had connections
ith Oporto since the middle of the 17th Century.

Immediately after luncheon in the British Factory it is to be
oticed that there is nothing in the least incongruous in going up
the Sé and making straight for the sacristy, for there is a
endency in old cities for the sacristy of a church to become
quivalent to a club and to have many of the amenities of a
omfortable meeting place. There could be no better example
an the cathedral sacristy at Oporto. The writer, himself, some-
hat of an amateur of sacristies, would number this among the
ur best that are known to him. One of its rivals is that of San
áolo Maggiore at Naples, a church built by a Theatine monk on
e site of a temple of Castor and Pollux, proving that the street
ven in classical times was a busy part of Naples. The portico of the
mple was *in situ* until destroyed by an earthquake in 1688; two
orinthian columns and a part of the architrave still remain, but
e sacristy with its brocaded chairs and looking-glasses is like a
rawing room, only it is a drawing room of old *monsignori* much
ddicted to taking snuff. The walls at either end are grandly
ainted in fresco with the Conversion of Paul and the Fall of
imon Magus, and there one may recognize the white horses of
olimena, called *l'Abate Ciccio*. Next on the list would be the
cristy of El Pilar at Zaragoza, "where the prettiest things,
earls and diamonds apart, are the vestments of the canons, tied
p in neat bundles, bound with green or red silk ribbons to
atch their colours, and worked with the initials of their

reverend owners". Closely rivalling it is that of La Seo, the o
cathedral of Zaragoza, "an enfilade of grand apartments, the er
one furnished like a drawing room with long pier-glasses ar
great vases of Chinese porcelain set upon the floor. The on
thing lacking is a China mandarin to nod his head and lift ar
let fall his outstretched hands"; the other contestant being th
Salón de la Sacristía at Toledo, with the *Expolio* by El Grecc
paintings by Goya and other masters, and a painted ceiling l
Luca Giordano, wherein, during the morning, a beam of sur
light shines across the ceiling from the figure of the Almighty.

The sacristy of the Sé at Oporto is now in imminent peril (
destruction and that is why these lines are written. What
beautiful old room it is! The patina of two centuries lies on i
The chests of drawers for the vestments are of magnificer
workmanship, there are lovely old mirrors, and the vaulte
ceiling is painted with architectural subjects in better style tha
most painted ceilings in Portugal. But it is precisely because (
this ceiling that the sacristy is in trouble, and the proposal is t
knock down all the plaster and reveal the bare stone vaultir
underneath. A beginning has been made already, and the ev
day is only postponed for a few months. When it comes, th
whole sacristy with its accumulation of the ages is to be de
troyed, all for the sake of a few bare stones. Then, one of th
most characteristic things in Oporto will be gone for ever, an
the authorities must not blame a friendly foreigner who tel
them that the sacristy is now, and for as long as it is spared, th
best part of the cathedral. For there is, in truth, not much els
there; a silver altar, but it has lost the gleam of silver; a delightfu
Baroque composition of urns and balconies over a door in th
principal front and under a rose window; and a cloister with th
usual *azulejos*. Such things are all over Portugal, but this uniqu
sacristy, with its echoes of city life over two centuries,
scheduled for destruction.

A better fate, at least, has befallen the church of São Francisc
even if it is now a national monument and services are no longe
held there (57)! This church is down near the river not far fror
the British Factory. The interior is a fantastic golden vision (54
Its Gothic structure, for it is a building of the 14th Century, ha

* Cf. *Spain*, London, B. T. Batsford Ltd., 1950, pp. 43 and 84.

51   Straw-coated Shepherds of Pinhão
        in the Douro Valley

52   A Water-carrier of the Lima Valley

53   Vila do Conde: Organ in the Church of Santa Clara

54   Interior of the Church of São Francisco

55, 56 Oporto: Interior, and *(below)* the Doorway of Santa Clara

een entirely overlaid with gilded woodwork, so that it has ecome a golden cavern. It is the masterpiece of the pelmet vorkers. You enter it by a 17th Century portal with Salomonic columns under a Gothic rose window; and the first effect, the urprise of entering, is as overwhelming as at the Jerónimos at Belém. There are chapels with golden gates to them that posiively glitter with gold. There are Manoelino archways; but they ave been given a golden cresting with golden drops or flounces s of some golden material, a waving cornice, and above that he broken pediment and all the ornament of the most coruscating of Chippendale mirror-cases, only the archway is thirty or forty feet high, and within what should be the mirror you look hrough to another golden structure which is the chapel altar. n every direction, wherever you look, there are these towering golden archways, best admired, perhaps, from low down under he wide arch of the *coro alto*. But the most glorious of all golden oroscenium arches is that framing the high altar, which is in pure Bibiena manner, as though by a hand and eye that had passed a ifetime, and all the ardour of youth, in a sacred theatre. This oroscenium arch has the prolixity of a Khmer temple, and its sacred figurants in their buskins and angelic garments, winged or unwinged, are the bayadères, or devadasis, of the temple. The interior of São Francisco, we repeat, is a fantastic golden vision, a thing only to be seen in Portugal and nowhere else, though, as we shall know in a few moments, there is in Oporto another gilded cavern of sacred purpose, glittering even more romantically, the ultimate, peerless specimen of its secluded kind.

To turn to more material needs there is also in Oporto a temple of gastronomy, one of only two in Portugal.* Naturally, it has walls of blue and white *azulejos* and high backed chairs. Here we tasted for the first time one of the legendary melons of the Minho, and I call them 'legendary' because I had been inclined not to believe in their existence. They are melons of a race apart, which effervesce, that is to say, they prickle the tongue as you eat them, and yet are not fermented. When cut into, it is said they make a 'fizzing' noise. These melons are only known in the Minho and do not produce this effect elsewhere, so that it must be some property in the soil in which they are grown. But

* The restaurant is called Escudidinho.

melons, however excellent, and these were very good indeed
are no qualification as to cooking. This is a famous restaurant fo
sea food, Atlantic fish being always better than the Mediterranean
but, also, it deserves three or four stars in every other respect
and a Frenchman who was a gourmet told me of going there ever
day for several days together, asking the wine waiter for som
exceptional wine every evening and being given, invariably, som
wine he had never heard of before, cheap in price, and first rat
of its kind. It is certainly true that there are wines in Portuga
unknown to foreigners, but which make the local wines, afte
the great wines of France and Germany, the best to be obtained
We ended our meal with gigantic peaches of unknown proven
ance, perhaps coming from Lamego, but even better than th
tawny peaches of Alcobaça. Then, returning to our hotel an
having a last drink before going to bed, a charming Irish pries
from Lisbon appeared out of nowhere and started arguments
religious and pagan, which lasted until late at night.

In the morning before my companions were fully awake
started off for the convent of Santa Clara. One of its delights i
that it is not easy to find, and when discovered is most difficul
to enter. We had tried the evening before. The door is immov
able, and at the barracks next to it we were shown a side doo
and told to knock there. We knocked and knocked, and heads
appeared at windows, but no one came down with the key. In
the morning it was the same story all over again, and in the end
I took a walk and returned at quarter-of-an-hour intervals to
resume the knocking. But it is a door on which it is difficult to
knock loudly, and you have to look in your pocket for some
metal object and knock on the door with that. A coin is the
most suitable weapon, but after a few raps it falls out of your
hand and rolls across the court. At the fourth attempt, and as
though she had but just heard it for the first time and had come
down immediately in response, an old woman opened the side
door by some invisible method, for it seemed to have neither
lock nor handle. The old woman came down into the court and
she was holding the key to Santa Clara in her horny hand.

To judge from its exterior no one would bother to enter
Santa Clara but would depart after the first disappointment,
entirely satisfied. For there is nothing exceptional in its façade.

There are no external signs of its fantastic golden interior.
The doorway of the convent from which the old woman emerged
has a pair of Salomonic pillars, and there are window grilles
which always have about them some little air of concealment
and expectancy (56). But the first moment of entering Santa Clara
fairly takes one's breath away. It is an aisleless chapel of mediaeval
construction transformed into a golden cavern (55). But the
transformation is not architectural. It is the art of the altar gilder
and scenographer, much influenced by the theatre, or, we could
say as well, under the influence of sacred music. This is an
entirely Portuguese manifestation, having nothing to do with
Italian architects who worked in Portugal, although affected by
Italian opera and scene painting. It is a final and culminating
ecstasy or delirium of the Baroque; and it is to be noticed that
there is something in the Portuguese temperament to which the
theme of the nun or sacred virgin—particularly if she was a
princess or lady of gentle birth and joined herself in spiritual
marriage to the Order of Poor Clares—was of transcendental
and overwhelming inspiration. We have seen this already at Beja,
where the convent of the Conceição was a nunnery of Santa
Clara, and we will meet it again, shortly, in the Convent of Jesus
at Aveiro, and in the convent at Arouca. They are among the
loveliest things in the whole of Portugal, and all of identical
inspiration. Under its auspices the fantasy and imagination of the
national style, the Manoelino, was born again. For the lover of
delirious and transcendental effects the convent chapel of Santa
Clara at Oporto is unexcelled.

There are five altars to each side, and above them great
window grilles from which you feel the eyes of the vanished nuns
looking down on you. Even the stone vaulting of the chapel has
great golden bosses depending from it, while golden floreations
spread themselves and flower upon the groining. Thus, a golden
rain seems to pour down from the roof. The high altar has an
enormous proscenium arch, the whole height of the chapel, with
golden lifesize figures standing guard under gilded canopies.
Behind this, the high altar is a golden grotto in this gilded cavern.
One could spend a long hour here studying the golden intricacy,
which in its ecstasy is prolix as the carvings of a Hindu temple
of the golden age. Up and behind the altar the golden coffers

diminish, tier by tier, and appear to climb, ceaselessly, as though
ascending on a ribbon, or like the glass waterfall in a clock that
winds up and moves, here applied in celestial argument for a
stair to heaven.

But the supreme beauty of Santa Clara is the *coro alto*. How
wonderfully 'managed' is the golden mystery! It is in this that
the poetical inspiration emanating from the theme of sacred
virginity comes to its climax. Only in the convent chapels of
Santa Rosa and Santa Clara at Querétaro, in Mexico, is it paral-
leled. And in those, as well, a particular importance, as of that
attaching to the queen bee in a beehive, has been imputed to the
screened balcony of the Mother Superior. In Santa Rosa the balcony for the Mother Superior has its elaborate golden base
supported by the carved *retablo* of an altar, while at Santa Clara
it stands like a bridge over a richly-carved doorway below. Let
us mention, in leaving this golden vision of Mexico, the con-
fessionals in Santa Rosa with their gilding sharpened with shrill
touches of metallic lustre, giving ruby and emerald-green effect
of much violence and brilliancy, and also, in the sacristy of Santa
Rosa, the fresco of the Hortus Conclusus, "an allegorical repre-
sentation of the nuns and their pupils at work in the garden of
the convent, combined with a symbolization of Santa Rosa in
which lambs receive white roses from the Virgin and bear them
to the feet of the crucified Saviour to be turned red by the blood
from His wounds. The angel with the vase of roses and lilies
receives the stream of water and of blood from the Saviour's side,
so that the water falls upon the white lilies and the blood upon the
red roses." This is a comparable ecstasy to that expressed in the
mystery of the *coro alto* in Santa Clara at Oporto. For the mystery
is impenetrable. From the floor of the chapel it is impossible to
get the detail. It is, indeed, a lesson in how to achieve effects of
mystery, except that there can be no precise knowledge as to how
it is done. There is only the impression of paler and paler golden
forms and recessions behind the latticed grille. There must be
stalls for the nuns and a throne for the abbess, and high golden
looking-glasses, but you cannot tell. An air of exquisite and soul-
ravishing music comes down from the nuns' choir.

What else there can be in the convent of Santa Clare we know
not. Perhaps in their vow of poverty the nuns spent all upon the

chapel. Or is the hidden part of the convent as romantic as the nunnery of Jesus at Aveiro? Another mystery of Santa Clara is how difficult it is to date in detail. The golden carvings seem to be of all periods from 1680 till the third quarter of the 18th Century. All things considered, it is a sacred theatre, or, more precisely, a sacred opera house. And after it, every other building in Oporto, even São Francisco, is drab and dull. There is, in fact, one other building that should be visited. It is the circular cloister at Vila Nova de Gaia, just across the Douro, a cloister of the Ionic order, and perhaps the most striking solution of this difficult architectural problem after Vignola's great circular courtyard at Caprarola.* At Leça do Balio, four or five miles north of Oporto, there is the fine and unspoilt church of the Knights Templar with a crenellated tower and parapet of the early 13th Century; while the only other monument that need be mentioned, in afterthought, is the six-storeyed granite tower of the Clérigos (58) built by the Florentine Nicolò Nasoni, bearing no particular resemblance, as has been alleged, to its unlikely prototype, the campanile of the cathedral of Lecce in Apúlia. The Quinta da Prelada, and the palace of Freixo with staircases, terraces and pavilions overlooking the Douro, neither of which villas I have seen, are also due to Nicolò Nasoni. There are also a number of *quintas*, some of them belonging to English families connected with the port wine trade, which have early 19th Century gardens where, doubtless, old and lost varieties of camellias could be found.

It was sad to leave Oporto and wonder how long it would be before one stood again in the golden cavern of Santa Clara! In a monastery or convent there is always the contrast between those few moments, or even an hour, of enjoyment and a long life led entirely shut away from other human beings. Part of the pleasure is, even, the compressed essence of those other, sheltered lives. We get the burden of their long days in a single sip of honey.

---

* Reynaldo dos Santos attributes this circular Ionic cloister to the Italian Filippo Terzi (d. 1597), of Bologna, who designed the church of São Roque at Lisbon. It has also been attributed to his pupil Leonardo Torriani of Cremona. We may think that this matter of pupils makes it even more probable that the exquisite church of the Conceiçao at Tomar may turn out, eventually, to be by an Italian pupil of Sansovino (see p. 132).

Santa Clara in its golden ecstasy is in a particular category
beside Frauenzell and Weltenburg which are works of Cosma
Damian and Egid Quirin Asam, and beside the Ursuline conven
church at Straubing by the same pair of brothers; and with Sa
Gregorio Armeno at Naples and the church of Tepozotlan i
Mexico. They are its peers; and all pertain to that same elevatio:
of the sensual feelings in religion which is comparable to thos
in music.

But we are now Southward bound and going to Aveiro, wit]
destination the Convent of Jesus. We pass nothing of interest o:
the way, which allows time to ponder on these mysteries an
prepare our minds for more. For the direct road avoids Ovar,
fishing town with a population of supposedly Phoenician origi:
whence come the *varinas* or fishwives of the Lisbon streets. An
having arrived at Aveiro, which is little more than an hour'
drive from Oporto, we go out first in order to look at the lagoor
with pyramids of salt gleaming in every direction like encamp
ments of tents. A long canal leads from the town down to th
coast, and the builders have given it a formal look by placin;
obelisks along it which echo the artificial hills of salt. It is of
different atmosphere altogether from the salt pans near Cádiz, fo:
those, also near a town of Phoenician forbears, are of som
ghostly military feeling as though haunted by the bugle call
whereas the salt hills of Aveiro suggest a lunar landscape. I
becomes stranger, and more strange still, for after passing on ;
long causeway through the lagoons we are suddenly, in a moment
in a sea-mist with the hooting of a loud fog-horn in our ears
and going a little further in this sinister half-darkness out o
the sun come to a lighthouse whence the noise emerges
apparently from the end of the world, and gladly make agair
for the sunlight in search of *esguichos* and *moliceiros* of Aveiro.*

Esguichos are shaped like a sickle or a half-moon and are boat

* There is a pair of beautifully produced books dealing with the *esguichos* an
moliceiros of Aveiro, in a series called *Estudos Etnográficos, Obra editada pel*
Instituto para a Alta Cultura, Oporto, 1943, by A. José de Castro. It has excellen
coloured lithographs by the author. Eighteen further volumes are advertised
presumably by different writers, but no special work seems to have beer
devoted yet to either the boats of Caparica or the sardine boats of Nazaré
although they have been drawn and painted times beyond number, and forn
so interesting a subject.

f the fishermen of Aveiro. The open Atlantic is about four or
ve miles away from the town so they are not seen so often as the
oliceiros, which are boats of the weed gatherers and salt collec-
ors on the lagoons. Both types of craft are of fascinating interest
nd are worth in themselves the journey to Aveiro. Just as at
ome in England you do not have to be an expert in order to get
omance and poetry from the 'long boat' on a canal or a Gypsy
aravan, so in Portugal it would be a dull mind that drew no
leasure from the boats of Nazaré or Aveiro. Portugal, for some
eason, is the country of all European lands to show the most
xtreme and curious development in small boats, and from the
right manner in which they are painted the direct comparison
s to canal barge or caravan, or to the painted carts of Palermo.
here would seem to be four or five main types of boat in
ortugal. *Esguichos* and *moliceiros* of Aveiro are two of them; the
thers are the river boats of the Douro which bring the wine
own to Oporto, the huge half-moon fishing boats of Caparica,
pposite Lisbon (see p. 141), and the sardine boats of Nazaré.
)n a first visit to Portugal in 1926, when communications were
o difficult and it was a day's journey from Lisbon to Coimbra or
o Oporto, all sorts of stories were rife as to the extraordinary
oats to be seen in the fishing towns along the Atlantic coast.
here were tales of strange craft at Povoa de Varzim and Espo-
ende, between Oporto and the frontier with Spain. If so, they
ave vanished and there is no trace of them. No one, even so late
s 1934, seemed to know anything about the lower coast between
)porto and Lisbon, and one had the idea that small fishing
illages nobody had ever heard of might have developed their
wn special and peculiar types of boat. This, also, has been
isproved, but what remains is more than remarkable.

The antecedents of these fishing folk is another and most
urious question. Just as there seems to be a Semitic strain in
rás-os-Montes, the most remote province of Portugal which is,
s it were, the wrong side of the mountains, so a more ancient
emitic ancestry, by far, has been suggested for the fishermen
f Povoa de Varzim, for the *varinas* of Ovar, and the fisherfolk
f Nazaré and Aveiro. They are said to be a Phoenician colony
rom Tyre and Sidon. Another theory is that the population of
ll fishing towns, the 'dark men and women' of Plougastel in

Brittany, those of Marken and Volendam on the Zuyder Zee, the
fishermen of the Claddagh in Galway, and even the fishwives of
Newhaven to be seen in their striped dresses in the streets of
Edinburgh, are all descendants of the same early race. What is
perhaps true is that early and primitive types have gravitated to
the fishing towns, and that as the Celtiberians who settled in
Brittany, Northern Spain, Portugal, and Ireland were dark, so a
large proportion of these fishermen are of the dark type. At the
same time the inhabitants of Nazaré are so individual in type with
their goat-like features that there may well be a Phoenician
strain in them. Do not let us forget that the great empire of
Carthage, itself a Phoenician colony, perished from the face of
the earth but must have left descendants, and that they had many
settlements in the Iberian peninsula. This, however, is a problem better argued among the cubical houses and patchwork
inhabitants of Nazaré.

Conditions are uniquely propitious at Aveiro owing not only
to the flat and sandy coast but to the wide extent of the lagoons.
In their total area these are thirty miles long by some five miles
in breadth. The *esguichos* are to be seen along about the same
extent of coast, and what were formerly mere fishing villages
like Espinho in this area are now full of summer hotels with
concerts and *thé-dansants*. The fishermen, however, are so con-
servative that they are little altered and cling to their own ways.
In their checked shirts, not so strident as those of Nazaré, and
black stocking caps they form a picturesque population, as do
the fishwives in little round black felt hats, wearing gaily
coloured shawls and with baskets on their heads. There is unend-
ing material for the sketcher, easier still for the amateur
photographer, in groups of these women, the older ones always
dressed in black, as they sit upon the sands. There is the hauling
in or launching of the boats, always to the accompaniment of
chanting, and the nets form primitive encampments hung up
tent-wise, with the floats and corks.

The *moliceiros* of the weed gatherers and salt collectors, lagoon
boats with prows shaped like a swan's neck, are even more
elegant in their long thin line. It is said that the boat-builders
have an unerring eye and can 'see' the form of a boat in a tree
trunk, with no need for stated measurements or drawings. The

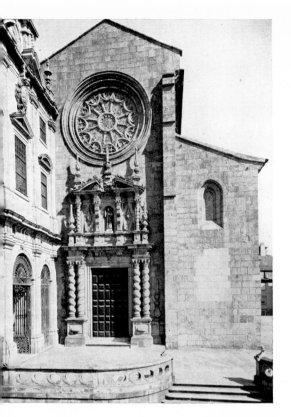

57   Church of São Francisco

58   Tower of the Clérigos

59   Arouca: one of the statues of nuns (1720–1725)
Jacinto Vieira, sculptor

60　Arouca: another of the statues of nuns

61   Vista Alegre: the tomb of Bishop Miranda,
by Claude Laprade

curve of the prow and the angle at which it bends back can only be the work of many generations of inherited skill. The boatmen working the *moliceiros* are more soberly clad in white, as though they had been in conference with the 'Roman soldiers' of Apúlia. A long row of *moliceiros* drawn up in line is an unforgettable sight; and more wonderful still must be a *moliceiro* on land and mounted on wheels when it is drawn down by a team of oxen to be launched on the lagoon, for then you can see the long sinuous line of the boat which is so thin in the middle, and would be swamped by the sea waves. In their line they are as thin looking as a birch bark canoe, but of incredible length, so that they call for admiration merely as carpenter's work. Perhaps they are not quite as impressive as the fishing boats of Caparica; but those, drawn up on the beach, are objects in another landscape, one of vastness and great expanses of sand and water, whereas the *moliceiros* ply to and fro on landlocked lagoons. The boats of Caparica seem to be about to start forth upon some dangerous expedition, as though the least they could do would be to engage tarpon or shark in combat, while the *moliceiros*, swan-like of type and bearing, have the line of boats of pleasure, gondolas of some forgotten lagoon-city. Both forms of boat, *esguichos* and *moliceiros*, lend a very special interest to Aveiro, and one could never tire of seeing their sickle-shapes or swan-necks above the low horizon.

But there is much in Aveiro over which to linger, of which a first intimation could be the *ovos moles* on sale in the station, if you are going by rail from Lisbon to Oporto, a sweetmeat made of eggs and sold in little wooden barrels, with a decided taste of the Orient as though confected in the harem, and resembling the more far-famed *yemas de San Isidro*, a sweet of undoubted Moorish origin, prepared and sold at the latchet in a convent of Seville. There can be little doubt that the *ovos moles* are a relic of the nuns of the Convent of Jesus in Aveiro. All over Portugal there is a profusion of little cakes and sweets of nunnish origin, now fast diminishing, which is a pity, as many of them are excellent and they are among the individual things of the country.* Before we reach the Convent of Jesus, however, there

* *Yemas*, as good as those of Seville, are on sale in a shop in Caldas da Rainha. Nunnish sweets, always with a taste of the Orient in the background, were

is another chapel which should be seen, that of the suitably named Senhor dos Barrocas, an octagon standing on a raised terrace or platform which is decorated with a pair of stone flower vases, or, in fact, flower-filled urns, that would be in place in a late Regency crescent, perhaps Pelham Crescent opening off Fulham Road. It seems sensible to attribute this octagonal chapel to João Antunes (see footnote), an architect who of predilection worked in rounded forms. There is a fine 'figured' frontispiece composed of door and window, with cupids galore, and saints perched on cornices and pediments, including St. Veronica kneeling as in the bull-fight and holding up her handkerchief.* Two flanking doorways are pretty, too, but the interior of the octagon, as nearly always, is a disappointment.

brought to perfection in the 18th Century, over a great part of Southern Europe. Salvatore de 'Giacomo is the authority for their history in Naples, and in Palermo, where, for instance, the nuns of Santa Catarina were famous for candied pumpkin and blancmange, and those of the nearby La Martorana, with its Byzantine mosaics, for imitation fruits of almond paste. The famous Sicilian ices were of this origin. The most horrific of all nunnish inventions is *Mole Poblana*, invented in the 18th Century by the nuns of Santa Rosa in the Mexican Puebla; twice-boiled turkey in a sauce of cacao, liquorice, sesame, chillis, amaranth, cinnamon, and eleven more ingredients. This dish is said to have been concocted by one of the nuns in the beautiful blue-tiled kitchen of Santa Rosa when preparing for a visit of the Archbishop. Furthermore, in the town of Oaxaca, where the churches built of *cantera verde*, unlike the tiled churches of Puebla, turn a beautiful green after rain, and the carnival is "celebrated with enthusiasm", green, yellow, red, and black *moles* are served, washed down with "devils' blood", a drink made of tequila, chillis, and orange juice; while if by good fortune you are at Tehuantepec, "weddings usually take place on Sundays, and anyone may attend at will, by simply paying the sum of one peso. For this, he is entitled to a glass of mezcal, a loaf of bread and a slab of chocolate, everything adorned with a coloured tissue-paper flag. He can also have the typical dish of beef, and dance the whole day!"

* Her 'opposite number', with scrolled volute waiting ready for foothold, has disappeared entirely, or been 'collected'. Amateurs of the octagon should certainly visit Portugal, where are to be seen the following: the Senhor da Cruz at Barcelos, also by Antunes, and the same architect's Menino de Deus at Lisbon; the china-lined chapel of the nuns of São Domingos at Elvas; and in the same category, the hexagonal chapel of Senhor da Pedra, outside Óbidos. There, too, a female painter, one of the only Portuguese painters, claims attention; Josefa d'Ayala y Cabrera, known as Josefa of Óbidos, half-Sevillian in origin, and in turns, painter, miniaturist, etcher, modeller in terracotta, silver worker, and calligraphist, but never to excess in point of talent. Paintings by her may be seen in the church at Cadaval near Lisbon, and improbably,

All else in Aveiro, even the craft along the lagoons, pales in beauty beside the Convent of Jesus. This is a Royal foundation that compares for Portugal with the fabulous Las Huelgas, outside Burgos, one of the glories of all Spain. It was here that Santa Joana, daughter of the King Dom Afonso V, professed in 1475 and she died in the convent in 1489. There are cloisters of her period with old doorways, but this ancient nunnery is of singular and touching beauty in many other ways. I had seen it before, and always remembered it, trying on more than one occasion to write my memories of it, but never can it have seemed more beautiful than on that early evening in August of last year when coming to the door we knew it was too late and that the museum was closed. It was half-past five, or after, knocking and ringing brought no answering footstep, the nunnery was empty and deserted, and it suddenly occurred to us to try the door ourselves, which was unlocked, and walk in. The long corridors were full of golden light and no one else was in the building. Following the maxims of military pursuit it is always better to push an advantage to the utmost, and so, finding the chapel open, we left that till later and went upstairs to the furthest corners of the convent.

This has unparalleled treasures in the matter of embroidered vestments and little painted shrines, the majority of the objects being the work of nuns of the convent, so that there is perhaps no such collection elsewhere of the finest works of women's hands. There are little carved figures of ravishing prettiness, painted and gilded; dressed figures, little shrines, and painted papers, essentially a feminine art, as can be seen in a group of the Flight into Egypt (?), where St. Joseph, the Virgin with pilgrims' staff, and the infant Jesus all wear black and gold *tricornes* set at a rakish angle, and the back of the shrine is painted with bunches of flowers of a dewy freshness.* There is room after room of altar cloths and vestments worked with the needle, and sumptuous

at Cascais, in the parish church, set among the fish restaurants and summer trippers. Another of the octagonal chapels is Senhor Jesus das Barrocas at Ponte de Rata, about six miles east of Aveiro, and described as being a neo-Manoelino version of the octagonal baptisteries at Florence and at Pisa. Its date is 1707–32.

* This particular group is illustrated in *Sacred and Profane Love*, Faber & Faber Ltd., London, 1940, p. 154.

materials giving a new meaning to the phrase 'of cloth-of-gold'. Seldom has a more exciting and thrilling experience fallen my way since long ago I spent a month in Granada and found a way of climbing into the Alhambra and walking about its courtyards in moonlight. There was the same sensation of intruding into part of a palace which was reserved for women. There is a little contemporary portrait of the Saint, by Nuno Gonçalves or a pupil, and this, one feels of instinct, must be the true portrait of her. This princess of Plantagenet descent, with her jewelled cap and long thin hands and long plain features, still haunts the convent. It has not the Moorish cupolas and stalactites which form so astonishing a feature of the Spanish convents of Las Huelgas and Tordesillas, because of the fantastic improbability of Moslem craftsmen being put to work in a nunnery, but there are wonders enough and to spare, here, at Aveiro.

This, in spite of the tomb of Santa Joana, in Florentine style of inlaid marbles, and as ugly as could ever be the tomb of St. Francis Xavier in the church of Bom Jesus in far Goa, given by Cosmo III, Grand Duke of Tuscany. This shrine of the Saint at Aveiro is by João Antunes, but it stands in the lower choir under a bad light. The *coro alto* is above this, with mysterious detail and alluring gilding, while the chapel beyond really and truly is *rutilante de dorures*, and, indeed, no other phrase so well describes it. Two portable organs, the acme of elegance, are in the upper choir.

But among the delights of Aveiro are a series of paintings of the life of Santa Joana. Some of these hang on the walls of the chancel. They appear all to be by the same hand and so entire is their naïveté that, at first, one is tempted to think the painter may have been a nun (65). Partly because of the feminine youthfulness of all concerned, for there is not an old face in the pictures. All are young with rounded features; and is not this true of female painters as unlike as Marie Laurencin and Kate Greenaway? Nearly all the characters in the paintings appear to be fifteen years old, and to have been painted by someone of their own age. There is a child-like innocence of any knowledge of past history, even down to the smallest detail, and a feminine shape to all the heads. Although the events depicted took place three centuries before, the innocence of the painter puts every

erson into contemporary dress of that exact time, not even
nto the fashions remembered from youth, but as though events
oncerning anyone as important as this Royal nun must be
clothed in the fashions of the hour.

The pictures are like fairy book illustrations to a forgotten
tory, and one goes from painting to painting trying to string
hem together in their right order. In the little low-ceilinged
oratory of the Saint, which is a golden cavern, there is a picture
over the altar of her deathbed. It must come, therefore, nearly
t the end of the narrative, and here we may begin to notice the
play made by the painter with the nuns' headdresses. It is at this
point, also, that one wonders if the pictures after all are by a
man and not a woman. For such an interest is shown in the sight
of a lot of nuns together, ethereal beings and inmates of the
acred harem. And now there seems to be no more reason why
he painter should not have been a man than there is excuse for
hinking that the carvers and gilders of the golden grotto of
Santa Clara at Oporto were nuns, and not men.

In the deathbed scene Santa Clara is dying in the arms of the
bbess, two nuns kneel weeping at the foot of the bed, and a part
of the regiment of nuns stand in the background. Or is it Santa
Clara who holds the dying abbess in her arms? But, already, the
pleated coifs of the nuns and their white habits are taking hold
of one, and looking round this golden oratory with its images of
aints in 'Chippendale' cases glittering and coruscating with the
gold of Brazil, one misses the nuns in the next picture, which
hows a child-king on his throne, with child-courtiers, and halberdiers in the background, examining a portrait which is held
up for him by a kneeling chamberlain in embroidered coat and
urcoat. This must be Dom Afonso V at some year before 1481,
vhen he died, looking at the portrait of his daughter, but she
vears Spanish court dress of about 1730–40, and now again one
eels certain that a nun painted the picture.

Perhaps the most delightful and naïf of the whole series is
hat showing the princess setting forth from her father's palace
o take her vows as a nun. She drives off in a golden coach like
hose at Belém, but with a negro coachman, who, henceforward,
becomes companion in imagination to the negro gondolier in
Carpaccio's scene on the Grand Canal (*Miracle of the Holy Cross*)

in Venice. Coaches, indeed, come into one or two more of th
paintings; and in another a company of youthful grenadiers i
drawn up. There is, as well, a curious painting in two storeys
as in a cloister. On the upper storey, the Saint talks to a priest o
a balcony; and in the lower, with nuns round her, she is speakin
to her father, still in the cloister, but near two flowerbeds and
fountain (65). The pictures are continued along the golde
chancel, where they appear to be by another and, perhaps, a
earlier hand, for the gentlemen wear longer coats and the ful
periwig. They may be by the painter at Santa Clara-a-Nova a
Coimbra, as will be evident when we reach that city. A figur
in black now appears dramatically among the nuns, probably th
King again, or if it is not her father Dom Afonso, it may be he
brother Dom João II; but with memories of the nuns of Odi
vellas still in mind from Augustus Hervey's *Journal*, written jus
at the time the pictures were painted, one must be forgiven fo
thinking of this black-clad figure as Casanova in a Venetian con
vent and he does, in fact, cut a sinister shadow against the nuns
white habits. Taking a last look round at these fairy tale picture
and at this golden chapel, we found the door again and opened i
to our relief, for we had thought we might be locked in, an
walked out into the sunlit street. The same old woman sat at th
corner, looking as if she could have been there on the day th
Saint drove up to the door in her golden coach with her negr
coachman, and going into the nunnery hand-in-hand with he
father, bade him good-bye, and was immured for ever with th
white-coiffed nuns.

One of the most beautiful, and remote, of the old convents c
Portugal must be that of Arouca, which we saw marked upon
signpost when about half-way between Oporto and Aveiro. I
lies inland some twenty miles, or about an hour's run from th
highroad, in the depths of the country. Arouca was anothe
Royal nunnery like that of Aveiro, being a Cistercian convent t
which Queen Mafalda, daughter of Dom Sancho I, and divorce
wife of Henry I of Castile, retired and became a nun in the middl
of the 13th Century. The church of Arouca is described a
having one of the most graceful and charming of the Portugues
gilded organ-cases; while the choir has over life-size granit
statues of Cistercian nuns with painted faces, statues of extrem

beauty to judge from the photographs, and unique in Portugal. We say 'over life-size' because surely no Portuguese nuns were over six feet in height, and of this proportion. One series is of saints of the Cistercian Order, and the other represents the most famous nuns of Arouca* (59, 60). The sculptor, by whom no other works are known, was Jacinto Vieira of Braga, and their date is about 1720–25. These recently discovered works are among the beautiful things of Portugal, and the remoteness of Arouca in no wise diminishes their beauty. The romantic conception of the Portuguese nun is to be seen here *in excelsis* in these statues, where, owing to the genius of a forgotten sculptor, something new is added to the repertory of poetry. The nuns of Arouca in their white coifs and white habits with the long sleeves, standing in granite niches, become one of the memories of Portugal. How much I long to have visited them, and their golden organ, in that bucolic valley!

But they were far away, and leaving Aveiro, nun-haunted, we came down the valley of the river Vouga and stopped for the night at Serem, in one of the most delightful of the *pousadas*, on the terraced hillside overlooking the main road from Lisbon to Oporto, and a little noisy from night traffic. Next morning, continuing through this Arcadian country, the highroad passes a region where for a mile or more there are little cabins by the road with tables set under trellises at which the local speciality of sucking-pig is consumed.† We stopped for a half-hour at one of these, run by a buxom peasant woman, and ate sucking-pig and drank a glass of wine from her vineyard, a foaming red wine not unlike the Valpolicella that is drunk in Venice. On summer evenings it must be a gay scene, and there is music and singing along the road.

We were nearing Coimbra, while Buçaco, not so much of a hallucination as before, lies close to hand, its repute dating from

* The authors of *The Selective Traveller* give the interesting information that during the Peninsular War there was a nun here, Clara Warre, who was visited in the convent by Field-Marshal Beresford and by her brother, later Lt.-Gen. Sir William Warre. One would like to know more of this English nun in this remote convent. It is probable that she was still living at the Dissolution in 1834.

† At Mealhada, about fifteen miles North of Coimbra. The sucking-pig is called Leitão de Bairrada, after the district.

the time not so long ago when there was no other good hotel in the country. It was begun as a Royal Palace for Dom Carlos, and designed by the scene painter of the São Carlos Opera House in Manoelino style. What are unique at Buçaco, its battlefield apart which will appeal to those who are following Wellington's campaigns, are the rare trees. Buçaco is like an inland Sintra, dripping with mists and waterfalls, with gigantic specimens of the hundred foot high *Cupressus lusitanicus*, or Mexican cedar, a tree which is extinct in its native habitat. These were growing here as long ago as 1690; and still earlier, in 1643, Pope Urban VIII, the Barberini pope and patron of Bernini, issued a Bill excommunicating persons who did any damage to the trees. The Barefooted Carmelites who planted the forest were a missionary Order with monasteries in Mexico and Brazil, and obviously they had influence in Rome. Their cells, gloomy as those of the Cork Convent in Sintra, give a yet more hallucinatory air to the comfortable beds and bathrooms of the hotel.

There are old convents of greater interest near Buçaco, Lorvão among them, in a deep valley, its famed inhabitants having been two nuns who were daughters of Dom Sancho I, in the 13th Century, their bodies lying in two silver coffins of much later date, and all the activity of the deserted buildings now taking the form of the whittling of toothpicks out of white willow-wood by village women. But in the church there are choir stalls of solid and splendid magnificence in the finest style of cabinet-making, choir stalls which could bear the stamp or signature of Vile and Cobb; two dozen of them to a row, with comfortable armchairs below for the novices and servants (68, 69). So much 'all of one piece' is this magnificent church furnishing, although the nuns have gone now, and so long ago, that one has the vision of them singing there, each in her stall, as upon a raft or platform of past luxury and privilege, and then cut loose and carried out to sea at the mercy of the waves, as in the Marx Brothers film, *A Night at the Opera*, when the orchestra, still playing their violins and other instruments, is cut adrift and borne away!

It is, perhaps, impossible for travellers who knew Portugal twenty-five years ago not to compare past adventures with present comfort. For Coimbra, where we are now bound, was almost inaccessible by road in those days. The dust and jolting,

62, 63   Coimbra: in the Parque de Santa Cruz

64   Small Oratory in the
Convent of Jesus

65   One of the Paintings in
the Convent of Jesus

AVEIRO

66, 67 Paintings in
Santa Clara

68   Choir stalls

69   The nuns' grille

LORVÃO

and dangerous food and damp beds, are memories which have to be insisted upon in order to draw attention to improvements that are now taken for granted. Recollections of arriving at Tomar so tired and aching that one wondered if one could continue the journey at all; of expecting to wake up in the morning at Leiria with rheumatic fever; of motoring, as I have said already, *backwards* for half an hour a day on the road to Buçaco so as to rest one's twisted neck; these now mingle with the sensation of rushing towards Coimbra, and by-passing it, for the sheer pleasure of the speed. Probably no other country has so improved and ameliorated itself in modern times; and it is only sad that in Portugal more than anywhere else in this generation the new and hideous has usurped the old. Unfortunately, Coimbra is a sad instance of this. It is even worse than the scraping of Alcobaça and Batalha. For in another hundred years, if left alone, those may recover something of their patina of age, though now bare as whited sepulchres. But at Coimbra not only has there been wanton and appalling destruction of what was old and beautiful, but new University buildings have been erected which are really shaming in their blatant ugliness. The sculptures, particularly, are of an insulting hideousness. It is a dreadful thought that they are dedicated to the youth of Portugal, and that they will be a memorial to the government of so wise and great a European as Dr. Salazar. His 'Augustan' features and cast of head call for architecture and sculpture of a nobler mould. Not that there is anything in the least Portuguese about these abominable buildings of Coimbra. But it is sad, too, because, Coimbra being the university town of Portugal, so many Portuguese retain memories of Coimbra and an affection for it all through their lives, as the Dutchmen do for Leyden, and those memories will now for ever more be tinged and coloured by the ugly buildings. There is no possible excuse for hideousness upon this scale; but it might, at least, be practised elsewhere and not in Coimbra.

The town, in the phrase of the guide book, is still 'seated in stately majesty above the Mondego', though hacked about and shorn of many of its beauties. And still, in spite of everything, it is one of the most charming towns of Portugal, with its own type of *fado*, or popular song, said to be quite different from that heard in Lisbon. They are romantic love songs tuned to the passions and sentiments of the students of Coimbra. And in fact the University buildings from below are almost as conspicuous as the Acropolis and dominate the town. It is a place which takes on another character in the heat of August, having seen it before on three occasions during the spring. Now, the new white buildings glared abominably, and the open square in front was so hot that one could not keep one's feet upon the ground. Coming out of the heat into shade was like stumbling out of a desert to a water well. It was even wonderful that the lizard could dart upon the wall.

The University of Coimbra was the one extravagance of Dom João V, which is of utility, apart from the aqueduct of the Aguas Livres that gives a Roman air to the outskirts of Lisbon. This is the Library with double-pillared entrance surmounted by a fine *stemma* of his arms. It is almost exactly contemporary with the Hof-Bibliothek of the Imperial Palace in Vienna, a work by J. B. Fischer von Erlach, and the fact that Dom João was married to a sister of the Kaiser Karl VI would appear to make it probable that both libraries were built in rivalry with each other, particularly as little or no other inducement can be discovered, Dom João being no booklover. The Library has three splendid halls opening out of each other; a light green, then a darker, and then a shade like that of orange Niger leather, these colours being given by the lacquering of galleries and bookshelves. A portrait of Dom João in a frame coruscating with gold faces the doorway and is, therefore, approached through what are, in effect, a pair of proscenium arches, one behind the other in fine Italian theatrical tradition (70, 71). But even in this portrait little is to be made of the King and he is never among those historical figures whom one would know by sight. The name of the designer of this Library has for long been uncertain, but it was probably Claude Laprade, by whom little else is known (71). Neither, would it seem, have the possible treasures in this Library been entirely inventoried and explored if it be true that in the music section there are unpublished MSS. by Domenico Scarlatti, catalogued, so it is said, under the Hispanicized form of his name, which was Escarlati, and so entered under 'E' instead of 'S'.*

* But Mr. Ralph Kirkpatrick in his recent book on Scarlatti, Princeton University Press, 1953, seems to suggest that he has seen the MSS. and that they only contain duplicates and not originals. Spaniards tell the same story

Reynaldo dos Santos mentions the golden organ in the University Chapel as among the finest in Portugal, but this I cannot recollect to have seen.

The other sights of Coimbra are in the lower town; and thinking of that one could find oneself on this hot day wishing one were in Bergamo! For in Bergamo with its Upper and Lower Towns it is a matter of paintings by Venetian masters; and in Portugal, comparatively, there are no paintings. At Bergamo, three churches in the Upper Town with pictures by Lorenzo Lotto, and the wonderful picture gallery with Madonnas by Giovanni Bellini, and incomparable Guardis and pictures by the later painters; in the Lower Town, the Cappella Colleoni of the early Renaissance, but with frescoes by Tiepolo, and near at hand, the glorious Lion of St. Mark upon its column! How can Coimbra, how can even Toledo be compared to Bergamo, that town in the Venetian *terra firma* in midst of the greatest school of colour the world has ever known! But such are profitless comparisons, and Coimbra has much in it that is beautiful. It has not, perhaps, in spite of the students as much life as Oporto, than which it is very much smaller in population, or as Évora, where the number of inhabitants is about the same. Perhaps the steep streets of Coimbra tire even adepts; and it is true that the heat here tends more to gentle melancholy than to uproarious song, as is audible in the *fados*. But, more especially, Coimbra is a town of learning and it may have possessed this character since Dom Diniz founded the University early in the 14th Century. It has not, although the demolishers have lent a hand, quite enough of a population to fill the heaped buildings sprawling up and down its hills.

The demolition squads have worked hard in the monastery of Santa Cruz and in the Sé Velha or Old Cathedral, the two most important buildings in Coimbra. Of the Romanesque Sé Velha it could be said, in the old phrase, that 'its own mother would not know it', and the scratchings and scrapings of the restorers have quite literally given it a new skin, destroying its old and natural

of unpublished Scarlatti MSS. at the library at Aranjuez. Dr. Robert C. Smith of the University of Pennsylvania, who has published a standard work on J. F. Ludovice, the architect of the palace of Mafra, has completed a study of Claude Laprade, designer of the Library at Coimbra.

surface most entirely and effectually in the process. It does not even look like an old and ugly building; it appears rather hideous and quite new. One work of art has been spared, unaccountably, the carved *retablo* by Olivier de Gand, late Gothic and exactly equivalent in style and treatment to numerous *retablos* by Flemish masters in cathedrals in Spain. For Coimbra was a great local centre for sculpture; as can be seen better still at Santa Cruz, where the pulpit is by a Frenchman, João de Ruão (Jean de Rouen), in Renaissance style, like richly elaborate French cabinet work of the reign of François premier. The tomb, also in Santa Cruz, of the Grand-Prior Dom João de Menêses, of Sephardic sound, is more interesting and more Portuguese, if only for its twisted pillars and interlacing ornament of seaweed fronds. The tomb of the founder Dom Afonso Henriques is old and glorious, in a happy muddle of late Gothic, Renaissance and Manoelino. This tomb, and the doorway of Santa Cruz, are by Nicholas Chantarène, the French sculptor of the kneeling figures of Dom Manoel and his wife upon the portal at Belém. Reynaldo dos Santos 'removes' the pulpit from João de Ruão and attributes it, too, to Chantarène, who must be elevated, then, to the same level as the best of the foreign sculptors who were at work during the same years in Spain. Wrecking is still going on apace at Santa Cruz, though, so far, the beautiful red and gold organ has been spared; but the double cloister has suffered fearful damage. The Machado de Castro Museum, not far away, appears in the guise of a hospital for statues and other works of art driven out of their homes, including some exceedingly curious pieces of silverwork, the only instances of Manoelino style in applied art, of which examples are nowhere else to be seen. There is a water jar, in particular, with a serpent handle and a spout in the form of an odd-shaped mask, which it would not be surprising to learn was the work of Diogo de Arruda, architect of the Chapter House at Tomar. It is more curious than beautiful. Of more certain appeal is the mediaeval stone figure of a mounted knight, his steed in long horse-cloths reaching to the ground; and the knight, visor on head, with spiked club or mace upon his shoulder. He is like an ivory chessman, magnified.

There are more churches at Coimbra, all worth entering for the sake of Salomonic columns and *azulejo* panels, if nothing earlier,* but the immensely long convent of Santa Clara-a-Nova, across the river, demands attention. Much here is romantic and beautiful. There are wooden polychrome carved panels over the side altars of the life of St. Elizabeth of Portugal, for this nunnery of Poor Clares is yet another Royal foundation. There is a red and gold portable organ in the choir; and another one like it in the upper choir where the nuns attended Mass and looked down through their grille into the church. The cloister is subtle and beautiful in shape, with a balustraded roof-line broken by obelisks, and compositions of Doric columns for the piers, which are elaborated on the upper storey into columns framing niches, with pediments above. This cloister of unusual and elegant design has lately been attributed to the Hungarian, Carlos Mardel. But it is, perhaps, of too subtle design to be by him. It is, in any case, a contribution by Dom João V to the luxury of the Poor Clares. One of the delights of Santa Clara-a-Nova is the set of six paintings in the chancel, showing the removal of the body of St. Elizabeth of Portugal to her new tomb in 1696. As works of art these are of the same order of merit as the paintings in the Convent of Jesus at Aveiro, though more sophisticated and beyond any question works of a masculine hand. In a pair of them, illustrated here, we see the opening of the Saint's old tomb, in a background of architecture that was the last word in elegance and is reminiscent of one of the side aisles of St. Peter's. Someone of importance—is it Dom Pedro II?—in a full black periwig, kneels, and with courtly gesture takes the corpse's hand, uncorrupted, in his own. In the other painting, courtiers or knights of some Order of Chivalry—could it be of Aviz?—process, holding a canopy over the heads of bishops and archbishops. They wear the cross of the Order on their left shoulders on a flowing white cloak or mantle, and stiff starched collars all of a pattern. All wear long periwigs of the latest fashion; and one of them walking towards us in the foreground, as though leading the procession and turning it in our direction, has a full black periwig of portentous size, holds a banner, and wears an expression of comical fervour and concentration. His must be a portrait. The influence

---

* The Colegio de Graça and the Colegio do Carmo, adjoining each other, are typical churches of Coimbra. These, and several more, contain sculptures of the local school.

of the court of Louis quatorze is strong in these pictures; and if they are not the work of a painter who has been to France they are by someone who, at least, has seen Gobelin tapestries and studied prints after Lebrun (66, 67).

In every direction from Coimbra there are old churches and convents in the quasi-Tuscan scene. The nunnery of Celas, just outside the town; or, at another tangent, São Marcos—were this convent in Italy it would not be unworthy of Tuscany, or among the vineyards of the Loire it would be not inappropriate to Touraine—with the late Gothic tomb of Fernão Teles de Menêses of irresistible name, from the hand of Diogo de Pires, and other and later tombs of the Silva family to which this noble-man of illustrious lineage pertained, tombs which could be in some church like Framlingham in Suffolk were it not for the vine-clad countryside. There is enough to see day after day from Coimbra; or going further afield and off the road from Pombal, which is on the way to Lisbon, the huge old convent at Louriçal, of later origin, last of the monasteries and convents in our con-text, for we were now returning at speed to Lisbon, only stopping at Leiria for long enough to note how that dead country town has woken into life; not even halting at Batalha, seen three times already; passing the gay chintz shops of Alcobaça, through Caldas da Rainha, taking the road through the Moorish-named and Moorish-looking Alenquer, down to the Tagus at Vila Franca de Xira, where is the bull-ring and bulls are run in the open street as at Pamplona; and so in the hot evening back to Lisbon as heavy drops of rain fell on the cannas, there was a stirring in the acacias and jacarandas, and a flash of summer lightning, but once more the thunder never came.

HISTORICAL NOTE

THIS historical note largely concerned with the kings of Portugal and their dates has a particular purpose, for while it is true that in the case of Spain most persons have some little knowledge of the Emperor Charles V, or of Philip IV, the patron of Velázquez, it is only the specialist who knows much of Portuguese history. This note is written, therefore, in order to place the kings of Portugal and the main events in the history of the country in their proper perspective against persons and figures who are known to all.

Roman Portugal was divided into three provinces with capitals at Braga, Santarém, and Beja. There followed barbarian invasions, chiefly by the Visigoths; and then in the 8th Century the Moorish occupation, up to the river Vouga which means as far North as Aveiro. The Moors were driven out of Lisbon in 1147, but remained in the Algarve in the extreme South down to 1249. Portugal was, meanwhile, part of the kingdom of León. It became independent early in the 12th Century when Count Henry of Burgundy, a French knight crusading against the Moors, married Theresa, daughter of the King of León, and was invested by him with the Duchy of Portugal. Their son, Dom Afonso Henriques, became King of Portugal and founder of its first dynasty of kings. Among their descendants was Dom Pedro I, lover of Inês de Castro (see p. 113). Their tombs are to be seen at Alcobaça. The wife of the last male of this dynasty had a daughter, married to the King of Castile, and there was danger that Portugal would revert again to Spain.

The illegitimate son of Dom Pedro, who was Master of the Knights of Aviz, was, therefore, put upon the throne. He defeated the Castilians at Aljubarrota in 1385, and became first of a new dynasty. It was this King Dom João I who built Batalha, and signed the Treaty of Westminster in 1386. He married Philippa of Lancaster, daughter of John of Gaunt, who bore him six sons, Prince Henry the Navigator among them, patron of the explorers. Three generations later, in the person of Dom Manoel I (1495–1521), Portugal attained its golden age. The Manoelino style is called after him, and his buildings include the Unfinished Chapels at Batalha and part of the Convent of Christ at Tomar. The over-chivalrous and crazy Dom Sebastião brought Portugal to ruin when he tried to conquer Morocco, and was killed in battle, leaving Philip II of Spain, whose mother was the beautiful Portuguese Infanta Isabella, free to claim the kingdom two years later in 1580. The Spanish domination followed, lasting for sixty years until 1640.

In that year Portugal regained its independence under Dom João IV,

Duke of Bragança, of illegitimate descent from the old kings, through a natural son of Dom João I, founder of the House of Aviz. A few years later the treaties with England were renewed and Charles II married Catherine of Bragança. Dom João V (1706–50) was the extravagant King of this dynasty, his wealth deriving from the gold and diamonds of Brazil. It was during the reign of his son Dom José I that Pombal was Prime Minister. Owing to the Napoleonic Wars the Royal family left Lisbon in 1807 and took refuge in Brazil, not returning to Portugal until 1821, and leaving one of the family behind as the first Emperor of Brazil. A period of Civil War then ensued between supporters of the young Queen D. Maria da Glória and the partisans of her uncle Dom Miguel. Though an extreme reactionary, it is impossible to deny to Dom Miguel that he was a romantic figure after the fashion of the Young Chevalier and Don Carlos. Retiring to Austria, he died in 1866, leaving six daughters all famous for their beauty. His grandson Dom Duarte Nuno and his family have now returned to Portugal at the invitation of the Government.

Queen Maria da Glória married Ferdinand of Saxe-Coburg, a cousin of our Prince-Consort. Their ultimate descendant, King Manoel, was driven from Portugal in 1910. Both he and his mother, Queen Amélie, left their large fortunes to the State. It only remains to add that, at the invitation of Marshal Carmona, Dr. Salazar became Finance Minister in 1928, and Prime Minister four years later. The return of prosperity to Portugal is mainly due to wise measures undertaken by him.

Postscript

Typical of the old monasteries so often mentioned in these pages is the church of Urilagres, near Leiria (see p. 93), wherein the authors of *The Selective Traveller* draw attention to "the unique manuscript *azulejo* panels" giving the legend of the local miracle "in delicate blue writing on a paler blue ground." This is certainly an original idea in *azulejos,* even if it reminds the present writer of a room in the house of an eccentric millionaire in England, the walls of which were papered with framed supertax demands, duly receipted.

70　Coimbra: portrait of Dom João V in the University Library

71   Coimbra: the University Library

POSTSCRIPT

M R. PETER PITT-MILLWARD, who lives at the beautiful Solar da Gloria, in the Upper Minho (44), was good enough to undertake a special expedition on my behalf in order to visit Castro Laboreiro, a little enclave near the Spanish frontier, where there is rumour of strange and primitive customs. There are several such isolated places in Portugal; Miranda do Douro, for instance, a village like Montalegre or Almofala (pp, 164, 154). A topic of minor interest was as to whether the hams of Melgaço, which is on the way to Castro Laboreiro, are as good as those of Chaves, that are perhaps the best in Europe. Mr. Pitt-Millward's account appears below.

> Solar da Gloria,
> Ponte de Lima,
> Portugal.
> 14 April, 1954.

"I have *you* to thank for the agreeable day I spent yesterday; never in this world should I have been likely to go to Castro Laboreiro if you hadn't hounded me into it. And it's fortunate that I got so much pleasure from the expedition, for I'm afraid it's going to give no satisfaction at all to anyone else.

"The main news is that it isn't at all the singular, isolated, 'enclave' that you supposed (and that the 'Guide Bleu' might lead anyone to suppose). It's just one more very high, very poor, very wretched Portuguese village, without anything at all that distinguishes it from the rest. Living at a devil of a height, in barren mountain country, imposes the same sort of life on everyone who lives on that sort of height and in that sort of country. Castro, to tell the truth, is less remote than many a village I could name: it's On The Telephone. And they have 28 subscribers, which is the most remarkable thing about the whole place, for there are only 32 houses.

"Another rather odd thing is that nearly all the houses are inhabited only by women and their children; the only men I saw were two policemen, and one or two in the dress of the 'Guarda Fiscal'; and one man with an ox-cart.

"The men of 'Castro', being freer to move than their women, have all moved. They've moved to France, and they work there usually as 'pedreirsos'—stone masons. If you'd seen the landscape you'd see at once why stone-masonry is bound to be second nature to any native of such parts; it's *all* stone. I never before—unless maybe in Spain, in the region of Almería, or in Italy at the top of Vesuvius—saw a countryside so totally desolate; and nowhere at all have I seen so much stone. Wisely, the men get out as soon as they can, and stay out. And as soon as her husband leaves, the wife puts on Widow's Weeds and keeps them for good; she knows she's lost her Man. If—and it does occasionally happen—he turns up again, they make a vast celebration of it; but the widow's soon back in her weeds again. This, by the way, isn't peculiar to Castro Laboreiro; it's current practice in the Minho, though usually the men go to Brazil or Venezuela; that the men's minds should always be bent on Paris, up there in Castro, is one of the few singularities the place offers.

"Except, of course, for the Dogs. I did my level best over those Dogs, but it was a poor best. They're dreary creatures to look at, being (though as big as an Alsatian) very much the Poor Relations of every other race of dog. They have ears that ought to stand straight, but they don't; and their coat is a nameless hue, which you might best describe as pepper-and-mud. Attempts to photograph them were nearly wholly thwarted by the speed at which they run away if you stand still and look at them. I ended with the sincere conviction that the sheep are there to defend *them*, and not they the sheep.

"For me, the principal astonishment was to find the place so very small. 32 houses, as I told you before; and 32 houses, if they're tiny houses and crammed close together, take up very little space. We'd sailed clean through Castro Laboreiro before I realized that we'd reached it, but as the road comes to an end 100 yards further on, I couldn't sail far. It's tiny, and it's ugly (and I'm not speaking, now, of the landscape, which might be considered excessively inhospitable even if you came across it on the far side of the Moon).

"As for costumes, almost the only male I saw—he served as our guide when we climbed to the Castello—was an Eskimo-faced youth in leggings and big boots, corduroy trousers, and a long water-proof jacket. The women wear woollen stuff bound round their legs, and they wear a combination of cap (padded with wool too) and cape, of rusty black material. I couldn't learn of any other costume known to them. They were indescribably ugly, one and all; most of them would have fitted neatly into any Brueghel, and the rest of them were straight out of any Hieronymus Bosch.

"I'm afraid I'm making it all sound drab and disappointing, but frankly that's just what that little cluster of hovels *is*. However, there's one more exciting feature to the place, and that is the Castle, on the very top of a precipitous peak that stands behind the village, high above a gorge that turns to Spain within a few miles. It's a 20-minutes scramble to get to the Castle, and from the village all you can see of it is an archway in the rock. Once you're through the archway there's a great deal more to be seen; the whole of the tip of the mountain has been walled in with a wall of granite well over 2 yards thick, and still largely intact. Who made it, and when, I couldn't guess; they call it Roman, of course, and the 'Castro' certainly bears that out; but why in the world should the Romans have built a 'castle' in such a desperate position? The Roman occupation of the peninsula wasn't, so far as I know, at all *that* sort of occupation. They didn't come all this way in order to shut themselves up on top of one of the most inhospitable, unprofitable mountains in Europe, and in as vile a climate as you could find anywhere on earth. (Until a few days before I went there, they'd been wholly blocked in by snow for weeks.) As for who the raiders were, it might have been anybody, I suppose, and at any time. Conceivably even Moors, for there's a village close by with the unlikely name of Alcobaça; the only 'Al—' that I remember to have encountered in these parts, and just possibly indicating the Furthest South that the Moors in N.W. Spain came.

"Mostly, up there, they live on sheep and goats, I take it, for that's all you see; they grow some wheat and some rye, but of course, no maize, at that height, and no olives and no vines. They're said to grow potatoes, but they grow them a long way from the village—down in the hollow, on the far side of a 'Roman' bridge that crosses their stream, somewhere between there and that improbable Alcobaça."

So ends this account of Castro Laboreiro; and on the return journey no less a person than the Chefe de Conservaçâo das Estradas awaited the travellers with a superb luncheon in a pensão, and had got a present for my informant in the shape of one of the famous hams of Melgaço, which should be sliced as thin as a rose-leaf, and are only lesser in repute than the smoked hams of Lamego, or of Chaves, the most excellent in all the Iberian peninsula.

INDEX

(The numerals in heavy type denote the *figure numbers* of illustrations)

239

INDEX